*This book is dedicated to the members
of the Chicago Fly Fishers*

CONTENTS

ACKNOWLEDGMENTS

I hesitate to mention all the members of the Chicago Fly Fishers who demonstrated or gave me patterns and recipes, because I know that I will forget to include everyone. However, my thanks to all the club members both past and present for all the support they gave me in making this book possible.

INTRODUCTION

The Chicago Fly Fishers, a Chicago-area fly-tying club, has promoted the art of fly tying to both beginners and experienced tiers since the organization was first started in 1977. The pages in this book are some of the instruction sheets used to demonstrate the patterns that were tied during the club's weekly meetings from 1984 to the present.

The pages represent a diverse selection, from simple patterns to the more complex. Each page includes general information about the pattern, including (if available) its origin, its originator's name, the club demonstrator, and the years it was demonstrated.

Each pattern was selected by the demonstrator to help members improve their tying skills or as a favorite pattern used by the demonstrator during his or her fishing endeavors.

In addition to existing known patterns, members (including myself) have submitted some of their own creations that illustrate their creativity and tying ability. I hope you enjoy as much as I did the many hours of fun and relaxation that the selections shown here can give as you put the hook in the vise and tie on the materials.

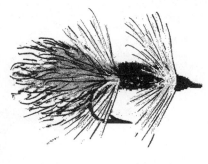

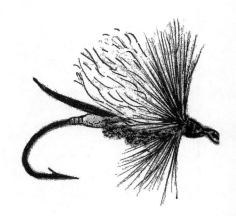

CHAPTER 1

Salmon and Steelhead Patterns

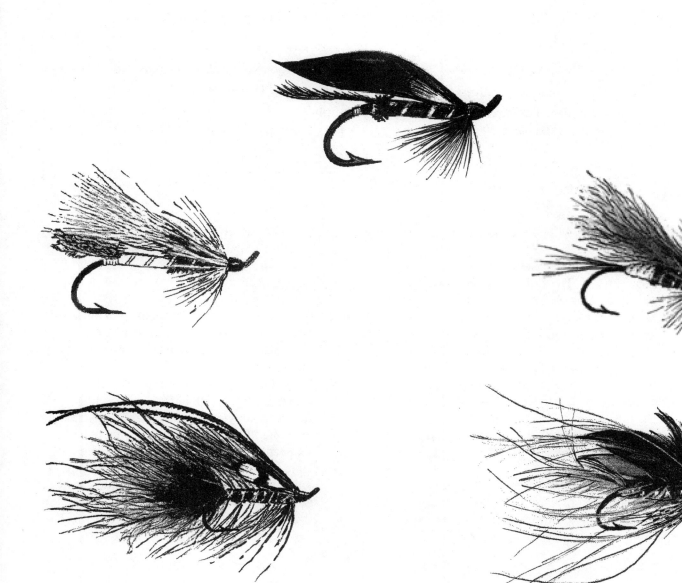

Black Power

Origin: Norway
Demonstrator: Gene Kugach 1988–89
Used for: Salmon, steelhead

A modern-day large Spey-type pattern for spring and fall salmon fishing. A nice-looking pattern designed in Norway for offshore trolling.

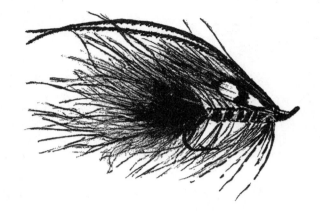

Thread	Black	**Body**	Black dubbing or ostrich herl
Hook	Mustad 36890, size 2/0 to 6/0	**Throat**	Silver Flashabou strands
Tail	Black marabou blood feathers	**Wings**	Black bucktail (sparse)
Rib	Silver Flashabou or wire, followed by a ring-necked pheasant's rump hackle stripped on one side and palmered Spey style.	**Topping**	3 or 4 peacock herls
		Cheeks	Jungle cock
		Head	Black thread

Step 1. Wrap the shank with black thread up to the hook bend.

Step 2. Tie in the black marabou blood feathers at the bend as the tail. The tail should be twice the length of the hook shank.

Step 3. Tie in the silver Flashabou or wire, followed by a ring-necked pheasant's rump hackle at the tail tie-in point. Both will be used later as ribbing over the body. *Note: The ring-necked pheasant's rump hackle should be stripped on one side so it can be palmered Spey style.*

Step 4. Tie in the black dubbing or ostrich herl and form the body to within 3/16 inch behind the hook eye. Secure the material with your thread, and snip off any excess.

Step 5. After the body is finished, rib the body with the silver Flashabou or wire followed by the ring-necked pheasant's rump hackle, using equally spaced wraps, and remove any excess.

Step 6. Tie in the silver Flashabou strands at the front of the body under the hook shank for the beard. *Note: The length of the strands should be longer than the hook.* After the beard is secured, snip off any excess.

Step 7. Tie in a sparse bunch of black bucktail as the wings on top of the hook shank. The wing length should be one and a half times the body length.

Step 8. After the wings are in place, top them with three or four peacock herls.

Step 9. Tie in the jungle cock cheeks on each side of the wings. The cheeks should be about half the body length with the second eye showing.

Step 10. Build a neat head with the thread, and tie off with a whip finish. Coat the head with head or epoxy cement.

Black Prince

Origin: Northwest United States
Demonstrator: Gene Kugach 1997–98
Used for: Salmon, steelhead

The Black Prince is an excellent steelhead pattern that is popular in both the Great Lakes region and the Northwest. It can be tied as a conventional hairwing or as a low-water version, depending on the tier's preference. The recipe below is for the conventional hairwing pattern, with a few options as to materials that can be selected during its construction.

Thread	Black prewaxed Monocord or Flymaster 6/0	**Body**	Rear half or third: Yellow wool or yellow floss Front half or two-thirds: Black wool or black chenille
Hook	Mustad 36890, Partridge N or M, or Eagle Claw 1197, size 2 to 8		
Tail	Red hackle fibers	**Throat**	Black hen hackle, collar style
Rib	Oval silver tinsel or flat fine silver tinsel	**Wing**	Black calf tail or squirrel
		Head	Black thread

Step 1. Lay down a base of thread, stopping just before the hook bend.

Step 2. Tie in the red hackle fibers for the tail. *Note: Tail fibers should be equal to the body length.*

Step 3. Tie in the ribbing material (flat or oval tinsel).

Step 4. Form the body using the material of your choice, as listed above, and rib the entire body with equally spaced turns using the flat or oval tinsel. *Note: Be sure to leave enough space behind the eye for the throat, wing, and head.*

Step 5. Tie in a black hen hackle and give it a few wraps (collar style) to form the throat.

Step 6. After you complete the body and throat, tie in the black calf tail or squirrel wing on top of the hook shank. *Note: Don't get carried away with the amount of hair you use for the wing; keep it sparse.*

Step 7. Form a neat head with the thread, and tie off with a whip finish. Give the head a few coats of lacquer, and you're ready to go steelheading.

Black Rat

Origin: Northwest United States
Demonstrator: Gene Kugach 1997–98
Used for: Salmon, steelhead

The Black Rat is an excellent wet-fly pattern for fall-run salmon. It can be tied as a conventional hairwing or as a low-water version, depending on the tier's preference. The recipe below is for a conventional hairwing pattern, with a few options as to materials that can be selected when constructing the pattern.

Thread	Black prewaxed Monocord or red Flymaster 6/0	**Body**	Peacock herl, tied full, or black seal fur dubbing
Hook	Mustad 36890 or Partridge N or M, size 2 to 10	**Throat**	Grizzly hen, collar style
		Wing	Gray fox guard hairs
Tag	Flat or oval silver tinsel or mylar	**Head**	Black or red thread
Tail (optional)	Golden pheasant crest or yellow hackle fibers		

Step 1. Lay down a base of thread, stopping just before the hook bend.

Step 2. Tie in a piece of mylar or oval or flat tinsel, making three to four wraps back around the bend, and returning to the tie-in point to form the tag.

Step 3. At this point, if you desire, you can tie in the tail, which should be equal to the body length.

Step 4. Form the body from three to four strands of black dubbing or peacock herl, tied in at the front of the tag and wound forward to within $1/8$ inch of the hook eye. If you use herl, wrap the herl with close wraps for a full body. *Note: For a more durable body, use a dubbing loop to form a noodle with the herl, or tie in a piece of fine wire prior to tying in the herl, and wrap it over the herl after the body is formed.*

Step 5. After you complete the body, tie in the gray fox guard hair wing on top of the hook shank. *Note: Don't get carried away with the amount of hair you use for the wing; keep it sparse.*

Step 6. After the wing is in place, tie in a grizzly hen feather in front of the wing, and give it a few wraps, collar style, to form the throat.

Step 7. Form a neat head with the thread, and tie off with a whip finish. Give the head a few coats of lacquer, and you're ready to go for the fall salmon.

Ingalls's Butterfly

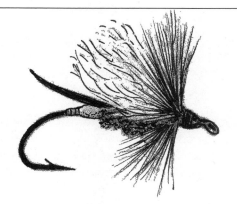

Origin: United States
Originator: Maurice Ingalls
Demonstrator: Gene Kugach 1990–91
Used for: Salmon, steelhead

An excellent wet-fly pattern for fall-run salmon developed by Maurice Ingalls of Florida. The pattern can be tied with various colored butts. The smaller sizes are excellent low-water patterns.

Thread	Black	**Body**	Peacock herl
Hook	Mustad 36890, size 4 to 10	**Wing**	Fine white hair (goat or calf), tied back at 45 degrees and divided
Tip	Oval silver tinsel		
Tag	Fluorescent green floss	**Hackle**	Brown (dry-fly style)
Tail	Fine red duck quill section	**Head**	Black thread

Step 1. Lay down a thread base to the point of the hook.

Step 2. Tie in a small piece of oval silver tinsel or Flashabou, and form the tip, which should be about $1/8$ inch wide from the bend of the hook.

Step 3. Tie in the fluorescent green floss, and form a tapered tag about $3/16$ inch wide.

Step 4. Tie in the tail, which is a small segment of red duck quill, on top of the shank in front of the tag. The tail should extend to the end of the hook.

Step 5. Tie in three or four pieces of peacock herl at the same point where the tail was tied in, and bring your thread forward. Wrap the remaining part of the hook shank with the herl.

Step 6. Select a sparse bunch of white calf tail as the wing, and even up the tips with your hair stacker. Tie it in at a 45-degree angle in front of the body, with the tips extending back to the end of the hook. Divide the wing into two equal bunches, using figure-eight wraps, with a few additional wraps around the base of each bunch.

Step 7. Select a brown hackle with barbules as wide as or slightly wider than the gap of the hook, and tie it in at the front of the wing. *Note: The hackle can be tied in either wet or dry style. Give the hackle a few wraps in front of the wing (wet style) or one wrap behind the wing and one in front (dry style), and secure it with the thread.*

Step 8. Form a neat head with your thread, and tie off with a whip finish.

McCleod's Ugly

Origin: Scotland
Originator: Ken J. McCleod
Demonstrator: Gene Kugach 1990–91
Used for: Salmon, steelhead, trout

An excellent wet-fly pattern for spring-run steelhead or fall-run salmon, or for trout when tied in smaller sizes. It can be tied as a conventional hairwing or as a low-water version, depending on the tier's preference. It can be fished with a sinking line during early spring or a slow-sinking line during the summer.

Thread	Black	**Rib**	Grizzly hackle
Hook	Mustad 9049, size 4 to 10	**Wing**	Black bucktail or equivalent
Tail	Fluffy fibers from base of orange feather	**Hackle**	Grizzly
Body	Black chenille	**Head**	Black thread

Step 1. Lay down a base of thread back to the point of the hook.

Step 2. Tie in the tail, using the fluffy fiber material at the base of an orange hackle feather. The tail should be the length of the hook shank.

Step 3. Tie in a piece of black chenille at the point where the tail was tied in.

Step 4. Tie in a grizzly hackle at the same point as the chenille. Tie in the hackle by the tip.

Step 5. Wrap the shank with the black chenille to about an $1/8$ inch from the hook eye. Snip off any excess material.

Step 6. Palmer the grizzly hackle over the chenille body, and secure it with your thread. Snip off any excess material.

Step 7. Tie in the wing of black bucktail on top of the shank. The length of the wing should extend up to the tail.

Step 8. After the wing is secured, tie in a grizzly hackle, give it two to three wraps in front of the wing, and collar it back.

Step 9. Form a neat head with your thread, whip-finish, tie off, and coat the head with cement.

The Sweep

Origin: United Kingdom
Demonstrator: Gene Kugach 1993–94
Used for: Salmon, steelhead

One of the many dark or black flies used today; others include Stoat's Tail, Black Dose, and the Black Bear series. Sometimes a jungle cock cheek is added, and often the fly is dressed with a black heron hackle or goose or turkey quill for the wing.

Thread	Black	**Body**	Black floss
Hook	Mustad 36890, size 12 to 3/0	**Beard**	Black hackle fibers
Tag	Fine gold tinsel	**Wing**	Black bear
Tip	Gold or yellow floss	**Horns** (optional)	Yellow-and-blue macaw fibers
Tail	Golden pheasant crest	**Cheeks**	Light blue hen hackle tips
Butt	Black ostrich herl	**Head**	Black thread
Rib	Fine gold tinsel		

Step 1. Lay down a base of thread about $3/16$ inch behind the hook eye, back to the bend of the hook

Step 2. Tie in a piece of flat gold tinsel, give it three to four wraps beyond the bend, and then wrap forward to the starting point, forming the tag. Secure the tinsel with your thread, and snip off any excess material.

Step 3. Tie in a short piece of gold or yellow floss in front of the tag, and form the tip using the floss. The tip should be about $1/8$ inch wide, tapered from the tag, going forward. Secure the floss with the thread, and snip off any excess material.

Step 4. Tie in the golden pheasant crest tail in front of the tip.

Step 5. After the tail is in place, tie in a black ostrich herl in front of the tip, and give it two to three tight wraps around the shank to form the butt. Secure the herl with your thread, and snip off any excess material.

Step 6. On the bottom of the shank, tie in a short piece of flat gold tinsel ribbing (just in front of the black ostrich herl butt), bringing your thread to the midpoint of the shank.

Step 7. Tie in a piece of black floss, and form the body by wrapping back to the butt and then forward, making it even with the thickness of the yellow floss tip. *Note: Don't wrap the body too close to the hook eye. Allow at least $3/16$ inch between the hook eye and the end of the body.*

Step 8. Rib the body with the flat gold tinsel, giving the tinsel four or five equally spaced wraps. Secure the tinsel with your thread, and snip off any excess material.

Step 9. After the body is completed, tie in the beard at the front of the body under the shank, using black hackle fibers.

Step 10. Take a sparse bunch of black bear hair and remove the underfur. Tie in the hair on top of the shank for the wing. *Note: The wing should end just short of the golden pheasant crest tail.*

Step 11. After the wing is in place, if you choose, you can tie in the optional yellow-and-blue macaw feather fibers as horns.

Step 12. Tie in the blue hen hackle tips as the cheeks on each side of the wing.

Step 13. Finish the pattern with a neat head of black thread, and tie off with a whip finish.

Munro's Killer

Origin: United Kingdom
Demonstrator: Gene Kugach 1996–97
Used for: Fall-run salmon

One of the most popular British hairwings of recent years. An excellent pattern for fall-run salmon because of the orange, yellow, and black color combination. The original pattern was tied using squirrel for the wing and blue-dyed guinea fowl or blue jay for the beard. The pattern can also be tied with a wing combination of black over brown or black over orange.

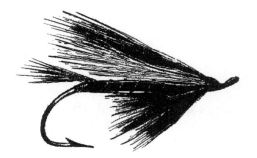

Thread	Black		**Rib**	Oval or flat gold tinsel
Hook	Mustad 36890, size 6/0 to 12		**Hackle/beard**	Orange hackle barbules with blue hackle barbules in front.
Tip	Oval or flat gold tinsel		**Wing**	Black calf tail over yellow calf tail
Tail	Orange hackle barbules			
Body	Black floss			

Step 1. Lay down a base of black thread, stopping just before the hook bend.

Step 2. Tie in a piece of oval or flat tinsel, making three to four wraps back around the bend, and returning to the tie-in point to form the tip. Don't snip off the excess material; it will be used later for the body ribbing.

Step 3. Tie in the tail (length equal to hook shank) in front of the tip on top of the hook shank, and bring your thread forward to within 1/8 inch of the hook eye.

Step 4. Tie in the black floss behind the eye, and form the body by wrapping the shank back to the tail and then forward to the tie-in point.

Step 5. Rib the body with the oval or flat tinsel, bringing it forward and securing it with the thread.

Step 6. Tie in a sparse bunch of orange hackle barbules under the shank, beard style, with a small bunch of blue hackle barbules in front of the orange.

Step 7. Tie in the wing (length equal to shank and tail) on top of the shank, using a sparse bunch of yellow calf tail, with a sparse bunch of black calf tail over the yellow. Form a neat head using the black thread, and tie off with a whip finish.

Renous Special

Origin: New Brunswick, Canada
Originator: E. Renous
Demonstrator: Gene Kugach 1992–93
Used for: Salmon, steelhead

The Renous Special, named after its originator, was created for spring salmon fishing on the Miramichi River in New Brunswick, Canada. This pattern supposedly represents a baitfish such as a smelt, which is the basic food fish for the spring salmon in the Miramichi. It is fished deep, using a sinking line, and is effective for both salmon and steelhead.

Thread	Black	**Rib**	Flat silver tinsel
Hook	Mustad 36890, size 1 to 6	**Beard**	Yellow bucktail or FisHair
Tag	Fine flat silver tinsel	**Underwing**	Chartreuse bucktail or FisHair
Tip	Bright red floss	**Overwing**	Yellow bucktail or FisHair
Tail	Chartreuse bucktail or FisHair	**Shoulders**	Jungle cock
Body	Green floss (dark)	**Head**	Bright red thread

Step 1. Lay down a base of thread about 3/16 inch behind the hook eye, back to the bend of the hook.

Step 2. Tie in the flat silver tinsel, give it three to four wraps beyond the bend, then wrap forward, forming the tag.

Step 3. Tie in the bright red floss, and form the tip in front of the tag, about 3/16 inch wide.

Step 4. Tie in a small bunch of chartreuse bucktail on top of hook shank in front of the tip as the tail (length equal to the shank of the hook).

Step 5. Tie in the flat silver tinsel under the hook shank in front of the tip, bringing the thread midway up the shank. Tie in the green floss, bringing the thread forward to the front of the shank. Form the body with the floss going back to the tip and then forward. Secure the floss with the thread, and snip off any excess. Rib the body going forward with the silver tinsel, secure it with the thread, and snip off excess.

Step 6. Tie in the yellow bucktail beard under the shank (beard should be equal to body length), and secure it with the thread.

Step 7. On the top of the hook shank, tie in a sparse bunch of chartreuse bucktail as the underwing, with the length of the wing ending at the end of the tail. On top of the underwing, tie in a sparse bunch of yellow bucktail as the overwing, slightly shorter than the underwing.

Step 8. Tie in the jungle cock shoulders on each side of the wing, making the shoulders approximately half the shank length, and tie off.

Step 9. Tie in the bright red thread, and form a neat head. Tie off with a whip finish, and coat the head with head cement.

Simplified Halloween Spey

Origin: United States
Demonstrator: Eric Heckman 1984–85
Used for: Salmon, steelhead

The unique identifying characteristic of Spey fly patterns is the long flowing body hackles, tied palmer fashion along the length of the body. The original Spey patterns were tied using heron feathers for the body. These are no longer available and are replaced by pheasant rump, guinea, mallard, teal, chicken, or burnt goose feathers. The pattern below uses burnt goose feathers in its construction.

Thread	Black	**Rib**	Oval silver tinsel	
Hook	Mustad 9049, size 4	**Wings**	Matched hen black hackle tips	
Body hackle	Burnt dyed hot orange domestic goose	**Beard**	Dark guinea hen fibers	
Body	Black rabbit dubbing	**Head**	Black thread	

Starting with white domestic goose wing feathers, dye the feathers hot orange. Then mix a solution of Clorox bleach and water (1/2 cup bleach to 1/2 gallon water) for the burning process, and immerse the feathers in the solution. When the feathers start to fan out (pucker) and begin to look thinner, remove them from this solution and immerse them in a second solution of vinegar and water (1/2 cup vinegar to 1 quart water) to stop the burning process. After the feathers dry, take the feather you plan to use for the pattern, and split it in half down the length of the stem, using a razor blade.

Step 1. Lay down a thread base to the hook bend, and tie in the split burnt dyed hot orange domestic goose feather by the tip, with the natural curve toward the back. Leave the butt end extending out behind the hook.

Step 2. Tie in the oval silver tinsel ribbing.

Step 3. Using black rabbit dubbing, dub the body forward to within 1/8 inch of the hook eye.

Step 4. Wrap the split goose feather forward to within 1/8 inch of the hook eye, securing it with the thread and removing any excess material.

Step 5. Rib the body with the oval silver tinsel ribbing, wrapping in the opposite direction from the hackle to within 1/8 inch of the hook eye. Secure the ribbing with the thread, and remove any excess material.

Step 6. Tie in a pair of matched hen black hackle tips on each side of the body for the wings.

Step 7. After the wings are in place, tie in the dark guinea hen fibers under the shank as the beard.

Step 8. Form a neat head using the black thread, and tie off with a whip finish. Coat the head with head cement.

Rusty Rat

Origin: United States
Originator: Dr. Orrin Summers
Demonstrator: George Cik 1986–87
Used for: Salmon, steelhead

The Rusty Rat is an excellent salmon pattern that is popular in both the Great Lakes region and the Northwest. The pattern is a variation on the original Rat series patterns created by Roy Angus Thompson in the early 1900s. The recipe below is for the conventional hairwing pattern.

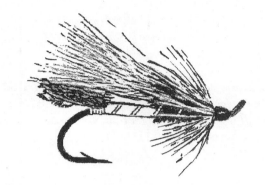

Thread	Red 6/0	Body	Rear half: Yellow floss
Hook	Mustad 36890, Partridge N or M, or Eagle Claw 1197, size 2 to 8		Front half: Peacock herl
		Veil	Yellow floss over rear half of body
Tag	Fine oval gold tinsel	Wing	Gray fox guard hair fibers
Tail	3 or 4 short peacock sword fibers	Hackle	Grizzly hackle, collar style
Rib	Fine oval gold tinsel	Head	Red thread

Step 1. Lay down a base of thread, stopping between the hook point and the barb, and then tie in the fine oval gold tinsel. Form the tag using three to four wraps to the back and three to four wraps forward. Secure the tinsel with the thread, then, with the tinsel under the hook shank, make an additional three to four wraps forward with the thread, allowing the tinsel to hang under the shank. *Note: The tinsel will be used later in the pattern as the ribbing.*

Step 2. Tie in three to four short peacock sword fibers for the tail, and bring your thread forward to a point midway between the tag and one eye length behind the eye. *Note: The tail fibers should be equal to the body length and tied in on top of the shank behind the tag.*

Step 3. Tie in the yellow floss on top of the shank midway between the tag and one eye length behind the eye. Then form the rear half of the body with the yellow floss, going back to the tag and returning forward to the tie-in point. Secure the floss on top of the shank, pulling back on the floss to form the veil. Using scissors, trim the floss veil over the rear half of the body to the middle of the tail or up to the tail, as shown in the pattern picture.

Step 4. Form a dubbing loop and tie in three or four strands of peacock herl, making a peacock chenille strand by twisting the loop and the peacock herl together. Advance your thread to within one hook eye length behind the eye, and form the front half of the body using the peacock chenille strand. Secure the strand with your thread, and remove any excess material.

Step 5. Using the fine oval gold tinsel ribbing material left at the tag end, rib the entire body, going forward with equally spaced turns. *Note: Do not wrap the ribbing over the floss veil.* Secure the tinsel under the shank with your thread, and remove any excess material.

Step 6. After you complete the body, tie in the gray fox guard hair fiber wing on top of the hook shank. The wing tips should extend about halfway into the tail. *Note: Don't get carried away with the amount of hair you use for the wing; keep it sparse, remove any guard hairs, and stack the tips prior to tying them in.*

Step 7. Tie in a grizzly hackle in front of the wing, and give it a few wraps to form the collar.

Step 8. Form a neat head with the thread, and tie off with a whip finish. Give the head a few coats of head cement to complete the pattern.

Renegade

Origin: Northwest United States
Demonstrator: Jerry Wasil 1989–90
Used for: Salmon, steelhead

The Renegade is an excellent dry-fly pattern for fall-run salmon or steelhead. It can also be tied in smaller sizes for most trout species. The rear hackle should be slightly smaller than the front hackle.

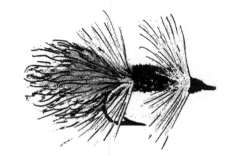

Thread	Black		**Rib**	Variegated metallic thread
Hook	Mustad 3135 or 34007, size 4 to 6		**Body**	Peacock herl, tied full
Tail	Red calf tail or polar bear		**Front hackle**	Soft white saddle
Rear hackle	Soft dark brown saddle		**Head**	Black thread

Step 1. Lay down a base of thread, stopping just before the hook bend.

Step 2. Tie in some red calf tail or polar bear hair fibers as the tail at the bend of the hook. *Note: The hair fibers should be equal to the body length.*

Step 3. At the same tie-in point as the tail, tie in the soft dark brown saddle hackle (fibers should be equal to the body length) and a short piece of the variegated metallic thread for the ribbing.

Step 4. Give the hackle two to three wraps in front of the tail, and secure it with your thread. Snip off any excess material.

Step 5. Tie in three to four strands of peacock herl at the front of the hackle, and wind them forward to within $1/8$ inch of the hook eye, using close wraps for a full body. *Note: For a more durable body, use a dubbing loop to form a noodle with the herl.*

Step 6. After you complete the body, rib the body going forward with the variegated metallic thread, using equally spaced wraps. Secure the rib with your thread, and remove any excess material.

Step 7. Tie in a white saddle hackle in front of the body, give it two to three wraps, and secure it with the thread. Remove any excess material.

Step 8. Form a neat head with the thread, and tie off with a whip finish. Give the head a few coats of lacquer, and your pattern is complete.

Gilly

Origin: United States
Originator: Gene Kugach
Used for: Salmon, steelhead

A simple hairwing pattern that can be used for both salmon and steelhead during their fall and winter spawning seasons.

Thread	Black and bright red	**Wing**	Sparse bunch of black bucktail with yellow bucktail on top
Hook	Mustad 36890, size 8 to 10	**Hackle**	Black, collared back
Tag	Fine flat silver tinsel	**Head**	Black thread with a red thread band in the center
Tail	Light green mallard flank feather fibers		
Body	Half yellow or gold floss, followed by one-quarter red floss, followed by one-quarter bright blue ostrich herl		

Step 1. Wrap the shank with thread up to the bend of the hook, and tie in a piece of flat silver tinsel. Form the tag by wrapping back three or four wraps and then returning to the starting point. Secure the tinsel with your thread.

Step 2. Tie in a few of the light green mallard flank feather fibers for the tail. *Note: The tail should be the length of the hook shank.*

Step 3. Tie in a piece of gold or yellow floss, and form the first half of the body, tapering it forward from the tag. Secure the floss with your thread, and snip off the excess.

Step 4. Tie in a short piece of bright red floss, and continue forming the body until three-quarters of the body is completed. Secure the floss with your thread, and snip off the excess.

Step 5. Tie in a bright blue ostrich herl, and wrap it around the shank until you have covered the remaining one-quarter of the body area. Secure the herl with your thread, and remove the excess.

Step 6. After you've finished the body, take a sparse bunch of black bucktail, even up the tips, and tie it in on top of the shank as the underwing. The bucktail should extend out to the tip of the tail.

Step 7. Take another sparse bunch of yellow bucktail, even up the tips, and tie it in on top of the black underwing. *Note: Make it slightly shorter than the underwing when you tie it in.*

Step 8. After the wing is finished, tie in a black hackle in front of the wing, and give it a few wraps around the shank. Secure it with your thread, snip off the excess, and then collar it back.

Step 9. Form a neat head with the black thread and tie off. Tie in the red thread at the center of the head, and then a red band in the center with the bright red thread. Tie off with a whip finish, and give the head a couple coats of head cement.

Ebony Knight

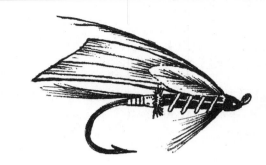

Origin: United States
Originator: Gene Kugach
Used for: Salmon, steelhead

The Ebony Knight is a black pattern that works well for both fall-run salmon and early-spring steelhead. The married wing is the most difficult part of the pattern construction.

Thread	Black	**Beard**	Black hackle fibers
Hook	Mustad 36890, size 8 to 1/0	**Wings**	Married dyed goose quill or duck segments: thin red segment, followed by a black segment twice as wide as the red, followed by a bright blue segment equal to the black, topped by another black segment
Tag	Fine flat silver tinsel		
Tip	Gold or yellow floss		
Tail	Yellow hackle fibers		
Butt	Black ostrich herl		
Body	Black floss, ribbed with fine flat silver tinsel	**Shoulders**	Bright blue hen feather tips
		Head	Black thread

Step 1. Wrap the shank with thread up to the bend of the hook, and tie in a piece of fine flat silver tinsel. Form the tag by wrapping back three or four wraps and then returning to the starting point. Secure the tinsel with your thread.

Step 2. Tie in a piece of gold or yellow floss and form the tip, making it about 3/16 inch wide. Secure it with the thread, and snip off the excess.

Step 3. Tie in a few yellow hackle fibers for the tail in front of the tip.

Step 4. Tie in a black ostrich herl, and form the butt by giving the herl two to three wraps forward. Secure it with your thread, and snip off the excess.

Step 5. Tie in another piece of fine flat silver tinsel at the front of the butt, along with a piece of the black floss, and bring the thread forward on the hook shank. Wrap the shank with the floss to form the body, and secure it with the thread. Rib the body with the silver tinsel, giving it three to four wraps. Again secure it with the thread, and snip off the excess materials.

Step 6. After you've finished the body, tie in some black hackle fibers on the bottom of the shank in front of the body as the beard.

Step 7. Now build the wings. Starting with a thin red segment from a goose or duck quill, marry a black segment, twice as wide as the red, to the top of the red segment. Then marry a bright blue segment, equal in width to the black, to the top of the black segment, then top off the wing with another black segment. Repeat the sequence for the second wing. After the wings are finished, tie them in on the top of the hook shank in front of the body, as shown in the pattern illustration.

Step 8. Select a pair of bright blue hen feathers, and strip them back until the tips are half the length of the floss body. Tie them in as the shoulders on each side of the wings.

Step 9. Form a neat head, and tie off with a whip finish. Give the head a couple coats of head cement.

Lord Amherst

Origin: United States
Originator: Gene Kugach
Used for: Salmon, steelhead

The Lord Amherst is a pattern that works well for fall-run salmon and early-spring steelhead. The wing construction of this pattern calls for feathers from the Amherst pheasant, which may not be easy to obtain.

Thread	Black	**Beard**	Blue hackle fibers
Hook	Mustad 36890, size 8 to 1/0	**Wing**	2 blue-and-black breast feathers from an Amherst pheasant, sandwiched by 2 shorter feathers
Tag	Fine flat silver tinsel		
Tip	Black floss		
Tail	Black pheasant rump fibers	**Cheeks**	2 thin white, black-tipped Amherst pheasant neck feathers
Butt	Blue ostrich herl		
Body	Rear two-thirds: Black floss, ribbed with fine flat blue Flashabou Front third: Blue ostrich herl	**Horns**	Blue-and-yellow macaw tail feather fibers
		Collar	Black hackle, tied collar style
		Head	Black thread

Step 1. Wrap the shank with thread up to the bend of the hook, and tie in a piece of fine flat silver tinsel. Form the tag by wrapping back three or four wraps and then returning to the starting point. Secure the tinsel with your thread.

Step 2. Tie in a piece of black floss and form the tip, making it about 3/16 inch wide. Secure it with your thread, and snip off the excess.

Step 3. Tie in a few black pheasant rump feather fibers for the tail in front of the tip.

Step 4. Tie in a blue ostrich herl, and form the butt by giving the herl two to three wraps forward. Secure it with your thread.

Step 5. Tie in the Flashabou at the front of the butt, along with a piece of the black floss, bringing your thread forward about two-thirds of the hook shank. Wrap the shank with the floss to form the body, and secure it with the thread. Rib the body with the Flashabou, giving it two to three wraps. Secure it with the thread, and snip off the excess materials. Tie in another blue ostrich herl, and form the remaining third of the body.

Step 6. Tie in some blue hackle fibers on the bottom of the shank in front of the body as the beard.

Step 7. Now build the wing. Select two equal blue-and-black Amherst pheasant breast feathers as long as the hook, and using a drop of cement at the base of each feather, glue them together back-to-back. After the cement dries, take two more feathers, about two-thirds the length of the first two, and cement them in place, sandwiching the first two feathers. Now add the cheeks, which are about one-third the wing length, cementing them in place on each side. After the wing dries, tie it in on top of the hook shank in front of the body.

Step 8. Tie in the blue-and-yellow macaw tail feather fiber horns on each side of the cheeks. (Their length should be equal to the body plus the tail.) Then tie in a black hackle, and give it a couple of wraps around the shank to form the collar, securing it collar-style with the thread.

Step 9. Form a neat head, and tie off with a whip finish. Give the head a couple coats of head cement or epoxy.

Lady Amherst

Origin:	United States
Originator:	Gene Kugach
Used for:	Salmon, steelhead

The Lady Amherst is a fall-run salmon and early-spring steelhead pattern. The wing construction calls for feathers from the Amherst pheasant, which may not be easy to obtain.

Thread	Black	**Wing**	2 white-and-black neck feathers (shaped with head cement) from an Amherst pheasant
Hook	Mustad 36890, size 8 to 1/0		
Tag	Fine flat silver tinsel		
Tip	Red floss	**Shoulders**	2 shorter blue-and-black breast feathers
Tail	Golden pheasant crest		
Butt	Yellow or golden ostrich herl	**Cheeks**	2 Amherst thin white, golden-tipped neck feathers
Body	Flat silver tinsel, palmered with a black saddle hackle and ribbed with fine gold oval tinsel	**Horns** (optional)	Blue-and-yellow macaw tail feather fibers
		Topping	Golden pheasant crest
Beard	Red and yellow hackle fibers tied in sequentially	**Head**	Black thread

Step 1. Wrap the shank with thread up to the bend of the hook, and tie in a piece of flat silver tinsel. Form the tag by wrapping back three or four wraps and then returning to the starting point. Secure the tinsel with your thread.

Step 2. Tie in a piece of red floss and form the tip, making it about 3/16 inch wide. Secure it with your thread, and snip off the excess.

Step 3. Tie in a golden pheasant crest for the tail in front of the tip on top of the hook shank.

Step 4. Tie in a yellow ostrich herl, and give it a few wraps to form the butt in front of the tip.

Step 5. Tie in another piece of flat silver tinsel, in front of the butt, along with a black saddle hackle and a piece of fine gold oval tinsel. Bringing your thread forward, wrap the silver tinsel forward to form the body. Palmer the body with the black saddle hackle, and rib it with the fine gold oval tinsel, being careful not to mat down the hackle fibers.

Step 6. After you've finished the body, tie in some yellow and red hackle fibers sequentially on the bottom of the shank in front of the body as the beard.

Lady Amherst continued

Step 7. Now build the wing. Select two equal white-and-black Amherst pheasant neck feathers (larger feathers found on the lower part of the neck), and shape them by using a little head cement and your fingers until they are slimmed down and are as long as the hook. *Note: Using the head cement and working it into the feathers will slim them down and give them a better shape.* After they dry, using a drop of cement at the base of each feather, glue them together back-to-back. After the cement dries, take two short blue-and-black breast feathers for the shoulders, one-third shorter than the wing, and cement them in place, sandwiching the wing feathers. Now take the cheek feathers, two slim white, golden-tipped Amherst pheasant neck feathers about one-third the wing length, and again using the head cement, shape them with your fingers. After they dry, cement them in place on each side. After the wing dries, tie it in on the top of the hook shank in front of the body.

Step 8. Tie in the blue-and-yellow macaw tail feather fiber horns (their length should be equal to the body plus the tail), and then add the topping, which is another golden pheasant crest feather, over the top of the wing. *Note: The end of the golden pheasant crest topping should meet the end of the tail.*

Step 9. Form a neat head, and tie off with a whip finish. Give the head a couple coats of head cement.

Black Reaper

Origin: United States
Originator: Gene Kugach
Used for: Salmon, steelhead

A simple hairwing pattern designed for fall salmon or steelhead fishing. It can be tied as a conventional hairwing, as shown above, or as a low-water version.

Thread	Black	**Wing**	Black squirrel tail, black bear hair fibers, or black calf tail
Hook	Mustad 36890, size 8 to 1/0	**Hackle**	Black neck hackle, collared back
Tail	Yellow hackle fibers	**Head**	Black thread
Body	Single strand floss Rear third: Bright red floss Front two-thirds: Black floss ribbed with fine flat silver Flashabou (single strip)		

Step 1. Wrap the shank with thread up to the bend of the hook, and tie in the yellow hackle fibers for the tail. *Note: The tail should be equal to one and a half times the length of the body.*

Step 2. Tie in a short piece of bright red floss and form a tapered butt one-third the body length. Secure the floss with your thread, and remove any excess.

Step 3. Tie in a piece of fine flat silver Flashabou and a piece of black floss. Finish wrapping the remaining two-thirds of the body with the black floss, forming a cigar-shaped body, and rib it with the silver Flashabou. Snip off any remaining excess materials.

Step 4. Now add the wing. Select a sparse bunch of black squirrel tail, black bear hair fibers, or black calf tail, and tie it in on top of the hook shank. *Note: The length of the wing should extend to the end of the tail.*

Step 5. Tie in a black neck hackle, and give it a couple wraps in front of the wing, securing it with the thread. Cut off any excess materials, and then, using the thread, collar it back and build a small neat head. Tie off with a whip finish.

Black Pheasant

Origin: United States
Originator: Gene Kugach
Used for: Salmon, steelhead

Another black hairwing pattern designed for fall salmon or steelhead fishing. It can be tied as a conventional hairwing, as shown, or as a low-water version.

Thread	Black and bright red	**Beard**	Black pheasant rump fibers
Hook	Mustad 36890, size 8 to 1/0	**Wing**	2 blue-and-black breast feathers from a black pheasant, sandwiched by 2 shorter feathers, sandwiched by another 2 shorter feathers
Tag	Fine oval silver tinsel		
Tip	Bright red floss		
Tail	Black pheasant rump fibers		
Butt	Black ostrich herl	**Shoulders**	2 white lesser covert feathers
Body	Black floss, ribbed with fine oval silver tinsel	**Cheeks**	Jungle cock or equivalent
		Head	Black thread with a red thread band in the center

Step 1. Wrap the shank with thread up to the bend of the hook, and tie in a piece of fine oval silver tinsel. Form the tag by wrapping back three or four wraps and then returning to the starting point. Secure the tinsel with your thread.

Step 2. Tie in a piece of red floss and form the tip, making it about 3/16 inch wide. Secure it with your thread, and snip off the excess.

Step 3. Tie in a few black pheasant rump fibers for the tail in front of the tip.

Step 4. Tie in a black ostrich herl and form the butt, giving the herl two to three wraps forward and securing it with the thread. Snip off the excess.

Step 5. Tie in another piece of fine oval silver tinsel at the front of the butt, along with a piece of black floss, bringing your thread forward. Wrap the shank with the floss to form the body, and rib it with the silver tinsel. Secure it with the thread, and snip off the excess materials.

Step 6. After you've finished the body, tie in some black pheasant rump fibers on the bottom of the shank in front of the body as the beard.

Step 7. Now build the wing. Select two equal blue-and-black breast feathers from a black pheasant, as long as the hook, and use a drop of cement at the base of each feather to cement them together back-to-back.

Step 8. Sandwich two shorter feathers (about two-thirds as long as the first) over the first two, using another drop of cement at the base of each feather. Repeat the same process with a third set of feathers (one-third the length of the first) sandwiched over the second set.

Step 9. Add two white lesser covert feathers (about one-third the wing length) for shoulders, cementing them in place on each side of the wing, followed by the jungle cock cheeks, which are as long as the shoulders. Tie in the wing on top of the hook shank in front of the body.

Step 10. Form a neat head with the black thread, then tie in a piece of bright red thread at the center of the head and give it a few tight wraps to form the center band. Secure it with the black thread, cutting off the excess, then finish off the head and tie off with a whip finish. Give the head a couple coats of head cement.

Coburn Special

Origin: Unknown
Demonstrator: George Cik 1985–86
Used for: Salmon, steelhead

One of the many newer salmon patterns that has proven to be very effective. It can also be tied in other color combinations such as red and black, yellow and black, or orange and black.

Thread	Black or fluorescent green	**Body**	Fluorescent green floss, built up cigar shape, with several turns of black ostrich herl in the middle
Hook	Mustad 36890, size 2 to 12		
Tag	Oval silver tinsel	**Wing**	Sparse black calf tail over green calf tail (length equal to end of tail)
Tail	Sparse black calf tail over green calf tail		
		Hackle	Yellow hackle, collared and tied back
		Head	Black or fluorescent green thread

Step 1. Lay down a base of thread, stopping just before the hook bend.

Step 2. Tie in a piece of oval or flat tinsel, making three to four wraps back around the bend, and returning to the tie-in point to form the tag. Snip off any excess material.

Step 3. Tie in some green calf tail with a sparse bunch of black calf tail on top of the green as the tail. *Note: The hair fibers should be about half the body length.*

Step 4. Tie in a piece of fluorescent green floss at the tail tie-in point, and start to form the body going forward. *Note: The entire body will be cigar shaped when finished.* When you reach the midpoint of the body, tie in a black ostrich herl using the green floss, and make several close turns with the herl. Snip off any excess material. Continue forming the remaining half of the body, going forward with the green floss to within 3/16 inch behind the hook eye.

Step 5. After you've completed the body, tie in a bunch of fluorescent green calf tail fibers, topped with a sparse bunch of black calf tail fibers, on top of the shank as the wing.

Step 6. Tie in a yellow hackle in front of the body, give it two to three wraps, and collar it back with your thread. Remove any excess material.

Step 7. Form a neat head with the thread, and tie off with a whip finish. Give the head a few coats of lacquer, and your pattern is complete.

Skykomish Sunrise

Origin:	Scotland
Originator:	Ken J. McCleod
Demonstrator:	George Cik 1987–88
Used for:	Salmon, steelhead

One of the many salmon patterns created in Scotland by Ken J. McCleod. It has proven to be very effective during the fall salmon runs.

Thread	Bright red		**Wing**	White calf tail or equivalent
Hook	Mustad 36890 or 9049, size 2 to 10		**Hackle**	Red and yellow, mixed, collared, and tied down
Tail	Red and yellow hackle fibers, mixed		**Head**	Bright red thread
Rib	Flat silver tinsel			
Body	Bright red chenille			

Step 1. Lay down a base of thread, stopping just before the hook bend.

Step 2. Tie in a sparse bunch of mixed red and yellow hackle fibers on top of the shank as the tail. *Note: Hackle fibers should be about half the body length.*

Step 3. Tie in a 6-inch-long piece of flat silver tinsel at the tail tie-in point as the ribbing, which will be used later. Also at the same point, tie in a 6-inch-long piece of bright red chenille, and bring your thread forward to within ⅛ inch of the hook eye.

Step 4. Use the red chenille to form the body, going forward to within ⅛ inch behind the hook eye. Secure it with the thread, and remove any excess material.

Step 5. Use the flat silver tinsel to rib the body, going forward with evenly spaced wraps. Secure it with the thread, and remove any excess material.

Step 6. After you've completed the body, tie in a bunch of white calf-tail fibers on top of the shank as the wing. The wing fibers should be slightly shorter than the end of the tail fibers.

Step 7. Tie in a yellow and a red hackle in front of the body, and give them two to three mixed wraps, pulling them down and collaring them back with the thread. Remove any excess material.

Step 8. Form a neat head with the thread, and tie off with a whip finish. Give the head a few coats of lacquer, and your pattern is complete.

Black Gordon

Origin: United Kingdom
Demonstrator: George Cik 1987–88
Used for: Salmon, steelhead

The Black Gordon is one of the classic patterns that have been around for many years. The recipe given here is a simplified hairwing version used in the United States.

Thread	Black		**Wing**	Black bucktail
Hook	Mustad 36890 or 9049, size 2 to 10		**Hackle**	Black, collared back
Rib	Narrow oval gold tinsel		**Head**	Black thread
Body	Rear third: Red floss Front two-thirds: Black floss			

Step 1. Lay down a base of thread, stopping just before the hook bend.

Step 2. Tie in a 6-inch-long piece of narrow oval gold tinsel to be used later in the pattern construction. Also at the same point, tie in a short piece of red floss, and bring your thread forward about one-third of the hook shank.

Step 3. Use the red floss to form a slightly tapered body, going forward about one-third of the hook shank. Secure the floss with the thread, and remove any excess material.

Step 4. Tie in a short piece of black floss in front of the red, and going forward, finish the remaining two-thirds of the body. Secure the floss with the thread, and remove any excess material. *Note: Allow space behind the hook eye to add the wing, collar, and head.*

Step 5. Using the narrow oval gold tinsel, rib the body going forward with evenly spaced wraps over both the red and black floss and secure it with the thread and remove any excess material.

Step 6. After you've completed the body, tie in a bunch of black bucktail on top of the shank as the wing. The wing fibers should be slightly longer than the bend of the hook.

Step 7. Tie in a black hackle in front of the body, and give it two to three wraps, collaring it back with the thread. Remove any excess material.

Step 8. Form a neat head with the thread, and tie off with a whip finish. Give the head a few coats of lacquer, and your pattern is complete.

Purple Peril

Origin: Scotland
Originator: Ken J. McCleod
Demonstrator: Roger Hetzke 1991–92
Used for: Salmon, steelhead

Another one of the many salmon patterns created in Scotland by Ken. J. McCleod that have proven to be very effective.

Thread	Black	**Body**	Purple floss or wool
Hook	Mustad 36890 or Eagle Claw 1197B, size 2 to 8	**Rib**	Flat silver tinsel
		Wing	Mottled brown bucktail
Tag (optional)	Flat silver tinsel	**Hackle**	Purple, collared back
Tail	Purple hackle fibers	**Head**	Black thread

Step 1. Lay down a base of thread, stopping just before the hook bend.

Step 2. Tie in a 6-inch-long piece of flat silver tinsel, making three to four wraps back around the bend, and returning to the tie-in point to form the tag. Move the remaining tinsel out of the way; it will be used later in the pattern construction.

Step 3. Tie in a sparse bunch of purple hackle fibers on top of the shank as the tail. After the tail is in place, at the same point, tie in a short piece of purple floss, and bring your thread forward about 1/4 inch from the hook eye.

Step 4. Use the purple floss to form the body, going forward. Secure the floss with the thread, and remove any excess material.

Step 5. Use the remaining flat silver tinsel to rib the body, going forward with evenly spaced wraps over the purple floss. Secure it with the thread, and remove any excess material.

Step 6. After you've completed the body, tie in a bunch of mottled brown bucktail on top of the shank as the wing. The wing fibers should be slightly longer than the bend of the hook.

Step 7. Tie in a purple hackle in front of the body and give it two to three wraps, collaring it back with the thread. Remove any excess material.

Step 8. Form a neat head with the thread, and tie off with a whip finish. Give the head a few coats of lacquer, and your pattern is complete.

Umpqua Special

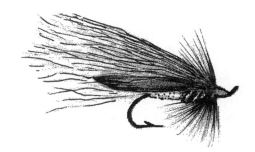

Origin:	United States
Originator:	Don Harter
Demonstrators:	Warren Wormann 1988–89
	Roger Hetzke 1992–93
Used for:	Salmon, steelhead

This pattern was developed in the state of Oregon about 1935 for fishing on the famed North Umpqua River.

Thread	Red	**Wing**	White bucktail with narrow red goose quill segments on each side; or white bucktail with red bucktail on top, with more white bucktail over the red bucktail
Hook	Mustad 36890 or Eagle Claw 1197, size 2 to 8		
Tail	White bucktail or calf tail		
Rib	Flat silver tinsel	**Hackle**	Coachman brown, collared back
Body	Rear third: Yellow floss Front two-thirds: Red wool	**Head**	Red thread

Step 1. Lay down a base of thread, stopping just before the hook bend, and tie in a sparse bunch of white bucktail or calf tail (length equal to the body) as the tail.

Step 2. Tie in a 6-inch-long piece of flat silver tinsel to be used later in the pattern construction. Also at the same point, tie in a short piece of yellow floss, and bring your thread forward about one-third of the hook shank.

Step 3. Use the yellow floss to form a slightly tapered body, going forward about one-third of the hook shank. Secure the floss with the thread, and remove any excess material.

Step 4. Tie in a short piece of red wool in front of the yellow floss, and going forward, finish the remaining two-thirds of the body. Secure the wool with the thread and remove any excess material. *Note: Allow space behind the hook eye to add the wing, collar, and head.*

Step 5. Use the flat silver tinsel to rib the body, going forward with evenly spaced wraps over both the yellow floss and the red wool. Secure it with the thread, and remove any excess material.

Step 6. After you've completed the body, tie in a bunch of white bucktail on top of the shank as the wing. The wing fibers should be slightly shorter than or equal to the tail. Also tie in a red goose quill segment (slightly shorter than the wing) on each side of the wing. *Note: The wing can also be tied using white bucktail with red bucktail on top, with more white bucktail over the red bucktail.*

Step 7. Tie in a Coachman brown hackle in front of the body, and give it two to three wraps, collaring it back with the thread. Remove any excess material.

Step 8. Form a neat head with the thread, and tie off with a whip finish. Give the head a few coats of lacquer, and your pattern is complete.

Krystal Bullet

Origin: United States
Demonstrator: Len Eckerly 1988–89
Used for: Salmon, steelhead

One of the many newer salmon patterns made with some of the newer materials used today. The pattern can be tied in an assortment of color combinations.

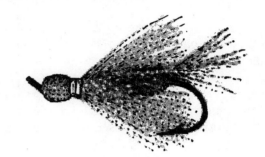

Thread	Black or tier's choice	**Body**	Chenille (color tier's choice)
Hook	Mustad 36890 or 9049, size 2 to 10	**Head/hackle**	Krystal Flash (color tier's choice), tied bullet style
Tail	Krystal Flash (color tier's choice)		

Step 1. Lay down a base of thread, stopping just before the hook bend.

Step 2. Tie in a few short (two-thirds of the hook shank length) strands of Krystal Flash.

Step 3. Tie in a short piece of chenille, and bring your thread forward about two-thirds of the hook shank. Wrap the shank forward with the chenille to form the body, and secure it with the thread. Snip off any excess material.

Step 4. Take about a dozen strands of Krystal Flash, double them over the thread, and tie them in on top of the shank in front of the body. *Note: The ends of the Krystal Flash should be forward of the hook eye.* Secure the Krystal Flash, going forward with the thread as close to the hook eye as possible, then bring the thread back to the tie-in point in front of the body.

Step 5. Bring the Krystal Flash strands back over the shank, and evenly spread them around the hook shank to form a neat bullet head. Pull the strands toward the back of the hook with one hand, and secure them with a few wraps of thread, forming a neat collar about one-third of the hook shank behind the hook eye.

Step 6. Tie off with a whip finish. Give the collar a few coats of lacquer, and your pattern is complete.

Gold Comet

Origin: United States or Canada
Demonstrator: Bob Dulian 1985–86
Used for: Steelhead, salmon

There are many variations of the comet-type pattern that vary in color and materials. They are all basically steelhead patterns that can also be used for salmon fishing.

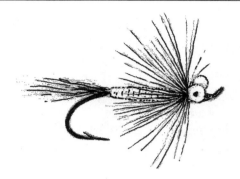

Thread	Orange	**Body**	Yellow floss, tapered
Hook	Mustad 36890 or Eagle Claw 1197B, size 2 to 6	**Hackle**	Yellow and hot orange, collared back
Tail	Yellow marabou fibers as long as the shank	**Eyes**	Brass bead chain
		Head	Orange thread
Rib	Oval gold tinsel		

Step 1. Lay down a base of thread, stopping just before the hook bend.

Step 2. Tie in a bunch of yellow marabou fibers (as long as the shank) on top of the shank as the tail.

Step 3. Tie in a 6-inch-long piece of oval gold tinsel at the tail tie-in, as well as a 12-inch-long piece of yellow floss.

Step 4. Use the yellow floss to form a tapered body, going forward to within 3/16 inch behind the hook eye. Secure the floss with the thread, and remove any excess material.

Step 5. Use the oval gold tinsel to rib the body, going forward with evenly spaced wraps over the yellow floss. Secure it with the thread, and remove any excess material.

Step 6. After you've completed the body, tie in a yellow and a hot orange hackle in front of the body, and give them two to three wraps, collaring them back with the thread. Remove any excess material.

Step 7. Add the bead chain eyes in front of the collared hackle on top of the shank, using several figure-eight wraps. After the eyes are secured in place, form a neat head with the thread, and tie off with a whip finish. Give the head a few coats of lacquer, and your pattern is complete.

Royal George

Origin: United States
Originator: Steve Almgreen
Used for: Salmon, steelhead

One of the salmon fly creations of Steve Almgreen, a member of the Chicago Fly Fishers.

Thread	Red	**Rib**	Medium French tinsel, gold
Hook	Mustad 90240, size 6	**Wing**	Silver fox or coyote
Tag	Medium French tinsel, gold	**Topping**	Golden pheasant crest feather
Butt	Peacock herl	**Hackle**	Yellow saddle, collared back
Body	Purple silk or rayon floss	**Head**	Red thread

Step 1. Lay down a thread base up to the hook point, and tie in a short piece of gold medium French tinsel. Wrap the tinsel back three or four turns past the hook bend, and return it back to the hook point, forming the tag. Secure the tinsel with the thread at the hook point, allowing the remainder of the tinsel to hang below the hook.

Step 2. Tie in a peacock herl at the hook point, and give it a couple of close wraps forward over the hanging tinsel, forming the butt. Secure it with the thread and remove the excess herl.

Step 3. Tie in a short piece of purple silk or rayon floss in front of the butt, and wrapping forward, form a smooth, neat body to about 1/8 inch behind the hook eye. Secure the material with the thread, and remove any excess.

Step 4. Using the remaining medium French tinsel, rib the body with five evenly spaced wraps. Secure the tinsel with the thread, and remove any excess material.

Step 5. Tie in a sparse bunch of silver fox or coyote fibers (about one and a quarter the hook length) as the wing in front of the body. *Note: Remove the underfur prior to tying in the wing.*

Step 6. After the wing is in place, tie in a golden pheasant crest feather (about one and a half the hook length) over the wing as the topping.

Step 7. Tie in a yellow saddle hackle in front of the wing, giving it two or three close wraps. Collar it back with the thread, and remove any excess material.

Step 8. Form a neat, oversize head with the thread, and tie off with a whip finish. Give the head a coat of cement, and your pattern is complete.

Babine Special

Origin: United States or Canada
Demonstrator: Bob Dulian 1990–91
Used for: Steelhead, salmon

The Babine Special is a simple pattern that is very effective for fall steelhead. It is designed to resemble a pair of red or orange salmon eggs, which steelhead eat during the fall salmon spawning season.

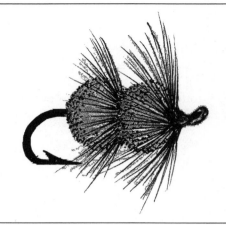

Thread	Black or red	**Hackle**	Center of body: Red
Hook	Mustad 36890, size 2 to 8		Front of body: White
Body	Fluorescent red or orange chenille	**Head**	Black or red thread

Step 1. Lay down a base of thread, stopping just before the hook bend.

Step 2. Tie in a 12-inch-long piece of fluorescent red or orange chenille, and form a ball-shaped body about half the shank length at the back of the hook, securing the chenille with your thread.

Step 3. Tie in a red hackle in front of the round body, and make a couple of close wraps. Secure the hackle with the thread, and snip off any excess material.

Step 4. Using the fluorescent red or orange chenille, form another ball in front of the red hackle as you did at the back of the hook. Secure the chenille with your thread, and snip off any excess material. *Note: Make sure you leave enough room behind the hook eye for the front hackle and the head.*

Step 5. Tie in a white hackle in front of the body, and make a couple of close wraps. Secure the hackle with the thread, and snip off any excess material.

Step 6. Form a neat head with the thread, and tie off with a whip finish. Give the head a few coats of lacquer, and your pattern is complete.

Boss

Origin: United States or Canada
Demonstrator: Greg Chambers 1988–89
Used for: Steelhead, salmon

The Boss is a variation on the Comet series of patterns. It is similar in its construction and is fished the same way. It is basically a steelhead pattern that can also be used for salmon.

Thread	Black	**Body**	Black chenille
Hook	Mustad 36890 or Eagle Claw 1197B, size 4 to 6	**Hackle**	Red or hot orange, collared back
		Eyes	Brass bead chain
Tail	Black squirrel tail fibers, twice the length of hook	**Head**	Black thread
Rib	Medium oval silver tinsel		

Step 1. Lay down a base of thread, stopping just before the hook bend.

Step 2. Tie in a sparse bunch of black squirrel tail fibers (twice the length of the hook) on top of the shank as the tail.

Step 3. Tie in a 6-inch-long piece of medium oval silver tinsel at the tail tie-in, as well as a 12-inch-long piece of black chenille.

Step 4. Use the black chenille to form the body, going forward to within 3/16 inch behind the hook eye. Secure the chenille with the thread, and remove any excess material.

Step 5. Use the oval silver tinsel to rib the body, going forward with evenly spaced wraps over the black chenille. Secure it with the thread, and remove any excess material.

Step 6. After you've completed the body, tie in a red or hot orange hackle in front of the body, and give it two to three wraps. Collar it back with the thread, and remove any excess material.

Step 7. Add the bead chain eyes in front of the collared hackle on top of the shank, using several figure-eight wraps. After the eyes are secured in place, form a neat head with the thread, and tie off with a whip finish. Give the bead a few coats of lacquer, and your pattern is complete.

Green Butt Skunk

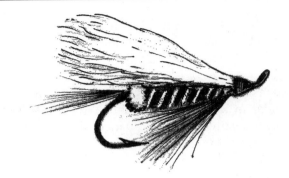

Origin: United States or Canada
Demonstrator: George Cik 1988–89
Used for: Steelhead, salmon

The Green Butt Skunk is a steelhead hairwing pattern that is simple to tie and very effective during the spring steelhead runs. It also works well for fall salmon.

Thread	Black	**Rib**	Flat silver tinsel
Hook	Mustad 36890, size 1 to 6	**Body**	Black chenille
Tail	Red hackle fibers	**Wing**	White bucktail or calf tail
Butt	2 or 3 turns of fluorescent green chenille	**Hackle**	Black, collared back
		Head	Black thread

Step 1. Lay down a base of thread, stopping just before the hook bend.

Step 2. Tie in a sparse bunch of red hackle fibers (about the length of the hook shank) on top of the shank as the tail.

Step 3. Tie in a short piece of fluorescent green chenille at the tail tie-in, and give it two or three turns around the shank to form the butt. Secure it with the thread, and snip off any excess material.

Step 4. Tie in a 6-inch-long piece of flat silver tinsel in front of the butt, as well as a 12-inch-long piece of black chenille.

Step 5. Use the black chenille to form the body, going forward from the butt to within 3/16 inch behind the hook eye. Secure the chenille with the thread, and remove any excess material.

Step 6. Use the flat silver tinsel to rib the body, going forward with evenly spaced wraps over the black chenille. Secure it with the thread, and remove any excess material.

Step 7. After you've completed the body, tie in a sparse bunch of white bucktail or calf tail on top of the shank as the wing. The wing should be slightly shorter than the body plus the tail.

Step 8. Tie in a black hackle at the wing tie-in point, give it two or three close wraps, and collar it back to form the beard.

Step 9. Form a neat head with the thread, and tie off with a whip finish. Give the head a few coats of lacquer, and your pattern is complete.

Lady Godiva

Origin: United States or Canada
Demonstrator: Warren Wormann 1988–89
Used for: Steelhead, salmon

The Lady Godiva is very effective during the winter steel-head runs. It also works well for fall salmon.

Thread	Black	**Rib**	Flat silver tinsel (wide)
Hook	Eagle Claw 1197B, size 1/0 to 6	**Body**	White yarn
Tip	Flat silver tinsel	**Wing**	Bright red polar bear or equivalent
Tail	Red and yellow mixed hackle fibers	**Head**	Black thread
Butt	2 or 3 turns of red chenille		

Step 1. Lay down a base of thread, stopping just before the hook bend.

Step 2. Tie in a short piece of flat silver tinsel, and make a few wraps beyond the bend and back to the tie-in point to form the tip. Snip off any excess material.

Step 3. Tie in a sparse bunch of mixed red and yellow hackle fibers (about the length of the hook shank) on top of the shank as the tail.

Step 4. Tie in a short piece of red chenille at the tail tie-in, and give it two or three turns around the shank to form the butt. Secure it with the thread, and snip off any excess material.

Step 5. Tie in a 6-inch-long piece of flat silver tinsel in front of the butt, as well as a 12-inch-long piece of white yarn.

Step 6. Use the white yarn to form the body, going forward from the butt to within 3/16 inch behind the hook eye. Secure the chenille with the thread, and remove any excess material.

Step 7. Use the flat silver tinsel to rib the body, going forward with evenly spaced wraps over the white yarn. Secure it with the thread, and remove any excess material.

Step 8. After you've completed the body, tie in a sparse bunch of bright red polar bear (or equivalent) on top of the shank as the wing. The wing should be slightly shorter than the body plus the tail.

Step 9. Form a neat head with the thread, and tie off with a whip finish. Give the head a few coats of lacquer, and your pattern is complete.

Steelhead Bee

Origin: United States or Canada
Demonstrator: Ray Podkowa 1990–91
Used for: Steelhead

One of the newer steelhead flies, developed recently as a divided hairwing pattern designed to represent a large bee.

Thread	Black		**Body**	One-third brown yarn, one-third yellow yarn, one-third brown fur dubbing
Hook	Mustad 90240, size 6 to 12			
Wing	Red fox squirrel tail fibers, divided		**Hackle**	Brown hen (sparse)
Tail	Red fox squirrel tail fibers		**Head**	Black thread

Step 1. Lay down a thread base, and return to approximately $\frac{1}{8}$ inch behind the hook eye.

Step 2. Tie in a bunch of red fox squirrel tail fibers (a little longer than the hook gape) with the tips extending beyond the hook eye. Then, using your thread, lift the fibers up and secure them in an upright position. Divide the hair fibers into two equal bunches, using figure-eight wraps to form a divided wing, and bring the thread back along the shank to the hook bend.

Step 3. Tie in a sparse bunch of red fox squirrel tail fibers (about the length of the hook shank) on top of the shank as the tail.

Step 4. Tie in a short piece of brown yarn at the tail tie-in, and wrap it forward about one-third of the shank, securing it with the thread and removing any excess material.

Step 5. Tie in a short piece of yellow yarn in front of the brown yarn, and wrap it forward about one-third of the shank, securing it with the thread and removing any excess material.

Step 6. Using brown fur dubbing, dub the remaining one-third of the shank going forward.

Step 7. After the body is complete, tie in the brown hen hackle behind the wing, and make a couple of wraps behind and in front of the wing, securing it with your thread and removing any excess material.

Step 8. Form a neat head with the thread, and tie off with a whip finish. Give the head a few coats of lacquer, and your pattern is complete.

Tickletailed Comet

Origin: United States or Canada
Demonstrator: Len Eckerly 1989–90
Used for: Steelhead, salmon

There are many variations of the Comet-type pattern that vary in color and materials. The recipe below gives the general construction of this pattern. The color selections are the tier's choice.

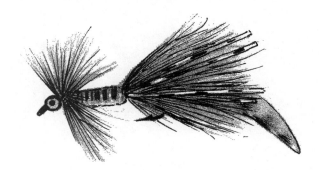

Thread	Black	**Rib**	Oval silver tinsel
Hook	Mustad 90240, size 4 to 10	**Body**	Ultra-Chenille
Tail	2 grizzly hackles (twice as long as the hook), with 6 to 8 strands of silver Flashabou (hook length) sandwiched by 2 marabou feathers (hook length)	**Collar**	Soft hackle or neck hackle, collared back
		Eyes	Brass bead chain
		Head	Natural or synthetic dubbing

Step 1. Lay down a base of thread, stopping just before the hook bend.

Step 2. Tie in two grizzly hackles (twice as long as the hook) with six to eight hook-length strands of silver Flashabou sandwiched by two hook-length marabou feathers as the tail.

Step 3. Tie in a 6-inch-long piece of oval silver tinsel at the tail tie-in, as well as a 12-inch-long piece of Ultra-Chenille.

Step 4. Use the Ultra-Chenille to form the body, going forward to within 3/16 inch behind the hook eye. Secure the Ultra-Chenille with the thread, and remove any excess material.

Step 5. Use the oval silver tinsel to rib the body, going forward with evenly spaced wraps over the Ultra-Chenille. Secure it with the thread, and remove any excess material.

Step 6. After you've completed the body, tie in a soft hackle or neck hackle in front of the body and give it two to three wraps, collaring it back with the thread. Remove any excess material.

Step 7. Add the bead chain eyes in front of the collared hackle on top of the shank, using several figure-eight wraps. After the eyes are secured in place, dub around and between them to form a neat head, and tie off with a whip finish.

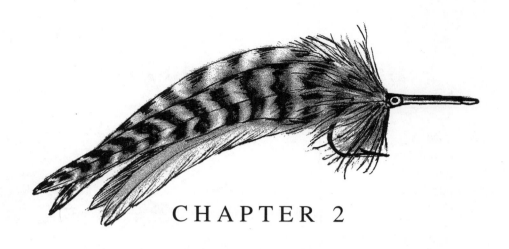

CHAPTER 2

Saltwater Patterns

Bonbright Tarpon Fly

Origin: United States
Originator: Howard Bonbright
Demonstrator: Gene Kugach 1989–90
Used for: Tarpon and most other saltwater game fish

One of the more popular tarpon flies fished during annual Florida tarpon tournaments. In addition, the pattern has been successful for other types of saltwater fish. It is fished slowly on a sinking line or trolled on a floater or slow-sink line.

Thread	Black	**Wing**	White saddle hackles, 2½ inches long	
Hook	Eagle Claw 254SS, size 3/0 to 5/0	**Shoulders**	Red swan	
Tail	Red and white saddle hackle tips, 1 inch long	**Cheeks**	Jungle cock	
Body	Silver tinsel	**Hackle**	White, collared	
		Head	Black thread	

Step 1. Lay down a base of black thread, and tie in the red and white hackle tips for the tail.

Step 2. After the tail is in place, bring the thread forward to within ⅛ inch of the hook eye, and tie in a piece of silver tinsel. Wrap the tinsel around the shank, back to the tail and then forward, to form the body. Secure it with your thread, and snip off the excess tinsel. *Note: Give the body a coat of head cement or epoxy to make it more durable.*

Step 3. Tie in the white hackles on top of the body to form the wing.

Step 4. After the wing is in place, tie in the shoulders on each side, using the red swan or substitute material, and then add the jungle cock (or substitute) cheeks over the red swan.

Step 5. Tie in the white hackle in front of the wing, and give it three or four wraps to form the collar. Using your thread, collar back the white hackle and form a neat head. Tie off with a whip finish, and coat the head with cement.

Wild Canary

Origin: United States
Originator: Larry Green
Demonstrator: Gene Kugach 1988–89, 1998–99
Used for: Kelp bass, Pacific yellowtail, skipjack tuna, albacore, Pacific mackerel, bonito

Typically used for offshore or inshore trolling, fishing kelp beds and flats. Although this pattern was designed for saltwater fishing, it can be used in freshwater for muskie or northern pike.

Thread	Red		**Underwing**	Fluorescent yellow FisHair, topped with 10 to 12 strands of peacock herl
Hook	Eagle Claw 66SSA, size 3/0		**Overwing**	2 long grizzly hackles
Tail	4 yellow hackles with six strands of silver Flashabou on each side		**Head**	Red thread
Body	Silver cloisonné		**Eyes**	Styrofoam or painted, white with black centers
Throat	Fluorescent yellow FisHair			

Step 1. Lay down a base of thread, stopping just before the hook bend.

Step 2. Tie in four yellow hackles (about one and a half times the hook length), and then add about six strands of silver Flashabou on each side of the hackles for the tail.

Step 3. Tie in a 6-inch-piece of Silver cloisonné. Form the body with the silver cloisonné, using tight wraps around the entire hook shank to about ³/₁₆ inch behind the hook eye.

Step 4. After the body is finished, tie in a sparse bunch of yellow FisHair fibers under the hook shank to form the throat. *Note: The throat should extend beyond the back of the hook about midway under the tail.*

Step 5. Tie in a sparse bunch of yellow FisHair as the underwing, and top it with ten to twelve strands of peacock herl. *Note: The length of the FisHair and the herl should be as long as or slightly longer than the body plus the tail.*

Step 6. Tie in two long grizzly hackles over the underwing as the overwing. *Note: The grizzly hackles should be slightly longer than the underwing.*

Step 7. Form a neat head with the thread, and tie off with a whip finish. Then paint or glue the eyes in place on each side of the head, and give the head a coat of epoxy cement. *Note: Also cover the eyes with the epoxy.*

Sea Arrow Squid

Origin: United States
Originator: Dan Blanton
Demonstrator: Gene Kugach 1989–90
Used for: Most saltwater game fish

The Sea Arrow Squid is one of the more popular patterns created by Dan Blanton, a West Coast fisherman and expert fly tier, and is considered a new standard by many saltwater fishermen. It is fished slowly on a sinking line or trolled on a floater or slow-sink line.

Thread	White	**Eyes**	Plastic amber doll eyes (8mm) on wire stems
Hook	Eagle Claw 254SS, size 3/0		
Butt	White chenille	**Body**	White marabou tufts tied in around the eyes, followed by white chenille wrapped around the hook shank
Tentacles	2 grizzly saddle hackles 5 inches long		
Tail	Eight white saddle hackles	**Head**	6 pieces of 3-strand white acrylic yarn, 1 1/2 inches long

Step 1. Wrap the hook shank with thread to the bend of the hook. Tie in a piece of white, medium chenille, and form a ball (butt) just before the bend of the hook. Snip off the excess chenille.

Step 2. Tie in the two 5-inch-long grizzly saddle hackles on each side of the hook shank just behind the butt to form the tentacles.

Step 3. Tie in the eight 3-inch-long white saddle hackles, splaying them in all directions around the hook shank just behind the butt to form the tail.

Step 4. Tie in the plastic eyes just behind the hackles on each side of the hook shank. Bend the wire stems close to each eye at a 90-degree angle before you secure them to the hook. After the eyes are in place, fill in the gaps around the eyes with white marabou tufts or short white hackles.

Step 5. Tie in a piece of white medium chenille behind the eyes, and wrap the shank to form the body. Leave about a 1/8-inch gap between the hook eye and the end of the body. Snip off the excess chenille.

Step 6. Attach six 1 1/2-inch pieces of acrylic fiber yarn behind the body. Add three pieces at a time, crisscrossing them and locking them in place with a figure eight. Tie off with a whip finish under the yarn.

Step 7. Remove the fly from the vise, and use a bodkin to separate the fibers in the yarn, forming an even circular flare. After separating the fibers, work a liberal amount of silicone cement into both sides of the fibers using your fingers. *Note: Make sure you retain the circular flare when you apply the cement.*

Step 8. After the cement dries, trim the head into a pentagon or arrow shape. *Note: Use a paper template to develop the desired shape prior to the actual trimming of the fly.*

Chico's Orange Grizzly

Origin: United States
Originator: Chico Fernandez
Demonstrator: Gene Kugach 1987–88
Used for: Tarpon and most other shallow saltwater species

Also known as Chico's Shallow Water Tarpon Fly, this pattern is used extensively by tarpon fishermen in Florida and Costa Rica. It's a simple pattern to tie and is

mostly fished in shallow waters during the tarpon season.

Thread	Fluorescent orange
Hook	Mustad 34007, size 2/0 to 5/0
Tail	2 hot orange saddle hackles flanked by 2 grizzly saddle hackles (one on each side)

Collar — Hot orange hackle and grizzly hackle wound together and collared

Body — Fluorescent orange thread

Eyes (optional) — Plastic doll eyes or painted white with black centers

Step 1. Starting at the bend of the hook, tie in your thread and the two orange hackles flanked by the two grizzly hackles (one on each side) as the tail. *Note: The hackles should be about 3 to 4 inches long.*

Step 2. Tie in a hot orange and a grizzly hackle at the same tie-in point. Wrap them together with two to three wraps to form the collar. Secure the hackles with thread, and snip off the excess.

Step 3. Going forward, wrap the remainder of the hook shank with the orange thread to within $1/16$ inch behind the hook eye. Tie off with a whip finish. *Note: When wrapping the shank, make sure you use close, neat wraps.*

Step 4. After you finish tying, coat the orange thread covering the shank with clear epoxy cement, and allow it to dry.

Step 5. (Optional) After the cement dries, add the eyes on each side of the head.

Frankie-Belle

Origin: United States
Originators: Frankie Albright and Belle Mathers
Demonstrator: Chuck Stoops 1988–89
Used for: Bonefish and most other
              shallow saltwater species

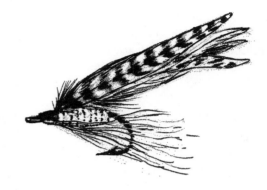

The Frankie-Belle was created by two very competitive fishing buddies from the Florida Keys area, Frankie Albright and Belle Mathers. It's an excellent bonefish pattern that can also be tied with the hook riding up by tying the wing below the shank.

Thread	Fluorescent Red	**Beard**	White bucktail or calf tail, fibers extending beyond the hook bend
Hook	Mustad 34007, size 2/0 to 6/0	**Head**	Fluorescent red thread
Body	Fluorescent white chenille		
Wing	2 grizzly hackle tips over 2 white hackle tips, splayed out		

Step 1. Lay down a thread base up to the bend of the hook, and tie in a short piece of fluorescent white chenille. Wrap the shank going forward with the chenille, using close, neat wraps.

Step 2. Tie in two grizzly hackle tips over two white hackle tips (splayed out) on top of the shank as the wing.

Step 3. Tie in the white bucktail or calf tail fibers for the beard. *Note: The fibers should extend beyond the hook bend and should be about half of the wing length.*

Step 4. Form a neat head with the fluorescent red thread, tie off with a whip finish, and give the head a couple coats of head cement.

Lefty's Deceiver

Origin: United States
Originator: Lefty Kreh
Demonstrators: George Cik 1985–86
                   Gene Kugach 1998–99
Used for: Tarpon and most other
                   shallow saltwater species

Developed by Lefty Kreh, this pattern is a favorite among saltwater fishermen. It is mostly fished in shallow waters and sinks quickly. It can be tied in many color combinations, including yellow and red, black and yellow, chartreuse and orange, white and grizzly, or any other combination you choose.

Thread	Color tier's choice	**Collar**	Bucktail (color tier's choice), spread evenly around the hook shank
Hook	Mustad 34007, size 2/0 to 5/0	**Topping**	Peacock herl over silver nylon tinsel or Krystal Flash
Tail	Bucktail (color tier's choice), inside 4 neck hackles (color tier's choice)	**Eyes**	Styrofoam or painted, white with black centers
Body	Silver mylar tinsel		

Step 1. Starting at the bend of the hook, tie in your thread and the bucktail, flanked by the four hackles (two on each side), extending one and a half times the shank length, as the tail.

Step 2. Tie in the silver tinsel at the tail tie-in, and bring your thread forward to within $3/16$ inch behind the hook eye. Form the body by wrapping the tinsel forward, covering the shank, and secure it with the thread. Snip off any excess material.

Step 3. Tie in the collar using bucktail spread evenly around the shank. *Note: The bucktail should extend nearly to the tip of the tail.*

Step 4. After you finish tying in the collar, add the topping, which consists of four to six stands of Krystal Flash over which are four to six peacock herls. *Note: The Krystal Flash and peacock herls should be as long as the collar.*

Step 5. Using your thread, form a neat head, and tie off with a whip finish.

Step 6. Cement in the Styrofoam eyes on each side of the head, and coat the entire head and eyes with epoxy cement. *Note: As an alternative to the Styrofoam eyes, the eyes can be painted after the head is coated with the epoxy and allowed to dry.*

Red and White Tarpon Streamer

Origin: United States
Demonstrator: Todd McCagg 1992–93
Used for: Tarpon and most other shallow saltwater species

This pattern is mostly fished in shallow waters and sinks quickly. It can be tied in many color combinations, including yellow and red, black and yellow, chartreuse and orange, white and grizzly, or any other combination you choose. In addition to being used in salt water, this pattern can be also used in fresh water for northern pike or muskie.

Thread	Bright red	**Hackle**	Red hackle, palmered forward, followed by a white hackle covering half of the hook shank
Hook	Mustad 34007, size 2/0 to 6/0		
Tail	2 red saddle hackles sandwiched by 2 white saddle hackles	**Body**	Bright red thread covering the remaining half of the hook shank

Step 1. Starting at the bend of the hook, tie in your thread and two red saddle hackles flanked by two white saddle hackles as the tail.

Step 2. Tie in another red saddle hackle, and palmer it forward along the hook shank with close wraps, covering one-quarter of the hook shank.

Step 3. Tie in a white saddle hackle in front of the red hackle, and palmer it along the shank, covering another one-quarter of the hook shank.

Step 4. After you finish tying in the hackles, remove any excess material, and cover the remainder of the hook shank with the red thread. Tie off with a whip finish, and give the thread a couple coats of head cement to complete the pattern.

Dan's Offshore Streamer

Origin: United States
Originator: Dan Blanton
Demonstrator: George Cik 1984–85
Used for: Billfish and most other saltwater species

Developed by Dan Blanton, this pattern is a favorite among saltwater fishermen. It is mostly fished as a trolling streamer for offshore billfish or other saltwater species. It can be tied in many color combinations, including yellow and red, black and yellow, chartreuse and orange, white and green, or any other combination you may choose. It can also be used in fresh water for pike and muskie. It's an attractor pattern as well as a bait-fish imitator, and when wet, it takes on a fish shape.

Thread	White and black
Hook	Mustad 34007, size 2/0 to 7/0
Tail	5 $\frac{1}{2}$-inch-long white FisHair with 3 $\frac{1}{2}$-inch-long red FisHair on top
Body	Braided silver mylar tubing
Collar	2 $\frac{1}{2}$-inch-long bright blue bucktail spread evenly around the hook shank, with 10 to 12 1 $\frac{1}{2}$-inch-long strands of silver Flashabou on each side
Head	Oversize, black thread
Eyes	Styrofoam or painted, white with black centers

Step 1. Lay down a white thread base to the bend of the hook. Starting at the bend of the hook, tie in the white FisHair on top of the hook shank, followed by the shorter red FisHair as the tail.

Step 2. Remove the core material from a piece of silver braided mylar tubing. Slip the tubing over the hook shank, secure the back end with your thread at the hook bend, and tie off. Tie in the black thread behind the hook eye, and secure the opposite end of the mylar tubing with the thread. *Note: Leave about $\frac{1}{2}$ inch of space behind the hook eye for the head.*

Step 3. Tie in the collar using the 2 $\frac{1}{2}$-inch-long bright blue bucktail spread evenly around the shank.

Step 4. Add ten to twelve 1 $\frac{1}{2}$-inch-long silver Flashabou strands on each side of the collar.

Step 5. Using your thread, form a neat oversize head, and tie off with a whip finish.

Step 6. Cement in the Styrofoam eyes on each side of the head, or paint on eyes, and cover the entire head and eyes with a coat of epoxy.

Bally Hoo Tail Streamer

Origin: United States
Demonstrator: Bill Somerville 1984–85
Used for: Most saltwater species

Developed to represent one of the many beak-type bait-fish found throughout the world and used for saltwater fishing. The pattern can be tied in other color combinations, such as blue and white or black and white.

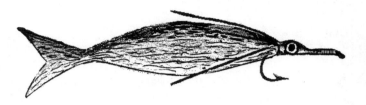

Thread	Lime green floss and bright red thread	**Collar**	4 to 6 pieces of $^1/_{16}$-inch flat silver and blue mylar tinsel, half body length
Hook	Eagle Claw 254CA, size 1/0 to 5/0	**Head**	Green floss
Body	4 to 6 inches long, green over white FisHair	**Beak**	Green floss tipped by $^3/_{16}$ inch of bright red thread behind the hook eye
Tail	Green over white FisHair, coated with epoxy and cut to shape after the cement dries	**Eyes**	Styrofoam or painted, white with red inner centers, topped by smaller black centers

Step 1. Starting at the bend of the hook, tie in the lime green floss and a bunch of white FisHair about 4 to 6 inches long under the hook shank.

Step 2. Tie in a bunch of green FisHair, the same length as the white, on top of the hook shank over the white FisHair.

Step 3. Tie in the collar using four to six strands of blue and silver mylar tinsel, tying two or three strands of each on each side of the FisHair.

Step 4. Form a neat head over the area where you tied in the FisHair and the tinsel (see pattern picture).

Step 5. Using the lime green floss, wrap the hook shank to within $^3/_{16}$ inch behind the hook eye using neat, close wraps, and tie off with a whip finish.

Step 6. Tie in the bright red thread behind the hook eye, and finish wrapping the remainder of the shank with the red thread. Tie off with a whip finish. Coat the head and the hook shank with epoxy cement, and allow it to dry.

Step 7. Using a piece of thread, tie the ends of the FisHair that protrude behind the hook bend together using a loose overhand knot, allowing about a 1-inch area behind the knot.

Step 8. Flatten and coat the 1-inch area using clear silicone cement, and allow it to dry. After the cement dries, remove the thread knot, and cut the tail to shape using a pair of scissors, as shown in the pattern picture.

Step 9. Cement in the Styrofoam eyes on each side of the head, or paint on eyes, and cover the entire head and eyes with another coat of epoxy.

Purple Pimpernel

Origin: United States
Demonstrator: Chuck Stoops 1991–92
Used for: Tarpon and most other shallow saltwater species

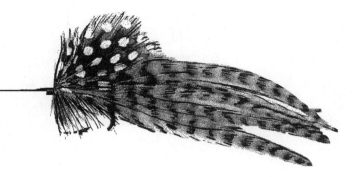

A large, colorful streamer pattern designed to represent a beak-type baitfish. It is simple to tie and is mostly fished in shallow waters during the tarpon season. It is an excellent tarpon pattern and also works well for other saltwater species.

Thread	Red single-strand floss	**Shoulders**	Natural guinea hen feathers (1 per side), with the concave side out so that they flare
Hook	Mustad 34007, size 2/0 to 6/0		
Tail	6 Grizzly hackles dyed purple	**Beak**	Red floss covering half of the hook shank
Hackle	Purple saddle, tied in and palmered at the tail		

Step 1. Starting at the bend of the hook, tie in red floss and the six purple grizzly saddle hackles as the tail.

Step 2. Tie in a purple saddle hackle at the tail tie-in, and give it a couple of close wraps. Secure it with the floss, and snip off any excess material. *Note: You may add a red saddle hackle at this point if desired.*

Step 3. Tie in the shoulders, which consist of a natural guinea hen feather on each side of the hook shank. The feathers should be tied in with the concave side facing out, so that they flare away from the shank.

Step 4. Using the red floss, wrap about half of the hook shank with close wraps to form the beak, and tie off with a whip finish.

Step 5. Give the red floss beak a coat of epoxy or head cement, and allow it to dry.

Tinsel Tail Squid

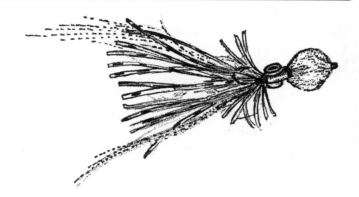

Origin: United States
Originator: Gene Kugach
Used for: Most saltwater game fish

A squid pattern developed for offshore or near-shore trolling, the Tinsel Tail Squid pattern should be fished slowly on a sinking line or trolled on a floater or slow-sink line.

Thread	White	**Head form**	Preshaped plastic or Styrofoam
Hook	Mustad 3193, size 1/0 to 2/0	**Body/head**	3 1/2-inch-long pearlescent mylar tubing (large), pulled over a precut head form and body area
Tentacles	6 to 8 strands of Krystal Flash		
Butt	White chenille or craft foam	**Eyes**	Movable plastic doll eyes (7mm)
Tail	8 12-inch-long silver tinsel strips (doubled over)		

Step 1. Wrap the hook shank with thread to the bend of the hook, and tie in the six to eight strands of Krystal Flash.

Step 2. Take a piece of white chenille or a strip of 1/8-inch-wide craft foam, and form a ball (butt) over the tie-in area of the Krystal Flash.

Step 3. Tie in the eight silver tinsel strips by doubling them over, forming sixteen strips, and splaying them in all directions around the hook shank just behind the butt to form the tail.

Step 4. Cut out a head form, using the pattern below. Tie it in behind the tail by slipping the hook eye through the hole in the pattern and securing the tab end at the tail tie-in point. *Note: Make sure that the form is parallel to the hook shank (flat on top of the shank) and that you allow about 1/16 inch behind the hook eye.*

Head Form Pattern
(Actual Size)

Step 5. Form a second ball with the craft foam or chenille over the tab area. *Note: The second ball should be large enough to hold the doll eyes when they are glued in as the final step.* After the ball is formed, tie off with a whip finish, and snip off any remaining excess material.

Step 6. Tie in your thread behind the hook eye. Remove the core material from the 3-inch-long mylar tubing, tie it in by slipping about 1/2 inch over the hook eye, and secure it with the thread. Tie off with a whip finish.

Step 7. Tie in the thread at the back end of the second ball formed in Step 5. Pull the mylar tubing over the head form, turning it inside out, and secure it with the thread behind the second ball. Tie off with a whip finish.

Step 8. Tie in the thread in front of the second ball, using a couple of loose wraps. Squeeze down the mylar with the thread, then use tight, neat, close wraps to secure it with the thread, and tie off again with a whip finish. Coat all the thread areas with epoxy. After it dries, unravel the mylar tubing behind the second ball area.

Step 9. Use epoxy to glue the movable eyes on each side of the second ball.

Big Eyed Beak

Origin: United States
Originator: Gene Kugach
Used for: All saltwater species

The Big Eyed Beak is a large saltwater streamer pattern that represents a beak-nosed baitfish. It is used extensively in Florida for fishing. In addition to being used in salt water, the pattern works very well for northern pike or muskie. It can also be used as a trolling streamer for salmon or trout in the Great Lakes region.

Thread	White and black	**Cheeks**	2-inch-long burnt orange marabou blood feather tips, tied in on each side of the hook shank
Hook	Eagle Claw 115, size 3/0 to 6/0		
Tail	Tied in at the bend, in this order: sparse bunch of white bucktail (3 inches long), topped by 2 white saddle hackles (3 inches long), sandwiched by 2 black saddle hackles (3 inches long), sandwiched by 2 olive green saddle hackles (3 inches long), sandwiched by 2 long grizzly saddle hackles (5 inches long)	**Head**	White thread, tapered from the tail-and-body tie-in point to the hook shank
		Beak	White thread along the hook shank to $1/4$ inch behind the hook eye, followed by black thread to the eye
		Eyes	Plastic doll eyes (7mm)
		Color markings	Yellow and green permanent markers
Collar	Olive green, 2-inch-long marabou blood feather tips, tied on the top, bottom, and sides of the hook shank		

Step 1. Starting at the bend of the hook, tie in the white thread and a sparse bunch of 3-inch-long white bucktail.

Step 2. Tie in, in the following order, two white saddle hackles (3 inches long), sandwiched by two black saddle hackles (3 inches long), sandwiched by two olive green saddle hackles (3 inches long), sandwiched by two long grizzly saddle hackles (5 inches long).

Step 3. Tie in the collar at the same tie-in point, using 2-inch-long olive green marabou blood feather tips on the top, bottom, and sides of the hook shank.

Step 4. Tie in the cheeks at the same tie-in point, using 2-inch-long burnt orange marabou blood feather tips on each side of the hook shank.

Step 5. Wrap a neat, tapered head using the white thread from the tie-in point to the hook shank.

Step 6. Going forward, wrap the remainder of the hook shank (beak) with the white thread to within $1/4$ inch behind the hook eye, and tie off with a whip finish.

Step 7. Tie in the black thread where you stopped with the white thread, and finish wrapping the shank to behind the hook eye. Tie off with a whip finish.

Step 8. Color the white thread with yellow and green permanent markers, coloring the beak, bottom of head, and sides yellow and the top of head and beak green.

Step 9. Cover the head and entire shank with clear epoxy cement, and allow it to dry.

Step 10. After the cement is dry, add the eyes on each side of the head, and give it another coat of epoxy, including the eyes.

Gene's Water Eel

Origin: United States
Originator: Gene Kugach
Used for: Most saltwater game fish

The Water Eel pattern is a long trolling-type streamer that can be used for off-shore or reef fishing. It was designed to represent a saltwater eel often used for bait. In addition to being a saltwater pattern, it also is very effective for both northern pike and muskie.

Thread	Black or white	**Body/head**	Tied in Thunder Creek style, in the following order: white bucktail under the shank, followed by a sparse bunch of red bucktail on top, with a sparse bunch of green and black bucktail over the red, followed by 6 to 8 strands of peacock herl.
Hook	Mustad 3193, size 1/0 to 2/0		
Tail	In the following order: 6 to 8 strands each of red and green Krystal Flash tied in at the hook bend; 2 3-inch-long white saddle hackles, sandwiched by 2 shorter 2-inch-long red saddle hackles, sandwiched by 2 shorter 1 1/2-inch green saddle hackle tips tied on top of the Krystal Flash.	**Eyes**	1/4-inch-diameter white Styrofoam with black centers

Step 1. Wrap the hook shank with thread to the bend of the hook, and tie in the six to eight strands of red and green Krystal Flash.

Step 2. Tie in the two white saddle hackles, followed by the red and green hackles as specified above.

Step 3. Starting behind the hook eye, tie in, Thunder Creek style, a bunch of 3 1/2-inch-long white bucktail hairs under the hook shank.

Step 4. Tie in, Thunder Creek style, six to eight peacock herls on top of the hook shank, followed by a sparse bunch of black, green, and red bucktail hairs on top of the hook shank.

Step 5. Use your bodkin to separate the white bucktail from the rest, and fold it back under the shank toward the hook bend, securing it at the bend with a few wraps of thread.

Step 6. Fold the remaining tail materials back over the top of the shank toward the hook bend, and secure them with the thread. *Note: At this point, the peacock herl should be on top, followed by the various bucktail colors as specified above.*

Step 7. Mix a batch of five-minute epoxy cement, and completely coat the bullet-head shape (top, sides, and bottom) up to the thread area. *Note: Be careful not to cover any of the thread with the cement.*

Step 8. After the cement starts to set, place the Styrofoam eyes in position, and apply a second coat of cement over the head and eyes. Allow it to dry.

Step 9. After the cement is dry, cut away the thread at the hook bend that held the materials in position. The pattern is now complete.

Gene's Feathered Eel

Origin:	United States
Originator:	Gene Kugach
Used for:	Most saltwater game fish; also muskie and northern pike

Designed to represent a saltwater eel, this pattern should be fished slowly on a sinking line or trolled on a floater or slow-sink line.

Thread	Black
Hook	Mustad 92676, size 1/0 to 2/0
Tail	2 6-inch-long grizzly saddle hackles, sandwiched by 4 (2 per side) 3-inch-long black saddle hackles, sandwiched by 2 more (1 per side) slightly shorter yellow saddle hackles
Cheeks	Orange marabou blood feather
Collar	Black hackle
Head	Oversize, black thread
Eyes	1/4-inch-diameter white Styrofoam with black centers

Step 1. Wrap the hook shank with thread to the bend of the hook, and tie in the two 6-inch-long grizzly saddle hackles.

Step 2. Add the four black saddle hackles (two per side) and a yellow saddle hackle on each side of the grizzly hackles.

Step 3. Add the orange marabou cheeks on each side of the tail.

Step 4. Tie in a black hackle, palmer it with a few close wraps, and tie it back collar style.

Step 5. Form a neat oversize head with the thread, and tie off with a whip finish.

Step 6. Give the head a coat of epoxy cement, and allow it to start setting. Once it thickens, add the Styrofoam eyes. Cover the eyes and the entire head with a second coat of epoxy.

Finger Mullet

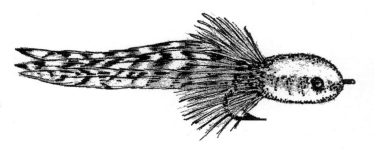

Origin: United States
Originator: Tom Lentz
Demonstrator: George Cik 1986–87
Used for: Tarpon, snook, and redfish

This pattern is fished on top of or just below the surface to imitate a small feeding mullet.

Thread	White	**Collar**	Deer-hair tips
Hook	Mustad 34007, size 1/0 to 2/0	**Head**	White or light-colored deer body hair, spun on the shank (entire length) and trimmed to shape
Tail	4 to 6 3-inch-long grizzly saddle hackles		
Eyes	Glass or bead chain painted black and tied in ¼ inch behind the hook eye	**Coloration**	Pantone permanent markers in olive green and cool gray

Step 1. Attach the thread at the bend of the hook, and tie in four to six 3-inch-long grizzly saddle hackles as the tail. Bring the thread forward to ¼ inch behind the hook eye.

Step 2. Tie in a pair of glass eyes or bead chain eyes (painted black) ¼ inch behind the hook eye, using figure-eight wraps to secure them to the shank.

Step 3. After the eyes are in place, return the thread to the tail tie-in point.

Step 4. Place a bunch of stacked deer body hair with the tips toward the back of the hook, and spin it around the hook shank. Repeat, adding bunches of spun deer hair with the tips removed, until the entire shank is filled, then tie off with a whip finish.

Step 5. Using a pair of scissors, trim the head to shape, exposing the eyes and being careful not to cut off the collar hairs.

Step 6. Color the head using the permanent markers, giving it a cool gray top and an olive stripe on each side.

Brooks Blonde

Origin: United States
Originator: Joe Brooks
Demonstrator: Todd McCagg 1990–91
Used for: Many saltwater species

The Blonde series of patterns was developed by one of the best saltwater fishermen of the twentieth century, Joe Brooks. The series includes the Argentine Blonde, Blushing Blonde, Honey Blonde, Hot Orange Blonde, Irish Blonde, and Platinum Blonde, just to mention a few. They are simple patterns to tie.

Thread	Black	**Wing**	White or yellow bucktail
Hook	Mustad 36890, size 3/0	**Head**	Black thread
Body	Wide embossed silver or gold tinsel		

Step 1. Lay down a thread base, stopping at the hook bend, and tie in a short piece of wide embossed silver or gold tinsel. Bring the thread forward about one-third of the hook shank.

Step 2. Wrap the wide embossed silver or gold tinsel, forward one-third of the hook shank.

Step 3. Tie in a sparse bunch of white or yellow bucktail on top of the shank, with the tips extending about half the shank length behind the hook bend.

Step 4. Continue wrapping the shank forward with the wide embossed silver or gold tinsel to about $^1/_8$ to $^3/_{16}$ inch behind the hook eye. Secure the tinsel with your thread, and snip off any excess.

Step 5. On top of the shank, tie in another sparse bunch of white or yellow bucktail, with the tips slightly shorter than the previous bucktail that was tied in.

Step 6. Form a neat head with the thread, and tie off with a whip finish. Give the head a couple coats of epoxy or head cement.

Mono Body Honey Blonde

Origin: United States
Originator: Joe Brooks
Demonstrator: Bill Somerville 1985–86
Used for: Many saltwater species

The recipe below is a modification of the basic Blonde pattern to give the fly a more durable body.

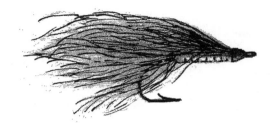

Thread	Black	**Body**	Mono over wide embossed gold tinsel	
Hook	Mustad 34007, size 1/0 to 3/0	**Wing**	Yellow bucktail	
Tail	Yellow bucktail	**Head**	Black thread	

Step 1. Lay down a thread base, stopping at the hook bend, and tie in a sparse bunch of yellow bucktail, followed by a short piece of wide embossed gold tinsel and a short piece of clear monofilament line. Bring the thread forward to about $1/8$ to $3/16$ inch behind the hook eye. *Note: The tail length should equal the hook length.*

Step 2. Wrap the wide embossed gold tinsel forward, and secure it with your thread. Remove any excess material.

Step 3. Wrap the monofilament line forward over the wide embossed gold tinsel, and secure it with your thread. Remove any excess material.

Step 4. Tie in a sparse bunch of yellow bucktail on top of the shank, with the tips extending slightly less than the tail tips.

Step 5. Form a neat head with the thread, and tie off with a whip finish. Give the head a couple coats of epoxy or head cement.

CHAPTER 3

Wet-Fly Patterns

Bloody Butcher

Origin: United Kingdom
Originator: Mr. Moon
Revised by: Mr. Jewhurst
Demonstrator: Gene Kugach 1992–93
Used for: Trout, panfish

The Butcher pattern originated in Tunbridge Wells, United Kingdom, around 1836 and was first tied by two gentleman who were great friends and ardent fly fishermen. The pattern was originally called Moon's Fly, named after Mr. Moon, its originator, who was a local butcher. Mr. Moon tied the pattern to represent the butcher's trade, with the red tail representing the meat the butcher cut and the blue-black wing the apron he wore.

The original Butcher pattern was tied with a black hackle beard, which was revised by Mr. Jewhurst (a friend of Mr. Moon's), who substituted red hackle for the black hackle at a later date to represent blood, giving rise to the name Bloody Butcher.

There are other variations of the Butcher pattern, such as the Kingfisher Butcher, Hardy's Gold Butcher, Irish Butcher, and Canary Butcher, which are also excellent trout flies. The Butcher patterns have been around for a long time and still work very well today when fished deep in the early part of the season.

Thread	Black	**Rib**	Oval silver tinsel
Hook	Mustad 3906B, size 10 to 16 or 8 for sea trout	**Beard**	Red hackle fiber or spun hackle
Tail	Red ibis, red quill segments, or red hackle fiber	**Wing**	Blue-black section of secondary wing feather from a mallard duck or crow
Body	Flat silver tinsel	**Head**	Black thread

Step 1. Lay down a base of thread about $3/32$ inch behind the hook eye back to the bend of the hook.

Step 2. Tie in the tail (length equal to hook shank).

Step 3. Take the thread back down the shank (midway), and tie in the flat silver tinsel and the oval tinsel rib, going back to the bend and then bringing your thread forward behind the eye.

Step 4. Wrap the shank with the flat silver tinsel, going forward, and rib it with the oval tinsel. Secure them with the thread.

Step 5. Tie in the red hackle fiber beard under the shank (beard length equal to body length), and secure it with the thread. *Note: In some pattern instructions, the beard can be tied in after the wing (using a red hackle feather), giving it a few wraps and then collaring it back.*

Step 6. On the top of the hook shank, tie in two wing segments (width equal to the gap of the hook), with the length of the wing ending just beyond the hook bend.

Step 7. Form a neat head with your thread, and tie off.

Grizzly King

Origin: United Kingdom
Originator: John Wilson
Demonstrator: Gene Kugach 1995–96
Used for: Trout, panfish

The Grizzly King is one of the many older patterns that have been around for a number of years and are still used extensively for trout fishing. It's a simple pattern that can be tied as a wet fly, dry fly, or streamer pattern. The recipe below is for the wet-fly version.

Thread	Black	**Body**	Green floss
Hook	Mustad 3906B, size 8 to 12	**Rib**	Oval gold tinsel
Tip (optional)	Oval gold tinsel	**Wing**	Gray mallard breast
Tail	Scarlet goose, swan, or hackle fibers	**Hackle**	Grizzly

Step 1. Lay down a base of black thread, stopping just before the hook bend.

Step 2. (Optional) Tie in a piece of oval tinsel, making three wraps back around the bend and returning to the tie-in point to form the tip. Don't snip off the excess; it will be used later for the body ribbing.

Step 3. Tie in the tail (length equal to hook shank) in front of the tip on top of the hook shank, and bring your thread forward to within 1/8 inch of the hook eye. *Note: If you didn't add the tip, tie in the oval tinsel after you tie in the tail. Then bring your thread forward.*

Step 4. Tie in the green floss behind the eye, and form the body by wrapping the shank back to the tail and then forward to the tie-in point.

Step 5. Rib the body with the oval tinsel, bringing it forward and securing it with the thread.

Step 6. Tie in the wing (length equal to shank and tail) on top of the shank, using sections of a mallard duck breast feather.

Step 7. Tie in a grizzly hackle beard style, and form a neat head, tying off with a whip finish.

Rio Grande King

Origin: United States
Demonstrator: Gene Kugach 1996–97
Used for: Trout, panfish

The Rio Grande King is one of the many older patterns that have been around for a number of years and is still used extensively for trout fishing. It's a simpler pattern that can be tied as a wet fly, a dry fly, or as a streamer. The following recipe is for the wet-fly version.

Thread	Black	**Body**	Black chenille	
Hook	Mustad 3906B, size 8 to 12	**Beard**	Yellow or brown hen hackle	
Tail	Yellow hackle fibers	**Wings**	White goose or duck matched wing quill segments	
Tip	Fine gold tinsel			

Step 1. Lay down a base of black thread, stopping just before the hook bend.

Step 2. Tie in the tail (yellow hackle fibers equal to length of hook shank) on top of the hook shank.

Step 3. Tie in a piece of gold tinsel at the same tie-in point as the tail, and form a tapered tip (going forward) about 3/16 inch long.

Step 4. Tie in a piece of black chenille in front of the tip, and bring your thread forward to within 1/8 inch of the hook eye. Form the body by wrapping the chenille forward around the shank. Secure it with the thread, then snip off the excess chenille.

Step 5. Tie in a yellow or brown hackle feather for the beard, using one of the following methods:

Method 1: Strip off the barbules and fluff on one side and the fluff on the bottom of the feather on the opposite side. Tie in the hackle by the tip end, and give it two to three wraps around the shank. Using your fingers, pull the hackle fibers down so they are below the hook shank, and then secure them with the thread. Cut away the remainder.

Method 2: Strip off a small bunch of hackle barbules from the feather and tie them in under the shank in front of the body.

Step 6. Tie in a pair of matched wing segments on top of the shank in front of the hackle. *Note: Wing segments should be the length of the hook and as wide as the hook gape, in the down position, with the tips pointing inward. Use two loose wraps over the wings, and pull down with your bobbin while holding the wings securely in position, then make a few additional wraps before releasing the wings.*

Step 7. Cut off the excess material, and form a neat head with your thread, tying off with a whip finish.

Zulu

Origin: United Kingdom
Demonstrator: Gene Kugach 1988–89
Used for: Trout, panfish

The Zulu wet-fly pattern was first developed in the United Kingdom and is considered a standard there. The pattern has been around for quite a number of years and is a proven fish catcher. It's a very dependable pattern to use for both trout and panfish, as well as other types of game fish, when most other patterns fail to produce. It's not a difficult pattern to tie, making it a favorite of many fly fishermen.

Thread	Black and bright red (optional)	**Body**	Black wool, seal, or ostrich herl
Hook	Mustad 3906B, size 10 to 16	**Collar**	Black saddle hackle
Tail	Red wool	**Head**	Black or bright red thread
Rib	Fine flat silver tinsel, followed with a palmered black hackle		

Step 1. Wrap the shank with thread up to the bend of the hook. Tie in a short piece (slightly past the hook bend) of red wool for the tail.

Step 2. At the same point, tie in a black hackle, followed by a short piece of fine silver tinsel. Both will be used later in the pattern construction.

Step 3. Form the body by using black wool, black seal dubbing, or black ostrich herl (tier's choice). Wrap the body to within 1/8 inch behind the hook eye.

Step 4. Rib the body with the silver tinsel, using equally spaced wraps. Secure it with the thread, and remove the excess.

Step 5. Fold back the barbules of the black hackle, and then palmer it through the body between the tinsel wraps. Secure it with the thread, and remove the excess.

Step 6. Tie in a black saddle hackle for the collar. Make about three or four wraps of the hackle around the shank, securing the wraps with the thread (collar style), and then cutting off the excess. *Note: At this point, if you elect to have a red head on the pattern, tie off and tie in the red thread.*

Step 7. Using the thread, build a small, neat head, and tie off with a whip finish. Coat the head with head cement or epoxy.

Blue Zulu

Origin: United Kingdom
Demonstrator: Gene Kugach 1988–89
Used for: Trout, panfish

The Blue Zulu wet-fly pattern was also developed in the United Kingdom and is a proven standard there. The pattern is different from the standard Zulu pattern in appearance as well as construction.

Thread	Black and bright red	**Body**	Black ostrich herl or black dubbing
Hook	Mustad 3906B, size 10 to 16	**Collar**	Bright blue saddle hackle with long fibers
Tag	Fine silver wire	**Head**	Bright red thread
Tail	Red wool		

Step 1. Wrap the shank with black thread up to the bend of the hook. Tie in a short piece of fine silver wire, and give it three to four wraps around the bend and then back to the tie-in point to form the tag. Secure the wire with the thread, and snip off the excess.

Step 2. Tie in a short piece of red wool (slightly past the hook bend) for the tail.

Step 3. Form the body by using the black ostrich herl or black dubbing. Use close wraps if you use the herl, and wrap the herl body to within $1/8$ inch behind the hook eye.

Step 4. Tie in the bright blue saddle hackle for the collar. Make about three or four wraps of the hackle around the shank, securing the wraps with the thread (collar style), and then cutting off the excess material. Tie off and tie in the red thread.

Step 5. Use the red thread to build a small, neat head, and tie off with a whip finish. Coat the head with head cement or epoxy.

Weeney Macsweeney

Origin: United Kingdom
Originator: Dick Walker
Demonstrator: Gene Kugach 1988–89
Used for: Trout, panfish

The Weeny Macsweeney wet-fly pattern was first developed in the United Kingdom from a similar pattern called the Sweeney Todd and is considered a standard in the U.K. It's not a difficult pattern to tie.

Thread	Black	**Body**	Rear two-thirds: Black floss, ribbed with silver wire
Hook	Mustad 3906B, size 10 to 16		Front third: Fluorescent magenta floss
Tag	Fine silver wire	**Wing**	Black squirrel tail (sparse)
Rib	Fine silver wire	**Collar**	Scarlet saddle hackle (long fibered)
		Head	Black thread

Step 1. Wrap the shank with black thread up to the bend of the hook. Tie in a 6-inch-long piece of fine silver wire, and give it three to four wraps around the bend and then back to the tie-in point to form the tag. Secure the wire with the thread.

Step 2. Tie in the black floss, and wrap the rear two-thirds of the hook shank with the floss. Rib the floss with the silver wire, and snip off the excess. *Note: Use evenly spaced wraps when ribbing the floss with the wire.*

Step 3. Tie in the magenta floss, and wrap the remaining third of the shank, stopping at about $1/8$ inch behind the hook eye. Secure the floss with your thread, and snip off the excess.

Step 4. Tie in a sparse bunch of black squirrel tail on top of the shank as the wing. Remove the excess, and give the tie-in point a drop of head cement.

Step 5. Tie in the scarlet saddle hackle, and give it two to three wraps in front of the wing to form the collar. Secure it back with the thread, and snip off the excess.

Step 6. Using the thread, build a small, neat head, and tie off with a whip finish. Coat the head with head cement or epoxy.

Red Tailed Invicta

Origin: United Kingdom
Originator: James Odgen
Demonstrator: Jerry Wasil 1987–88
Used for: Trout

The Red Tailed Invicta pattern is a variation of original Invicta, which was designed by James Ogden to represent an adult sedge fly. Extra thick hackling, body and throat, forces the fly to the surface, which creates a surface disturbance, making it an excellent attractor pattern.

Thread	Olive	**Body**	Yellow seal fur or wool
Hook	Mustad 3906B, size 8 to 14	**Throat**	Blue jay or dyed guinea hen fibers
Tail	Red floss or wool	**Wing**	Hen pheasant tail segments
Rib	Fine oval gold tinsel	**Head**	Olive thread
Hackle	Ginger brown or light red cock body hackle, palmered over the body		

Step 1. Lay down a thread base, stopping just before the hook bend.

Step 2. Tie in the red floss or wool tail (length equal to hook shank).

Step 3. Tie in a piece of oval gold tinsel and a ginger brown or light red cock body hackle at the tail tie-in point.

Step 4. Using yellow seal fur or wool, dub in the body, going forward to within $1/8$ inch of the hook eye.

Step 5. Rib the entire body forward with the oval tinsel, using equally spaced wraps, followed by the ginger brown or light red cock body hackle over the tinsel rib. Secure both with the thread, and snip off any excess material.

Step 6. Tie in the blue jay or dyed guinea hen fibers (length of fibers equal to body length) under the shank in front of the body as the beard. *Note: The beard can also be tied in using the entire feather collar style rather than feather segments.*

Step 7. Tie in the wing (length equal to shank and tail) on top of the shank, using sections of a hen pheasant tail feather.

Step 8. Form a neat head, and tie off with a whip finish.

Spitfire

Origin: United States
Originator: Dan Gapen
Demonstrators: Scott Hodlmair 1985–86
Jerry Wasil 1988–89
Used for: Trout, panfish

The Spitfire pattern is a wet fly that can be used for both trout and panfish. It has proven to be an excellent producer for those who have used it and is worth the time involved to tie it.

Thread	Black		**Body**	Black chenille
Hook	Mustad 3906B or 79580, size 8 to 14		**Hackle**	Guinea hen (collared)
			Head	Black thread
Tail	Red goose or duck quill segment			
Rib	Fine oval gold tinsel with a dark brown hackle, palmered over the body			

Step 1. Lay down a thread base, stopping just before the hook bend.

Step 2. Tie in the red goose or duck quill segment tail (length equal to hook shank).

Step 3. Tie in a piece of fine oval gold tinsel and a dark brown hackle at the tail tie-in point.

Step 4. Using black chenille, wrap in the body, going forward to within $1/8$ inch of the hook eye.

Step 5. Rib the entire body forward with the fine oval tinsel, using equally spaced wraps, followed by the dark brown hackle over the tinsel rib. Secure both with the thread, and snip off any excess.

Step 6. Tie in the guinea hen feather (length of fibers equal to body length) in front of the body, and give it a few wraps. Pull back on the feather fibers, and collar them back with your thread. Snip off any excess material.

Step 7. Form a neat head, and tie off with a whip finish.

Porcupine

Origin: United States
Originator: Don Reinhardt
Demonstrator: Don Reinhardt 1991–92
Used for: Trout, panfish

The Porcupine pattern was developed by Don Reinhardt of the Chicago Fly Fishers. It can be tied as either a floater or a sinker-type wet fly and can be used for both trout and panfish. The pattern has proven to be an excellent producer for those who have used it and is worth the time involved to tie it.

Thread	Black	**Hackle**	Badger hackle, palmered over the body
Hook	Mustad 3261 (floater) or 9672 (sinker), size 8 to 12	**Body**	Dark brown lamb's wool spun along the shank like deer hair
Weight (optional)	.025 lead wire	**Collar**	Guinea hen
Tail	Guinea hen fibers	**Head**	Black thread

Step 1. Lay down a thread base, stopping just before the hook bend. If you choose to weight the pattern, wrap in the .025 lead wire at this point, and secure it with your thread.

Step 2. Tie in the guinea hen fiber tail on top of the shank at the hook bend (length equal to one-third the hook shank).

Step 3. Tie in a badger hackle at the tail tie-in point.

Step 4. Spin the dark brown lamb's wool along the shank like deer hair, going forward to within $1/8$ inch of the hook eye.

Step 5. Rib the entire body forward with the badger hackle, using equally spaced wraps. Secure it with the thread, and snip off any excess.

Step 6. Tie in the guinea hen feather (length of fibers equal to body length) in front of the body, and give it a few wraps. Pull back on the feather fibers, and collar them back with your thread. Snip off any excess material.

Step 7. Form a neat head, and tie off with a whip finish.

Don's Gill Bug

Origin: United States
Originator: Don Reinhardt
Used for: Trout, panfish

top view

The Gill Bug pattern was developed by Don Reinhardt of the Chicago Fly Fishers. The pattern was not designed to represent any specific insect. However, it does resemble a water spider or water walker, found on most lakes, streams, or rivers. It can be fished as a floater or as a subsurface-type wet fly for both trout and panfish.

side view

Thread	Black	**Legs**	Fine chenille or braided dacron backing (diameter depends on hook size)
Hook	Tiemco TMC 101, size 8 to 12		
Tail	Philoplume	**Head**	Black thread
Body	Black chenille		

Step 1. Lay down a thread base, stopping just before the hook bend.

Step 2. Tie in the Philoplume tail (length equal to hook shank) at the bend.

Step 3. Tie in a short piece of black chenille at the tail tie-in point, and bring your thread to about midshank.

Step 4. Tie in two pieces of fine chenille or braided dacron, using a square knot as the legs. *Note: The fine chenille or dacron diameter can vary depending on hook size.* Adjust the legs, and secure them with the thread, using a couple of figure-eight wraps, then bring your thread forward behind the hook eye.

Step 5. Using the black chenille, wrap in the body, going forward to the hook eye. Secure the chenille with your thread, and remove any excess material.

Step 6. Form a neat head, and tie off with a whip finish. Apply a coat of head cement to the head. Adjust and trim the legs to the proper length, as shown above in the illustration.

Gilly

Origin: United States
Originator: Gene Kugach
Used for: Trout, panfish

The pattern does not represent any specific insect. It's basically an attractor pattern that works well for evening-feeding panfish or trout.

Thread	Black	**Wings**	Blue-black sections from a mallard duck's secondary wing feather (left and right)
Hook	Mustad 3906B, size 8 to 10		
Tail	Mallard flank feather fibers (light green)	**Hackle**	Black neck hackle
Body	Read two-thirds: Yellow or gold floss Front third: Bright red floss	**Head**	Black thread

Step 1. Wrap the shank with thread up to the bend of the hook, and tie in the light green flank feather fibers for the tail (tail equal to one and a half times body length).

Step 2. Tie in a short piece of yellow or gold floss, and form a tapered area two-thirds of the body length. Secure the floss with your thread, and remove any excess.

Step 3. Tie in a piece of red floss, and finish wrapping the remaining third of the body. Snip off any excess materials.

Step 4. Select two segments, left and right, from a pair of duck quills (segments the width of hook gap). Align the tips, shiny sides out, and tie the segments on top of the shank with the tips going back toward the hook bend. Trim off any excess materials, and bring your thread forward.

Step 5. Tie in a black neck hackle (fibers the width of hook gap), and make about two to three wraps around the shank in front of the wings. Secure the wraps with your thread, and cut off any excess. Using the thread, collar back the hackle and build a small neat head. Tie off with a whip finish.

Black Reaper

Origin: United States
Originator: Gene Kugach
Used for: Trout, panfish

The pattern was designed to represent any small, black insects often seen flying over the water surface. It's an excellent pattern for evening-feeding panfish or trout.

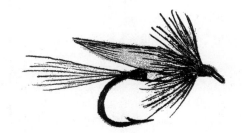

Thread	Black	**Wings**	Gray duck quill segments
Hook	Mustad 3906B, size 8 to 10	**Hackle**	Black neck hackle
Tail	Yellow hackle fibers	**Head**	Black thread
Body	Rear third: Bright red floss Front two-thirds: Black floss, ribbed with a fine flat silver Flashabou strand		

Step 1. Wrap the shank with thread up to the bend of the hook, and tie in the yellow hackle fibers for the tail (tail equal to one and a half times body length).

Step 2. Tie in a short piece of bright red floss, and form a tapered butt one-third of the body length. Secure the floss with your thread, and remove any excess.

Step 3. Tie in a piece of fine flat Flashabou and a piece of black floss. Finish wrapping the remaining two-thirds of the body with the black floss, forming a cigar-shaped body, and rib it with the silver Flashabou. Snip off any excess materials.

Step 4. Now add the wings. Select two segments, left and right, from a pair of gray duck quills (segments the width of hook gap). Align the tips, shiny sides out, and tie the segments on top of the shank with the tips going back toward the hook bend. Trim off any excess materials, and bring your thread forward.

Step 5. Tie in a black neck hackle (fibers the width of hook gap), and make about two to three wraps around the shank in front of the wings. Secure the wraps with your thread, and cut off any excess. Using the thread, collar back the hackle and build a small neat head. Tie off with a whip finish.

Red Hackle

Origin: United Kingdom
Demonstrator: Gene Kugach 1989–99
Used for: Trout, panfish

The Red Hackle wet-fly pattern has been around for years and is a very dependable pattern for trout, panfish, and other types of game fish. It's not difficult to tie.

Thread	Black and bright red 6/0 prewaxed thread	**Body**	Bronze peacock herl
		Collar	Furnace hen hackle
Hook	Mustad 3906 or Tiemco TMC 3769, size 12 to 14	**Head**	Bright red thread
Rib	Fine flat gold tinsel		

Step 1. Starting with the black thread, wrap the shank up to the bend of the hook.

Step 2. Tie in a short piece of fine gold tinsel, which will be used later in the pattern construction.

Step 3. Form the body from a bronze peacock herl, wrapping the body to within $1/8$ inch behind the hook eye.

Step 4. Rib the body with the gold tinsel, using equally spaced wraps. Secure it with the thread, and remove the excess.

Step 5. Tie in a furnace hen hackle for the collar. Make about three or four wraps around the shank, securing the wraps with the thread (collar style), and then cutting off the excess.

Step 6. Tie off the black thread with a whip finish, and tie in the red thread.

Step 7. Use the red thread to build a small, neat head and tie off with a whip finish. Coat the head with head cement or epoxy.

The Patriot

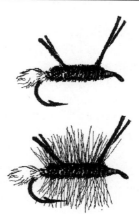

Origin: United States
Originator: Don Reinhardt
Used for: Panfish, trout

The Patriot was designed by Don Reinhardt of the Chicago Fly Fishers as a bluegill pattern. It can be tied weighted or unweighted, fully dressed or partially dressed. When tied weighted, the fly swims upright. When tied unweighted, it stays just below the surface, even when thoroughly soaked. The partially dressed version is tied by eliminating the hackle palmered over the body.

Thread	Black and bright red		**Body**	Silver Doctor blue fine chenille or acrylic rug yarn
Hook	Mustad 9671, size 10		**Legs**	Braided dacron backing (20 pound-test), colored red with a red permanent marker
Weight	Fine lead wire			
Tail	White Philoplume			
Hackle	Fine white saddle		**Head**	Bright red thread

Step 1. Lay down a thread base from above the barb to within $1/8$ inch of the hook eye.

Step 2. Apply four turns of the lead wire, ending about $3/16$ inch behind the hook eye. Secure the wire with your thread at the front and the back, and return the thread to above the hook barb.

Step 3. Tie in a wisp of white Philoplume as the tail, extending about $1/4$ inch beyond the hook bend, and bring your thread back behind the hook eye.

Step 4. Tie in a piece of the Silver Doctor blue fine chenille or acrylic rug yarn behind the eye on top of the lead wire and shank, bringing the thread back to the tail tie-in point. Allow it to hang until it is used later in the pattern construction to form the body.

Step 5. Tie in a fine white saddle hackle by the tip $1/32$ inch forward of the tail, and allow it to hang until it is used later in the pattern.

Step 6. Take two 3-inch pieces of 20 pound-test braided dacron backing for the legs, and tie them in at the center of each piece on the sides of the shank behind the lead wire. Then color each strand with a red permanent marker.

Step 7. Wind the body material forward, ending one or two turns ahead of the front legs. Secure the material with your thread, and remove any excess.

Step 8. Palmer the white hackle over the body, again ending one or two turns ahead of the front legs. Secure the material with the thread, and remove any excess.

Step 9. Tie off the black thread, and replace it with the bright red thread. Use the red thread to form a neat, prominent head, and tie off with a whip finish.

Step 10. Give the head a coat of head cement or epoxy, and allow it to dry. Then trim the legs with a pair of scissors, leaving the front legs slightly longer than the rear legs.

McRey's Honey

Origin: United States
Demonstrator: Jerry Wasil 1987–88
Used for: Panfish, trout

A very simple pattern to tie that works well for both trout and panfish. The source of the pattern was the October 1986 issue of *Flyfishing*.

Thread	Yellow	**Thorax**	Two turns of fine orange chenille
Hook	Mustad 9672, size 8 to 14	**Hackle**	Badger (very dark center, dry-fly grade)
Rib	Fine silver mylar tinsel	**Head**	Yellow thread
Body	Yellow floss		

Step 1. Lay down a thread base to a point midway between the hook point and the barb.

Step 2. Tie in a short piece of fine silver mylar tinsel, which will be used to rib the body.

Step 3. Tie in a piece of yellow floss and form a tapered body, going forward to within ¼ inch of the hook eye. Secure the floss with your thread, and snip off any excess material.

Step 4. Use the fine silver mylar tinsel to rib the body, going forward with evenly spaced wraps. Secure it with the thread, and remove any excess material.

Step 5. Tie in a short piece of fine orange chenille, and make two close wraps in front of the body to form the thorax. Secure it with the thread, and remove any excess material.

Step 6. Tie in a dry-fly-grade badger hackle in front of the thorax, and give it a couple of close wraps. *Note: Select a badger hackle with a very dark center.* Secure the hackle with your thread, and snip off any excess material.

Step 7. Form a small, neat head with the yellow thread, and give it a coat of head cement or epoxy. Allow it to dry.

Coachman

Origin: United Kingdom
Demonstrators: Warren Wormann 1987–88
Jerry Wasil 1990–91
Used for: Trout

A very old pattern that was devised in England and is still
one of the most popular patterns used for trout.

Thread	Black		**Body**	Bronze peacock herl tied full
Hook	Mustad 3906 or 3906B, size 6 to 16		**Wings**	White duck quill sections
Tag (optional)	Gold flat tinsel		**Hackle**	Coachman brown tied collar style
Rib (optional)	Fine gold wire		**Head**	Black thread

Step 1. Lay down a base of black thread, stopping just before the hook bend.

Step 2. (Optional) Tie in a piece of gold tinsel, and form the tag by wrapping slightly back past the bend with a couple of wraps and returning with another couple of wraps to the tie-in point. Snip off any excess material.

Step 3. (Optional) Tie in a short piece of fine gold wire, which will be used to rib the body, at the same tie-in point as the tinsel.

Step 4. Tie in a couple of bronze peacock herls, and form the body by wrapping the herls forward around the shank to within $3/16$ inch of the hook eye. Secure the herl with the thread, and snip off the excess material.

Step 5. Using the fine gold wire, rib the body with evenly spaced wraps over the herl. Wrap the wire in the opposite direction from the way you wrapped in the herl.

Step 6. Tie in a pair of matched white duck quill sections on top of the shank in front of the body. *Note: Wing segments should be the length of the hook and as wide as the hook gape, in the down position, with the tips pointing inward. Use two loose wraps over the wings, and pull down with your bobbin while holding the wings securely in position, then make a few additional wraps before releasing the wings.*

Step 7. Tie in a Coachman brown hackle in front of the wings, and make a couple of close wraps. Secure it with your thread, snip off any excess material, and collar back the hackle.

Step 8. Form a neat head with your thread, and tie off with a whip finish.

Rubber Hackle Bluegill

Origin: United States
Demonstrator: Len Eckerly 1987–88
Used for: Panfish

A simple wet-fly pattern that works well for bluegill and most any other panfish. The rubber hackle tail and wings give it a lot of movement when fished with the short jerks that most panfish can't resist.

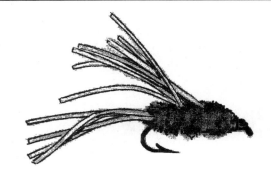

Thread	Body color	Body	Medium chenille (color tier's choice)
Hook	Mustad 79580, size 2 to 6	Hackles	Fine white rubber hackle strands
Tail	Fine white rubber hackle strands	Head	Body-color thread

Step 1. Lay down a thread base to the bend of the hook.

Step 2. Fold two or three 4-inch strands of fine white rubber hackle in half around the thread, and tie them in as the tail.

Step 3. Tie in a 6-inch-long piece of chenille (color tier's choice) at the tail tie-in point, and advance the thread forward about one-third of the shank length.

Step 4. Fold two or three 4-inch strands of fine white rubber hackle in half around the thread, and tie them in on top of the shank, securing them in place with a couple of figure-eight wraps. Advance the thread forward to about $^{3}/_{16}$ inch behind the hook eye, and repeat the same process. *Note: Once the hackles are secured, you can pull them into a side position (two or three on a side) or leave them on top as a wing.*

Step 5. Wrap the shank with the chenille, going forward with tight, close wraps to form the body. Secure the chenille with your thread, and remove any excess material.

Step 6. Form a neat head, and tie off with a whip finish. Give the head a coat of head cement or epoxy, and allow it to dry. You can trim the rubber hackles (tail and wing) to the shank length if necessary.

Silver Doctor

Origin: United States
Demonstrator: George Cik 1986–87, 1987–89
Used for: Trout

A very old pattern that dates back to the 1860s or '70s, when bright, colorful flies were extremely productive on wild fish. The married wings on this pattern are the classic style of tying for both trout and salmon flies.

Thread	Black	**Wings**	4 married quill segments layered from top to bottom as follows: mottled turkey quill, Silver Doctor blue goose quill, scarlet goose quill, yellow goose quill
Hook	Mustad 3906 or 3906B, size 6 to 14		
Tail	Golden pheasant tippets		
Body	Flat silver tinsel		
Beard	Silver Doctor blue hackle fibers	**Head**	Black thread

Step 1. Lay down a base of thread to the bend of the hook.

Step 2. Tie in a bunch of golden pheasant tippets as the tail (length equal to hook shank).

Step 3. Tie in the flat silver tinsel at the tail tie-in point, and then bring your thread forward behind the hook eye.

Step 4. Wrap the shank with the flat silver tinsel, going forward. Secure it with the thread, and remove any excess material.

Step 5. Tie in the blue hackle fiber beard under the shank (beard equal to body length), and secure it with the thread. *Note: In some pattern instructions, the beard can be tied in after the wings, giving it a few wraps and then collaring it back.*

Step 6. Using narrow segments from a mottled turkey quill, Silver Doctor blue goose quill, scarlet goose quill, and yellow goose quill, build a pair of wings by marrying the quill segments together. Each segment is married to the other in the following order:
Top segment: Mottled turkey quill
2nd segment: Silver Doctor blue goose quill
3rd segment: Scarlet goose quill
Last segment: Yellow goose quill

Step 7. After the two wings are assembled, tie them in on the top of the hook shank, with the length of the wing ending to the end of the tail.

Step 8. Form a neat head with your thread, and tie off with a whip finish.

Parmachene Belle

Origin: United States
Originator: Henry P. Wells
Demonstrator: George Cik 1985–86, 1988–89
Used for: Panfish, trout

The pattern was designed by Henry P. Wells back in 1878 and was named for the lake it was used in: Parmachene Lake in the state of Maine. The married wings on this pattern are the classic style of tying for both trout and salmon flies.

Thread	Black	**Body**	Yellow floss
Hook	Mustad 3906 or 3906B, size 6 to 14	**Beard**	Red and white hackle barbules, mixed
Tail	Red and white hackle barbules, mixed	**Wings**	Married quill segments: top quarter red, bottom three-quarters white
Rib	Flat gold tinsel	**Head**	Black thread

Step 1. Lay down a base of thread to the bend of the hook.

Step 2. Tie in a bunch of red and white hackle barbules (mixed) as the tail (length equal to hook shank).

Step 3. Tie in the flat gold tinsel at the tail tie-in point, as well as a short piece of yellow floss, and then bring your thread forward behind the eye.

Step 4. Wrap the shank with the yellow floss, going forward. Secure it with the thread, and remove any excess material.

Step 5. Rib the body with the flat gold tinsel, using equally spaced wraps. Secure it with the thread, and remove any excess.

Step 6. Tie in a bunch of mixed red and white hackle barbules under the shank as the beard (beard equal to body length), and secure it with the thread. *Note: In some pattern instructions, the beard can be tied in after the wings, giving it a few wraps and then collaring it back.*

Step 7. Build a pair of wings by marrying red and white quill segments together as follows: top quarter red, bottom three-quarters white.

Step 8. After the two wings are assembled, tie them in on the top of the hook shank, with the length of the wings ending just short of the tail end.

Step 9. Form a neat head with your thread, and tie off with a whip finish.

Partridge & Orange Soft Hackle

Origin: United Kingdom
Demonstrators: Scott Hodlmair 1985–86
Todd McCagg 1990–91
Used for: Trout

This pattern is an example of a soft-hackle fly, used and recommended by many fly fishermen. It is also popular in other colors, such as green or yellow body tied with a matching thread.

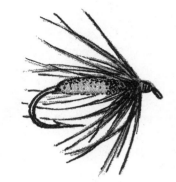

Thread	Orange	**Hackle**	Brown partridge
Hook	Mustad 3906 or 3906B, size 6 to 14	**Head**	Orange thread
Body	Rear two-thirds: Orange floss Front third: Mixed black and brown hare's mask dubbing		

Step 1. Lay down a base of thread to the bend of the hook.

Step 2. Tie in a short piece of orange floss, and form a tapered body, going forward and covering approximately two-thirds of the hook shank. Secure the floss with your thread, and snip off any excess material.

Step 3. Using a mixture of black and brown hare's mask dubbing, cover the remaining hook shank, going forward to within 1/8 inch of the hook eye.

Step 4. Tie in a brown partridge hackle by the tip in front of the body, and give it a couple of wraps around the shank. Collar it back, secure it with the thread, and snip off any excess material.

Step 5. Form a neat head with your thread, and tie off with a whip finish.

Professor

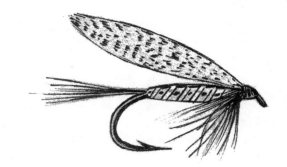

Origin: United States
Demonstrators: Roger Hetzke 1991–92
                   Steve Almgreen 1998–99
Used for: Trout

The Professor wet-fly pattern has been around for many years and is a proven fish catcher. It's dependable for use on both trout and salmon, and its bright colors make it easy to see when sight fishing in clear streams or lakes.

Thread	Black	**Body**	Yellow floss
Hook	Mustad 3906, size 10 to 16	**Beard**	Brown hen
Tail	Red hackle fibers	**Wing**	Barred mallard duck flank feather fibers
Rib	Fine flat gold tinsel	**Head**	Black thread

Step 1. Lay down a base of thread to the bend of the hook.

Step 2. Tie in a bunch of red hackle fibers as the tail (length equal to hook shank).

Step 3. Tie in the fine flat gold tinsel at the tail tie-in point, as well as a short piece of yellow floss, and then bring your thread forward behind the hook eye.

Step 4. Wrap the shank with the yellow floss, going forward and forming a tapered body. Secure it with the thread, and remove any excess material.

Step 5. Rib the body with the fine flat gold tinsel, using equally spaced wraps (about five). Secure it with the thread, and remove any excess.

Step 6. Tie in a bunch of brown hen hackle fibers under the shank as the beard (beard length equal to body length), and secure it with the thread. *Note: In some pattern instructions, the beard can be tied in after the wing, giving it a few wraps and then collaring it back.*

Step 7. Tie in a bunch of barred mallard duck flank feather fibers on top of the shank in front of the body as the wing. The length of the wing should extend to the tip of the tail.

Step 8. Form a neat head with your thread, and tie off with a whip finish.

Ke-He

Origin: Scotland
Originators: Mr. Kemp and Mr. Heddle
Demonstrator: Gene Kugach 1998–99
Used for: Trout

A very old pattern that was devised in Scotland around 1932 and is still one of the most popular patterns used for trout. It was designed to imitate a small bee, which is often blown into lakes and streams.

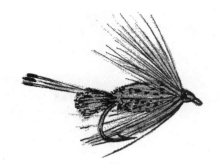

Thread	Black	**Rib**	Fine gold wire
Hook	Mustad 3906 or 3906B, size 10 to 12	**Body**	Bronze peacock herl tied full
		Hackle	Rhode Island black or red tied collar style
Tag	Red yarn or wool		
Tail	Golden pheasant tippet fibers over the red tag	**Head**	Black thread

Step 1. Lay down a base of black thread, stopping just before the hook bend.

Step 2. Tie in a short piece of red yarn or wool as the tag, and snip off any excess material.

Step 3. Tie in a few golden pheasant tippet fibers over the red tag as the tail.

Step 4. Tie in a short piece of fine gold wire, which will be used later to rib the body.

Step 5. Tie in a couple of bronze peacock herls, and form the body by wrapping the herls forward around the shank to within $3/16$ inch of the hook eye. Secure the herl with the thread, and snip off the excess material.

Step 6. Using the fine gold wire, rib the body with evenly spaced wraps over the herl. Wrap the wire in the opposite direction from the way you wrapped in the herl, and snip off the excess material.

Step 7. Tie in a Rhode Island black or red hackle in front of the body, and make a couple of close wraps. Secure it with your thread, snip off any excess material, and collar back the hackle.

Step 8. Form a neat head with your thread, and tie off with a whip finish.

Royal Coachman

Origin: United Kingdom
Demonstrator: Warren Wormann 1987–88
Used for: Trout

A very old pattern that was devised in England and is still one of the most popular patterns used for trout. This pattern can be tied as a dry fly, streamer, nymph, or wet fly.

Thread	Black	**Hackle**	Coachman brown tied down collar style
Hook	Mustad 3906 or 3906B, size 10 to 14	**Wings**	Matched white duck quill sections
Tail	Golden pheasant tippet fibers	**Head**	Black thread
Body	Bronze peacock herl and red floss		

Step 1. Lay down a base of black thread, stopping just before the hook bend.

Step 2. Tie in a few golden pheasant tippet fibers as the tail.

Step 3. Tie in a couple of bronze peacock herls and a short piece of red floss. Starting with the peacock herl, form a ball (butt) at the tail tie-in point, and secure the herl with the thread, bringing the thread forward to within 3/16 inch of the hook eye.

Step 4. Using the red floss, wrap forward over the remaining herl, forming an even body from the rear butt to within 3/16 inch of the hook eye. Secure the floss with the thread, and remove any excess floss. *Note: Do not remove the peacock herl.*

Step 5. Using the remaining peacock herl, form another ball in front of the body. Secure it with the thread, and remove the excess material.

Step 6. Tie in a Coachman brown hackle in front of the body, and make a couple of close wraps. While using one hand to pull the fibers back and down, secure the hackle with your thread collar style. Snip off any excess material.

Step 7. Tie in a pair of matched white duck quill sections on top of the shank in front of the body. *Note: Wing segments should be the length of the hook and as wide as the hook gape, in the down position, with the tips pointing inward. Use two loose wraps over the wings, and pull down with your bobbin while holding the wings securely in position, then make a few additional wraps before releasing the wings.*

Step 8. Form a neat head with your thread, and tie off with a whip finish.

McGinty

Origin: United States
Demonstrator: Steve Almgreen 1997–98
Used for: Trout

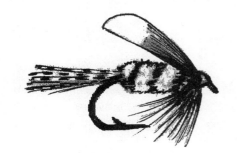

An old American pattern that was devised to represent a wasp. It's still one of the more popular patterns for trout. Also can be tied with a brown or white hairwing.

Thread	Black	**Hackle**	Coachman brown tied collar style
Hook	Mustad 3906 or 3906B, size 8 to 12	**Wings**	Matched sections of white-tipped blue-black mallard duck secondary wing feathers
Tail	Scarlet or red hackle fibers with teal flank feather fibers over the red	**Head**	Black thread
Body	Yellow and black chenille		

Step 1. Lay down a base of black thread, stopping just before the hook bend.

Step 2. Tie in a sparse bunch of scarlet or red hackle fibers, followed by a sparse bunch of teal flank feather fibers over the red fibers as the tail.

Step 3. Tie in a short piece of yellow and a piece of black chenille at the tail tie-in point, and bring your thread forward to within 3/16 inch of the hook eye. Starting with the yellow chenille, make a single wrap forward, followed by a single wrap of the black chenille. Continue alternating the chenille wraps until you complete the body. Then secure the chenilles with your thread, and snip off any excess materials.

Step 4. Tie in a Coachman brown hackle in front of the body, and make a couple of close wraps. Secure the hackle collar style with your thread, and snip off any excess material.

Step 5. Tie in a pair of matched white-tipped blue-black mallard duck secondary wing feather sections on top of the shank in front of the body. *Note: Wing segments should be the length of the hook and as wide as the hook gape, in the down position, with the tips pointing inward. Use two loose wraps over the wings, and pull down with your bobbin while holding the wings securely in position, then make a few additional wraps before releasing the wings.*

Step 6. Form a neat head with your thread, and tie off with a whip finish.

Butcher

Origin: United Kingdom
Demonstrator: Jerry Wasil 1987–88
Used for: Trout

A very old pattern that was devised in England and is still one of the most popular patterns used for trout.

Thread	Black	**Body**	Flat silver tinsel
Hook	Mustad 3906 or 3906B, size 10 to 16	**Hackle**	Black cock or hen tied collar style
Tail	Red hackle fibers	**Wings**	Matched sections of blue-black mallard duck secondary wing feathers
Rib	Oval silver tinsel	**Head**	Black thread

Step 1. Lay down a base of black thread, stopping just before the hook bend.

Step 2. Tie in a sparse bunch of red hackle fibers as the tail.

Step 3. Tie in a short piece of oval silver tinsel (which will be used to rib the body) at the same tie-in point as the tail. Also tie in a short piece of flat silver tinsel at the same point, bringing the thread forward to the hook eye.

Step 4. Starting with the flat silver tinsel, wrap the shank, going forward to within $3/16$ inch of the hook eye. Secure it with your thread, and snip off any excess material.

Step 5. Using the oval silver tinsel, rib the body with evenly spaced wraps over the flat silver tinsel. Wrap the flat silver tinsel in the opposite direction from the way you wrapped in the herl.

Step 6. Tie in a black cock or hen hackle in front of the body, and make a couple of close wraps, collaring back the hackle. Secure it with your thread, and snip off any excess material.

Step 7. Tie in a pair of matched blue-black mallard duck secondary wing feather sections on top of the shank in front of the body. *Note: Wing segments should be the length of the hook and as wide as the hook gape, in the down position, with the tips pointing inward. Use two loose wraps over the wings, and pull down with your bobbin while holding the wings securely in position, then make a few additional wraps before releasing the wings.*

Step 8. Form a neat head with your thread, and tie off with a whip finish.

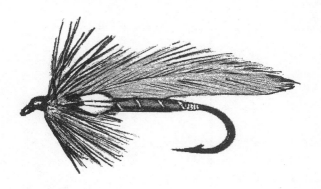

CHAPTER 4

Streamer Patterns

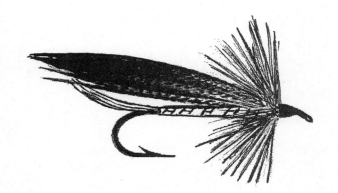

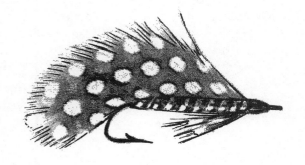

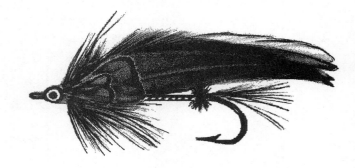

Chief Needabeh

Origin: United States
Originator: Chief Needabeh of the Penobscot tribe
Demonstrator: Gene Kugach 1989–90
Used for: Trout, salmon, steelhead

Excellent pattern for spring trout and fall salmon fishing. A nice-looking pattern that's been around for a while and is not too difficult to tie. It can also be used for largemouth and smallmouth bass.

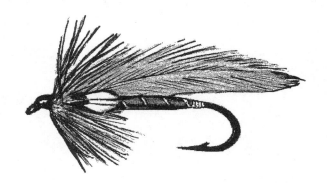

Thread	Black	**Wings**	2 yellow saddle hackles (back-to-back) inside, 2 orange saddle hackles outside
Hook	Mustad 9575, size 2 to 10		
Tag	Flat silver tinsel	**Cheeks**	Jungle cock
Tail (optional)	Red goose fibers	**Hackle**	Yellow hackle with red hackle in front, both wound and collared
Rib	Fine flat silver tinsel		
Body	Red floss	**Head**	Black thread

Step 1. Wrap the shank with black thread up to the hook point. Tie in a 6-inch long piece of flat silver tinsel, and give it three to four wraps going back, and return to the tie-in point to form the tag. Secure the tinsel with the thread.

Step 2. (Optional) Tie in the red goose fibers as the tail in front of the tag (tail length half of body length).

Step 3. Tie in a piece of fine flat silver tinsel at the tail tie-in point to use later as ribbing over the body.

Step 4. Tie in the red floss, and form the body to within 3/16 inch behind the hook eye. Secure the material with your thread, and snip off the excess.

Step 5. Rib the body with the fine flat silver tinsel, using equally spaced wraps, and remove the excess.

Step 6. Tie in the two yellow saddle hackles (back-to-back) inside and the two orange saddle hackles outside as the wings.

Step 7. Tie in the jungle cock cheeks on each side of the wings. The cheeks should be about half the body length with the second eye showing.

Step 8. Tie in the yellow hackle and red hackle in front of the wings. Give both hackles two to three wraps in front of the wing to form the collar. Secure the hackles back collar style with the thread, and snip off the excess.

Step 9. Using the thread, build a neat head, and tie off with a whip finish. Coat the head with head cement or epoxy.

Golden Demon

Origin: New Zealand
Originator: Fred Burnham
Demonstrator: Gene Kugach 1987–88
Used for: Trout, salmon, steelhead

The Golden Demon pattern was first developed in the United Kingdom and brought to the Carns River, New Brunswick and later to the United States in the 1920s. It was later modified by Fred N. Peet of Chicago and C. J. Pray of Eureka, California, into the Demon series of patterns, which includes the Gold, Black, and Silver Demons. The pattern has been around for quite a number of years and is still used on the East Coast around New Hampshire and Connecticut. It's a proven fish catcher

and is a very dependable pattern to use for both trout and salmon. It's not a difficult pattern to tie, making it a favorite of many fly fishermen.

Thread	Black	**Body**	Golden yellow wool or floss
Hook	Mustad 33665A or 9575, size 4 to 12	**Throat**	Hot orange hackle (collared)
		Wings	Bronze mallard flank feathers
Tail	Golden pheasant crest	**Head**	Black thread
Rib	Gold flat tinsel		

Step 1. Wrap the shank with black thread up to the bend of the hook. Tie in the golden pheasant crest as the tail (tail length half of body length).

Step 2. Tie in a piece of gold flat tinsel to use later as ribbing over the body.

Step 3. Tie in the yellow wool or floss, and form a tapered body to within 3/16 inch behind the hook eye. Secure the material with your thread, and snip off the excess.

Step 4. Rib the body with the gold flat tinsel, using equally spaced wraps, and remove the excess.

Step 5. Tie in the hot orange hackle, and give it two to three wraps in front of the body to form the collar. Secure it back collar style with the thread, and snip off the excess.

Step 6. Tie in a pair of bronze mallard flank feathers as the wings on top of the hook shank (wing length equal to length of body plus tail).

Step 7. Using the thread, build a neat head, and tie off with a whip finish. Coat the head with head cement or epoxy.

Crappie Minnow

Origin: United States
Demonstrator: Gene Kugach 1987–88
Used for: Trout, panfish

Excellent pattern for spring crappie or trout fishing. Also can be used for other species, such as striped bass and bluegill. A simple pattern to tie, requiring very few special materials.

Thread	Black	**Body**	White floss or chenille (thin to medium)
Hook	Mustad 3665, 4X long, size 2 to 6	**Throat**	White hackle (collared down)
Tail	Peacock herl to end of hook	**Wings**	2 grizzly hackles
Rib	Medium oval tinsel and one peacock herl	**Topping**	3 or 4 peacock herls
		Head	Black thread

Step 1. Wrap the shank with black thread up to the hook point. Tie in three or four peacock herls as the tail (tail half of body length).

Step 2. Tie in a piece of oval tinsel and one peacock herl at the tail tie-in point to use later as ribbing over the body.

Step 3. Tie in the white floss or chenille, and form a tapered body to within 3/16 inch behind the hook eye. Secure the material with your thread, and snip off the excess.

Step 4. Rib the body with the single peacock herl, using equally spaced wraps, and remove the excess. Then do the same with the single oval tinsel.

Step 5. Tie in the white hackle, and give it two to three wraps in front of the body. Pull down the hackle fibers with your fingers to form the beard under the hook shank, and secure them with the thread. After the beard is secured, snip off the excess.

Step 6. Tie in a pair of grizzly hackle tips as the wings on top of the hook shank (wing length equal to length of body plus tail).

Step 7. Top the wings with three or four peacock herls.

Step 8. Using the thread, build a neat head, and tie off with a whip finish. Coat the head with head cement or epoxy.

Evening Shadow

Origin: United States
Demonstrator: Gene Kugach 1987–88
Used for: Trout

Excellent pattern for spring trout and fall salmon fishing. A nice-looking pattern that's been around for a while and is not too difficult to tie.

Thread	Black	**Throat**	Golden yellow hackle (collared down)
Hook	Mustad 3665A or 9575, size 2 to 6	**Underwings**	Fox squirrel
Tag	Gold mylar tinsel	**Wings**	2 black saddle hackles
Tail	Black hackle fibers	**Topping**	3 or 4 peacock herls
Rib	Gold mylar tinsel	**Cheeks** (optional)	Jungle cock
Body	Black chenille (thin)	**Head**	Black thread

Step 1. Wrap the shank with black thread up to the hook bend. Tie in a 6-inch-long piece of gold mylar tinsel, and give it three to four wraps around the bend and then back to the tie-in point to form the tag. Secure the tinsel with the thread.

Step 2. Tie in black hackle fibers as the tail in front of the tag (tail length half of body length).

Step 3. Tie in a piece of gold mylar tinsel at the tail tie-in point to use later as ribbing over the body.

Step 4. Tie in the black chenille, and form a tapered body to within 3/16 inch behind the hook eye. Secure the material with your thread, and snip off the excess.

Step 5. Rib the body with the gold mylar tinsel, using equally spaced wraps, and remove the excess.

Step 6. Tie in the golden yellow hackle, and give it two to three wraps in front of the body. Pull down the hackle fibers with your fingers to form the beard under the hook shank, and secure them with the thread. After the beard is secured, snip off the excess.

Step 7. Tie in a sparse bunch of fox squirrel as the underwings on top of the hook shank and two black saddle hackles flanking the squirrel as the overwings (wing length equal to length of body plus tail).

Step 8. Top the wings with the three or four peacock herls.

Step 9. (Optional) Tie in the jungle cock cheeks on each side of the wings (cheeks half of body length).

Step 10. Using the thread, build a neat head, and tie off with a whip finish. Coat the head with head cement or epoxy.

Mrs. Dooley

Origin: United States
Originator: Wendell Folkins
Demonstrator: Gene Kugach 1991–92
Used for: Trout

Excellent pattern for spring crappie or trout fishing. Also can be used for other species, such as striped bass and bluegill. Simple pattern to tie, requiring very few special materials.

Thread	Black and red	**Throat**	Red hackle under white bucktail
Hook	Mustad 3907B, size 2 to 6	**Underwing**	Peacock herl
Tail	Red goose or swan quill segment	**Wing**	2 white hackles over 2 black hackles
Body	Black silk, yarn, floss, or chenille	**Shoulder** (Optional)	Jungle cock
Rib	Flat silver tinsel	**Head**	Black thread with a red thread band in middle

Step 1. Lay down a thread base to the bend of the hook.

Step 2. Tie in a small segment of red goose or swan quill as the tail, extending about 1/2 inch beyond the bend.

Step 3. Tie in the flat silver tinsel ribbing at the point where the tail was tied in under the hook shank.

Step 4. If you're using chenille or yarn, also tie it in at the same point as the tinsel and tail, and then bring the thread forward to within 1/4 inch of the eye. Form the body by wrapping forward. If you're using floss, tie in behind the eye and form the body with a double wrap, starting from behind the eye and going back to the tail and then forward.

Step 5. Rib the body with the silver tinsel.

Step 6. Tie in the white bucktail throat under the shank, with the hairs extending beyond the bend of the hook. Then, under the white bucktail, tie in some red hackle fibers.

Step 7. Select six to eight strands of peacock herl, and tie them in as an underwing on top of the hook shank. They should extend just beyond the tail.

Step 8. Tie in the wing, which consists of two black hackles (back-to-back), sandwiched between two white hackles that are a little shorter than the underwing.

Step 9. Tie in the jungle cock shoulders on each side, if desired.

Step 10. Form a neat head with the black and red thread. The head should have a red band in the center.

Aztec

Origin: United States
Originator: Dick Nelson
Used for: Trout

Excellent pattern for trout fishing that can also be used for other species, such as smallmouth and largemouth bass. The pattern requires very few special materials and is not that difficult to tie.

Thread	Black or body yarn color	**Wing yarn**	2 pieces of 1 1/2-inch-long, four-ply acrylic knitting yarn separated into single one-ply strands (color tier's choice)
Hook	Mustad 7957BX, size 4 to 10		
Tail yarn	4 1/2-inch-long, four-ply acrylic knitting yarn (color tier's choice)		
Body yarn	6-inch-long, four-ply acrylic knitting yarn (color tier's choice)	**Head**	Black or body yarn color

Step 1. Lay down a thread base to a point 1/32 to 1/16 inch behind the bend of the hook, and bring the thread forward to behind the eye.

Step 2. Tie in a 6-inch-long piece of four-ply acrylic knitting yarn (body yarn), starting about 1/16 inch behind the eye and under the shank. Secure it under the shank up to the bend, then apply a coat of cement to the shank.

Step 3. Tie in a 4 1/2-inch-long piece of tail yarn on top of the shank by folding it in half around the thread and securing it with tight wraps. Then bring the thread forward to behind the eye.

Step 4. Twist the body yarn about sixteen to twenty times to make it tight, and attach a pair of hackle pliers to the loose end to keep the yarn from untwisting. Apply a coat of thinned cement to the entire shank.

Step 5. While the cement is still wet, wrap the yarn around the shank, covering the thread at the tie-in behind and in front of the tail yarn, while keeping the tail perpendicular to the shank. *Note: If the cement dries before or during the construction of the wing, apply more cement during the tie-in of each wing segment.*

Step 6. Tie in a piece of wing yarn, using the same method as for the tail (except that the body yarn, rather than the thread, will be used to secure it), and advance the yarn a couple of wraps forward for the next wing segment.

Step 7. Repeat, adding seven wing segments at equal intervals, using the body yarn, until the wing is completed. Secure the last body yarn wrap underneath the shank with the thread, and remove the excess.

Step 8. Build a neat, tapered head with the thread, and tie off with a whip finish. Give the head a coat of cement.

Step 9. Remove the pattern from the vise, and use your bodkin to separate the fibers in the wing and tail segments. Then use a fine-toothed comb to comb out the fibers in both the tail and the wing.

Step 10. Trim the wing crest from the front to the back at an angle, using a pair of scissors.

Ducky Darling

Origin: United States
Demonstrator: George Carcao 1988–89
Used for: Trout

Excellent pattern for trout fishing that can also be used for other species. A simple pattern to tie, requiring very few special materials.

Thread	Black		**Throat**	Orange hackle fibers
Hook	Mustad 38941, size 8 to 12		**Wing**	Black squirrel tail or calf tail hair fibers
Tail	Orange hackle fibers		**Shoulders**	Jungle cock
Butt	Orange ostrich herl		**Head**	Black thread
Rib	Fine flat gold tinsel			
Body	Black silk, yarn, or floss			

Step 1. Lay down a thread base to the bend of the hook.

Step 2. Tie in the orange hackle fibers as the tail.

Step 3. Tie in a single orange ostrich herl, and form the butt by giving the herl a couple of wraps. Secure it with the thread, and remove any excess material.

Step 4. After the butt is secured, tie in the flat gold tinsel ribbing under the hook shank, securing it with the thread in front of the butt. Also at the same point, tie in a short piece of black silk or yarn and bring the thread forward to within ¼ inch of the eye. Form the body by wrapping forward. If you're using floss, tie in the floss behind the eye and form the body with a double wrap, starting from behind the eye and going back to the tail and then forward.

Step 5. Rib the body with the gold tinsel.

Step 6. Tie in the white orange hackle fibers under the shank as the throat.

Step 7. Select either a sparse bunch of black squirrel tail or calf tail hairs and tie them in on top of the shank as the wing.

Step 8. Tie in the jungle cock shoulders on each side, if desired.

Step 9. Form a neat head with the black thread and tie off with a whip finish. Give the head a few coats of lacquer to finish the pattern.

Mrs. Simpson

Origin: New Zealand
Demonstrator: George Carcao 1988–89
Used for: Trout

The Simpson pattern is a variation of the Killer pattern originated by Lionel Walker of New Zealand. It's an excellent pattern for trout fishing that is simple to tie and requires very few special materials.

Thread	Black	**Wing**	2 sets of cock ring-necked pheasant body feathers tied on each side of the hook (one set midshank and the other forward behind the eye)
Hook	Mustad 3906B, size 6 to 10		
Tail	Black squirrel tail under cock ring-necked pheasant body feather		
Body	Red or orange wool or floss	**Head**	Black thread

Step 1. Lay down a thread base to the bend of the hook.

Step 2. Tie in a sparse bunch of black squirrel tail hair fibers, over which are tied a pair of small cock ring-necked pheasant body feather tips (one on each side) as the tail.

Step 3. Tie in a short piece of red or orange wool or floss, and wrap the shank midway.

Step 4. Tie in another pair of cock ring-necked pheasant body feather tips (one on each side) that are slightly larger than those used for the tail. *Note: The tips should overlap the tail tie-in point.*

Step 5. Continue wrapping the shank forward to within $1/8$ inch of the hook eye with the red or orange wool or floss. Secure it with the thread, and remove any excess.

Step 6. Tie in another pair of cock ring-necked pheasant body feather tips (one on each side) that are slightly larger than those used at the midway point on the shank. *Note: The tips of these feathers should also overlap the previous set tied in at the midway point.*

Step 7. Form a neat head with the thread, and tie off with a whip finish.

Marvel Matuka

Origin: United States
Demonstrator: Len Eckerly 1984–85
Used for: Trout

A Matuka-style streamer pattern developed to represent various baitfish. It can be tied in assorted colors. The original pattern has been modified here by using an alternative material (marabou) for the wing rather than golden pheasant crests.

Thread	Black	**Wing**	Marabou tufts (color tier's choice)
Hook	Mustad 3665A, size 2	**Beard**	Red hackle fibers
Tail	Red hackle fibers	**Head**	Black thread
Body	Silver tinsel chenille (cloisonné)		

Step 1. Lay down a thread base to the bend of the hook.

Step 2. Tie in a sparse bunch of red hackle fibers (about half length of hook shank) at the bend as the tail.

Step 3. Tie in a 6-inch-piece of silver tinsel chenille (cloisonné) at the tail tie-in point, and bring your thread forward to within $1/8$ inch behind the hook eye.

Step 4. Give the tinsel chenille (cloisonné) a couple of close wraps going forward.

Step 5. Take a sparse bunch of marabou fibers, and tie them in on top of the shank, using the tinsel chenille to secure them in place with a couple of close wraps.

Step 6. Continue adding bunches of marabou tufts along the shank, as in Step 5, until you are within $3/16$ inch behind the hook eye.

Step 7. Tie in a sparse bunch of red hackle fibers under the shank as the beard (beard length half of body length).

Step 8. Form a neat head with the thread, and tie off with a whip finish.

Guinea Fowl Matuka

Origin: United States
Demonstrator: George Cik 1986–87
Used for: Trout

A Matuka-style streamer designed to represent a bait-fish, with seldom used guinea fowl feathers as the wing material. A simple pattern to tie, requiring very few special materials.

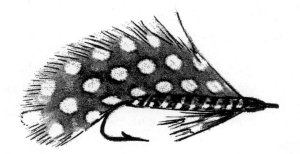

Thread	Black	**Body**	Black chenille or black dubbing
Hook	Mustad 79580, size 4 to 10	**Beard**	Guinea hen feather fibers
Rib	Medium flat silver tinsel over the body with fine copper wire through the wing	**Wing**	Matched pair of guinea hen feathers
		Head	Black thread

Step 1. Lay down a thread base to the hook point, and tie in a piece of medium flat silver tinsel and a piece of fine copper wire. Both will be used later to rib the body and secure the wing.

Step 2. Tie in a piece of black chenille or use black dubbing, and form the body by wrapping the chenille or dubbing forward to about $3/16$ inch behind the hook eye. Remove any excess material.

Step 3. Rib the body with the medium flat silver tinsel, using equally spaced wraps, and remove any excess.

Step 4. Tie in some guinea hen feather fibers as the beard under the hook shank in front of the body (beard fibers equal to hook gape). Remove any excess material.

Step 5. Select a matched pair of guinea hen feathers (length equal to twice the body length), and strip off the fluff at the base. Tie them in on top of the shank in front of the body. Pull the feathers down over the top of the body, and while holding them in position, wrap the fine copper wire forward through the feathers, securing them on top of the body. When you reach the front end of the body, secure the wire with the thread, and remove any excess.

Step 6. Form a neat head with the thread, and tie off with a whip finish. Coat the head with head cement or epoxy.

Zonker

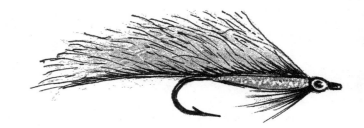

Origin: United States
Demonstrator: George Cik 1984–85
Used for: All larger species

A baitfish imitation that can be used for most large game fish species (bass, pike, muskie, trout, salmon, etc.). Can be tied in various color combinations.

Thread	Black, white, or red		**Beard**	Hackle fibers (color tier's choice)
Hook	Mustad 9674, size 2 to 6		**Wing**	Rabbit fur strip
Underbody options	Tapered yarn, piece of aluminum cut out of a pop can, or Zonker Tape		**Head**	Thread
			Eyes (optional)	White Styrofoam with black centers
Body	Mylar tubing		**Body markings**	Permanent markers

Step 1. Lay down a thread base to the hook point.

Step 2. Form a tapered underbody using yarn, or cut a piece of aluminum from a pop can about ¹/₂ inch wide and as long as the hook shank, with a couple of tabs in the center, as shown below, or use Zonker Tape. *Note: The tabs should be about ³/₁₆ inch long and ¹/₈ inch wide. Tabs are not necessary if you're using Zonker Tape.*

Step 3. If you're using a piece from a pop can, secure the back tab of the underbody with your thread in front of the bend, and return the thread under the foil to within ³/₁₆ of an inch behind the hook eye. Fold the aluminum piece in half over the shank, and crimp it tightly with pliers under the full length of the shank. Secure the front tab with your thread. If you're using Zonker Tape, return your thread to behind the hook eye, and fold the tape in half over the shank.

Step 4. If you're making the underbody from aluminum or Zonker Tape, use scissors to cut the area under the shank to the shape shown below. *Note: The rounded area at the front should be as wide as the mylar tubing when it has the core removed and is flattened.*

Step 5. Take a piece of mylar tubing about ¹/₂ inch longer than the shank, and remove the core material. Slip the tubing over the hook eye and the underbody, and secure the tubing at the front behind the hook eye with your thread.

Step 6. Tie in a rabbit fur strip (about twice the hook length) on top of the shank behind the eye.

Step 7. At the same location, tie in the hackle fibers under the shank as the beard.

Step 8. Using your thread, form a neat, oversize head, and tie off with a whip finish.

Step 9. Tie in your thread at the hook bend. Pull back on the mylar tubing, and secure it with a couple of close, neat wraps. *Note: At this point, you can unravel the tubing at the back end behind the thread.*

Step 10. Pull back on the rabbit fur strip, and secure it on top of the mylar body at the same location as the thread. *Note: Use close neat wraps, and avoid tying down the hair fibers.* After the strip is secured, tie off with a whip finish.

Step 11. Coat the head and the thread at the back with epoxy cement. While the glue is drying, add the Styrofoam eyes, and color the mylar tubing with permanent markers to the desired color pattern. Once it all dries, give the head and the body another coat of epoxy cement.

Gray Ghost

Origin: United States
Originator: Carrie Stevens
Demonstrator: Warren Wormann 1987–88
Used for: Trout

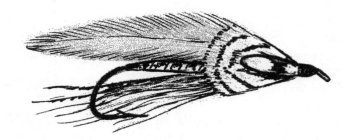

Originated in Maine by Carrie Stevens as a smelt imitation in 1924, this pattern is still a favorite for early-season trout in the northern New England states.

Thread	Black		**Underwing**	Golden pheasant crest full length of body
Hook	Mustad 9575 or 9672, size 2 to 12		**Wing**	4 gray saddle hackles
Rib	Fine flat silver tinsel		**Shoulders**	Silver pheasant body feather, about one-third of the wing length
Body	Golden yellow floss		**Cheeks**	Jungle cock
Beard	4 or 5 peacock herls next to body, followed by white bucktail, then a shorter golden pheasant crest			

Step 1. Lay down a thread base to the bend of the hook.

Step 2. Tie in the fine flat silver tinsel at the bend (under the shank) for the ribbing, which will be used later, and bring your thread forward to the middle of the shank.

Step 3. Tie in a piece of golden yellow floss at mid-shank, and then bring the thread forward to within 3/16 inch behind the hook eye. Form a neat, tapered body by going back and forth with the floss, and then secure it behind the eye with the thread. Remove any excess material.

Step 4. Rib the body with the fine flat silver tinsel, using evenly spaced wraps, and secure it with the thread. Remove any excess material.

Step 5. Add the beard by tying in four or five peacock herls next to body under the shank, followed by a sparse bunch of white bucktail, followed by a shorter golden pheasant crest. *Note: The peacock herl and bucktail should extend beyond the hook bend.*

Step 6. Tie in the underwing, which consists of a golden pheasant crest feather that extends the full length of the body.

Step 7. Tie in the four gray saddle hackles as the wing (saddles about 1 1/2 times the body length).

Step 8. Add the shoulders, using silver pheasant body feathers on each side of the wing. The feathers should be about one-third of the wing length.

Step 9. Add the cheeks, which consist of two jungle cock feathers (one on each side), on top of the shoulders.

Step 10. Form a neat head with the thread, and tie off with a whip finish. *Note: The head should have a red band in the center.*

The Thief

Origin: United States
Originator: Dan Gapen
Demonstrators: Warren Wormann 1988–89
Jerry Wasil 1992–93
Used for: All species

The Thief pattern was designed by Dan Gapen for crappie and bass fishing in northern Minnesota lakes. It imitates a variety of dark-bodied minnows and large aquatic insects when tied in smaller sizes. In addition to working well for crappie or bass, it's an excellent pattern for trout and other species.

Thread	Black	**Body**	Flat silver tinsel
Hook	Mustad 9672, size 2 to 12	**Wing**	Gray squirrel tail fibers with fairly wide sections of dark turkey wing or tail feather on each side
Tail	Red duck wing segment		
Rib	Oval silver tinsel	**Head**	Black chenille

Step 1. Wrap the shank with thread up to the bend of the hook, and tie in a red duck wing segment in the upright position on top of the shank as the tail (tail length equal to gape of hook). Wrap the butt end of the segment along the shank, going forward and then returning back to the tie-in point to eliminate any bumps along the shank when you add the body.

Step 2. Tie in a piece of oval silver tinsel under the shank at the same tie-in point as ribbing to be used over the body.

Step 3. Tie in a piece of flat silver tinsel at the same tie-in point, and wrap the shank, going forward to within ¼ inch of the hook eye, as the body. Secure the tinsel with your thread, and remove any excess material.

Step 4. Rib the body, going forward with the oval silver tinsel, using equally spaced wraps. Secure it with the thread, and remove any excess material.

Step 5. Tie in a stacked bunch of gray squirrel tail hair fibers on top of the shank in front of the body. *Note: The hair fibers should extend slightly beyond the tail.*

Step 6. Cut out a pair of matched, fairly wide sections from a turkey wing or tail feather, and tie them in on each side of the squirrel hair fibers.

Step 7. Tie in a short piece of black chenille in front of the wing, bringing the thread forward to the hook eye. Form an oversize head with the chenille, using close wraps up to the hook eye. Secure it with the thread, and remove any excess material. Make a few additional wraps with the thread behind the eye, and tie off with a whip finish.

Black Reaper

Origin: United States
Originator: Gene Kugach
Used for: Trout, panfish

This pattern was designed to represent any small dark baitfish or minnow. It's an excellent pattern for evening-feeding panfish or trout.

Thread	Black	**Wings**	Black hackle tips
Hook	Mustad 38941, size 6 to 16	**Hackle**	Black neck hackle
Tail	Yellow hackle fibers	**Head**	Black thread
Body	Rear third: Bright red floss Front two-thirds: Black floss, ribbed with a fine flat Flashabou strand		

Step 1. Wrap the shank with thread up to the bend of the hook, and tie in the yellow hackle fibers for the tail (tail length half of body length).

Step 2. Tie in a short piece of bright red floss, and form a tapered butt one-third of the body length. Secure the floss with your thread, and remove any excess.

Step 3. Tie in a piece of a fine flat Flashabou strand and a piece of black floss. Finish wrapping the remaining two-thirds of the body with the black floss, forming a cigar-shaped body, and rib it with the Flashabou. Snip off any excess materials. *Note: Allow at least a 1/8-inch area behind the hook eye.*

Step 4. Now add the wings. Select two equal black saddle hackles, and strip them back until they are as long as the shank plus the tail. Tie them in on top of the shank, with the shiny sides facing out.

Step 5. Tie in a black neck hackle. Make two to three wraps around the shank in front of the wings, securing the wraps with your thread. Cut off any excess materials. Using the thread, collar the hackle back, and build a small, neat head. Tie off with a whip finish.

Orange/Black Maribou Matuka Minnow

Origin: United States
Originator: Gene Kugach
Used for: All species

This pattern was designed to represent any small, dark baitfish or minnow. It's an excellent pattern for evening-feeding steelhead and salmon, and can also be used for most game fish species.

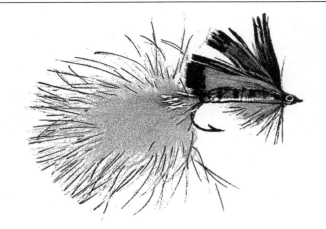

Thread	Black	**Wing**	2 black turkey feather tips sandwiched with 2 shorter orange turkey feather tips
Hook	Mustad 3261, size 1/0 to 2/0		
Tail	Orange marabou blood feather	**Head**	Black thread
Rib	Copper wire	**Eyes**	Styrofoam or painted, yellow with black centers
Body	Medium-size silver mylar tubing		
Throat	Orange marabou under black hackle fibers	**Markings**	Orange and black permanent markers

Step 1. Wrap the shank with thread up to the bend of the hook, and tie in the orange marabou tail. *Note: The tail feather should be about 2 1/2 inches long behind the tie-in point.*

Step 2. Tie in a 12-inch-long piece of copper wire at the tail tie-in point, which will be used later.

Step 3. Remove the core material from a 2-inch-long piece of silver mylar tubing. Using the core material, build an underbody around the hook shank to within 3/16 inch behind the hook eye. Remove any excess material, and tie off with a whip finish.

Step 4. Slip the tubing over the underbody, and tie it in behind the hook eye. Tie off with another whip finish.

Step 5. While pulling the back end of the mylar tubing, tie in your thread at the tail tie-in point, and secure it with a few close wraps. Tie off with a whip finish. *Note: At this point, about 1/2 inch of the tubing should be extending beyond the hook bend and should be unraveled as shown in the pattern picture.*

Step 6. Tie in your thread behind the hook eye, and tie in the orange marabou with the black hackle fibers under the hook shank as the beard.

Step 7. Tie in two black turkey feather tips (back-to-back), sandwiched with two shorter orange turkey feather tips on top of the shank behind the eye. Pull the feather ends down over the body, and secure them to the body by ribbing through them with the copper wire from the tail tie-in point to the hook eye. Secure the wire with the thread, and snip off any excess, then build a neat head, and tie off with a whip finish.

Step 8. Give the head a coat of epoxy cement. After it is dry, paint in eyes or use Styrofoam eyes, and cover them with a second coat of cement.

Step 9. Add the color markings to the body using orange and black permanent markers.

Gilly

Origin: United States
Originator: Gene Kugach
Used for: Trout

This pattern was designed to represent any small bait-fish or minnow. It's an excellent pattern for evening-feeding trout.

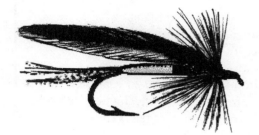

Thread	Black	**Wings**	Black hackle tips
Hook	Mustad 38941, size 6 to 16	**Hackle**	Black neck hackle
Tail	Mallard flank fibers (light green)	**Head**	Black thread
Body	Rear two-thirds: Gold or yellow floss		
	Front third: Red yarn or floss		

Step 1. Wrap the shank with thread up to the bend of the hook, and tie in the light green mallard flank fibers (tail length half of body length).

Step 2. Tie in a short piece of gold or yellow floss, and form a tapered butt two-thirds of the body length. Secure the floss with your thread, and remove any excess.

Step 3. Tie in a piece of red yarn or floss. Finish wrapping the remaining third of the body with the yarn or floss, forming a cigar-shaped body. Snip off any excess materials. *Note: Allow at least a 1/8-inch area behind the hook eye.*

Step 4. Now add the wings. Select two equal black saddle hackles, and strip them back until they are as long as the shank plus the tail. Tie them in on top of the shank, with the shiny sides facing out.

Step 5. Tie in a black neck hackle. Make two to three wraps around the shank in front of the wings, securing the wraps with your thread. Cut off any excess materials. Using the thread, collar the hackle back, and build a small, neat head. Tie off with a whip finish.

Peacock Matuka Minnow

Origin: United States
Originator: Gene Kugach
Used for: All species

This pattern was designed to represent any small dark baitfish or minnow. It's basically tied with peacock material, with the exception of the body.

Thread	Black	**Beard**	Blue peacock body feather barbules, followed by a few green peacock sword barbules, followed by a few rust-colored peacock body feather barbules
Hook	Mustad 3665A, or 9575, size 2 to 6		
Tail	8 peacock herls, 2 1/2 inches long		
Rib	Fine copper wire		
Body	Lime green floss	**Head**	Black thread
Wing	2 peacock sword feathers	**Eyes**	White Styrofoam with black centers
Cheeks	Peacock body feather tips		

Step 1. Wrap the shank with thread up to the bend of the hook, and tie in eight peacock herls as the tail. *Note: The tail should be about 2 1/2 inches long behind the tie-in point.*

Step 2. Tie in a 12-inch-long piece of fine copper wire at the tail tie-in point; this will be used later.

Step 3. Tie in a piece of lime green floss, and form a neat, slightly tapered body, going forward. *Note: Allow about 3/16 inch behind the hook eye.* Remove any excess material.

Step 4. Tie in two peacock sword feathers on top of the shank as the wing. The sword feathers should be slightly shorter than the tail.

Step 5. While pulling back on the sword feather ends (down over the body), secure them to the body by ribbing through them with the copper wire from the tail tie-in point to the hook eye. Secure the wire with the thread, and snip off any excess.

Step 6. Tie in the peacock body feather tip cheeks on each side of the wing.

Step 7. Tie in the beard under the hook shank, starting with some short blue feather barbules, followed by some green sword feather barbules, followed by a few rust-colored body feather barbules.

Step 8. Form a neat, oversize head with the thread, and tie off with a whip finish.

Step 9. Give the head a light coat of epoxy cement, and place the Styrofoam eyes in position on each side of the head. Apply a second coat of cement over the head and the eyes, and allow it to dry.

Brown Streamer

Origin: United States
Originator: Gene Kugach
Used for: All species

This pattern was designed to represent a small, dark bait-fish or minnow. It works well as a trolling streamer for most species.

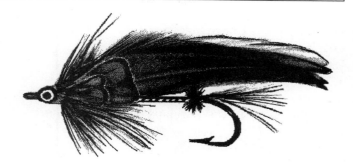

Thread	Black	**Shoulders**	Ring-necked pheasant neck feather (brown with black tips)
Hook	Mustad 38941, size 6 to 16	**Cheeks**	Ring-necked pheasant neck feather
Tag	Fine gold tinsel or Flashabou	**Beard**	Brown hackle fibers
Tail	Brown hackle fibers	**Hackle**	Furnace hackle collared back
Butt	Black ostrich herl	**Head**	Black thread
Body	Fine gold tinsel or Flashabou, ribbed with a fine red Flashabou strand	**Eyes**	Styrofoam, white with black centers
Wings	4 furnace saddle hackle tips		

Step 1. Wrap the shank with thread up to the bend of the hook, and tie in a piece of fine gold tinsel or Flashabou. Form the tag by wrapping beyond the bend and returning to the tie-in point. *Note: Do not remove the remaining tinsel or Flashabou; it will be used later.*

Step 2. Tie in the brown hackle fibers for the tail (tail length half of body length).

Step 3. Tie in a black ostrich herl, and form the butt by giving the herl two to three close wraps (the herl should be wrapped over the gold tinsel or Flashabou used to form the tag). Secure the herl with your thread, and remove any excess.

Step 4. Tie in a red fine flat Flashabou strand in front of the butt. Using the gold tinsel or Flashabou, wrap the entire shank, going forward to within 1/4 inch of the hook eye, and rib it with the red Flashabou strand to form the body. Remove any excess materials.

Step 5. Now add the wings. Select four equal furnace saddle hackles, and strip them back until they are as long as the shank plus the tail. Tie them in on the top of the shank, with the shiny sides facing out.

Step 6. Tie in the shoulders (ring-necked pheasant neck feathers), followed by the cheeks (shorter ring-necked pheasant neck feathers).

Step 7. Tie in the beard (brown hackle fibers), followed by the collar (furnace saddle hackle feather) collared and tied back.

Step 8. Cut off any excess materials. Using the thread, build a neat head, and tie off with a whip finish.

Step 9. Coat the head with epoxy cement, and when it starts to set, add the Styrofoam eyes. Give it a second coat of cement, covering the eyes, and allow it to dry.

Furnace Wing Streamer

Origin: United States
Originator: Gene Kugach
Used for: All species

This pattern was designed to represent a small, dark bait-fish or minnow. It works well as a trolling streamer for most species.

Thread	Bright red	Beard	Red hackle fibers
Hook	Mustad 7766, size 2 to 4	Wings	2 furnace saddle hackle tips
Tag	Fine silver tinsel or Flashabou	Topping	3 or 4 peacock herls
Tail	Peacock sword segments	Head	Oversize—bright red thread
Body	Bright red floss ribbed with fine silver tinsel or Flashabou strand	Eyes	Styrofoam, white with black centers

Step 1. Wrap the shank with thread up to the bend of the hook, and tie in a piece of fine silver tinsel or Flashabou. Form the tag by wrapping beyond the bend and returning to the tie-in point. *Note: Do not remove the remaining tinsel or Flashabou; it will be used later as ribbing.*

Step 2. Tie in four or six peacock sword segments for the tail (tail length half of body length).

Step 3. Tie in a piece of bright red floss in front of the tail, and wrap the entire shank, going forward to within 1/4 inch of the hook eye to form the body. Rib the body with the silver tinsel or Flashabou strand used to form the butt, and remove any excess materials.

Step 4. Tie in the beard under the shank in front of the body, using red hackle fibers.

Step 5. Now add the wings. Select two equal furnace saddle hackles, and strip them back until they are as long as the shank plus the tail. Tie them in on top of the shank, with the shiny sides facing out.

Step 6. Tie in the three or four peacock herls on top of the wings as the topping (topping equal to wing length).

Step 7. Cut off any excess materials. Using the thread, build a neat, oversize head, and tie off with a whip finish.

Step 8. Coat the head with epoxy cement, and when it starts to set, add the Styrofoam eyes. Give it a second coat of cement, covering the eyes, and allow it to dry.

Mega Streamer

Origin: United States
Originator: Gene Kugach
Demonstrator: Gene Kugach 1990–91
Used for: Northern pike

This is a large streamer pattern that works very well for northern pike or muskie. It can also be used for salt-water fishing (all species) or as a trolling streamer for salmon or trout. Designed as an attractor or baitfish pattern, it can be tied in a number of color combinations, including green and yellow, blue and white, and orange and white.

Thread	Black		**Underwing**	White bucktail
Hook	Eagle Claw 254, size 2/0 to 4/0		**Wing**	2 white saddle hackles
Tail	8 to 10 strands of red Flashabou or Krystal Flash tied in first, with 2 long grizzly saddle hackles sandwiched by 2 white saddle hackles over the Flashabou or Krystal Flash		**Shoulder**	Red hen feather tips
			Cheek	Black-tipped ring-necked pheasant breast feathers
			Collar	White hackle (collared)
Body	Silver cloisonné		**Head**	Black thread
Beard	White bucktail extending beyond the bend, with short red hackle fibers over the white		**Eyes** (optional)	Styrofoam or painted, white with black centers

Step 1. Wrap the shank with thread up to the bend of the hook, and tie in eight to ten strands of red Flashabou or Krystal Flash. Tie in two long grizzly saddle hackles (dull sides in), sandwiched by two ($^3/_4$ inch shorter) white saddle hackles.

Step 2. Tie in a 6-inch-long strip of silver cloisonné, and wrap the entire shank with close wraps to form the body. *Note: Stop about $^1/_8$ inch behind the eye.*

Step 3. Tie in the beard using white bucktail with a sparse bunch of shorter red hackle fibers over the white.

Step 4. Tie in some white bucktail on top of the shank for the underwing.

Step 5. Tie in the wing, which consists of two white saddle hackles (dull sides in), with two red hen feathers (on each side) as the shoulder and two black-tipped ring-necked pheasant breast feathers (on each side) over the red hackles as the cheeks.

Step 6. Tie in a white hackle, and give it a couple of wraps in front of the wing. Collar it back with the thread, and snip off the excess.

Step 7. Build a neat head with your thread, and tie off with a whip finish. Glue the Styrofoam eyes in position with some Goop cement. Coat the head with epoxy cement, entirely covering the eyes on each side, and allow it to dry.

Flashabou Minnow

Origin: United States
Originator: Gene Kugach
Used for: Northern pike or muskie

The Flashabou Minnow is a large streamer pattern that works very well for northern pike or muskie. It can be used for saltwater fishing (all species) or as a trolling streamer for salmon or trout and can be tied in a number of color combinations, such as green and yellow, blue and white, and orange and white.

Thread	Black	**Body**	Mylar Flashabou tubing
Hook	Eagle Claw 66SS, size 3/0	**Eyes**	Plastic doll eyes (7mm)
Tail	2 long grizzly saddle hackles, sandwiched by 2 red hackles with a bunch of red bucktail on each side and a bunch of white deer body hair spun around the shank	**Collar**	Bright red thread

Step 1. Place your hook in the vise. Wrap the shank with thread up to the bend, and tie in the two long grizzly saddle hackles (shiny sides out).

Step 2. Tie in the two bright red saddle hackles (1 inch shorter than the grizzly hackles) on each side.

Step 3. Tie in a bunch of red bucktail on each side of the hackles (tips should extend about half the length of the red hackles). Wrap the butt ends with your thread down the entire length of the hook shank, and trim off the excess behind the hook eye.

Step 4. Spin a bunch of white deer body hair around the hook shank. Spread the hairs evenly around the shank, also tying down the butt ends as you did with the red bucktail.

Step 5. Remove the core from a 2½-inch to 3-inch piece of mylar Flashabou tubing.

Step 6. Tie a single strand of the core material on the top and one on the bottom of the hook shank, rounding it off at the front and back of the shank with your thread after you trim off the excess. Then bring the thread forward behind the hook eye.

Step 7. Tie in the mylar Flashabou tubing material by slipping it over the hook eye and securing the end with the thread behind the eye. Tie off with a whip finish.

Step 8. Push the secured material back over itself onto the hook shank. Then, using bright red thread, make a few wraps over the material at the bend of the hook. Using one hand, pull the material back tightly, and secure it to the shank with the red thread, making a neat band of red at the back of the body. Tie off with a whip finish, and give the band a coat of head cement.

Step 9. Remove the hook from the vise, and glue the eyes into position with Goop or epoxy cement. Color the body various baitfish shades using permanent markers, if desired.

Ray's Minnow

Origin: United States
Originator: Ray Podkowa
Used for: Walleye

This pattern was designed by Ray Podkowa of the Chicago Fly Fishers. It's one of his own creations, which he developed to simulate a minnow when he fishes for walleye. It can also be used for most any game fish and is a simple pattern to tie. It should be fished deep with a slow, jerking motion.

Thread	White	**Body**	Woven strand of gold tinsel chenille and chartreuse chenille, with the gold chenille on the bottom
Hook	Mustad 9575, size 4		
Tail	Chartreuse marabou blood feather		
Underbody	Plastic nymph body form or art foam, built up and covered with chartreuse floss	**Dorsal fin**	Chartreuse rabbit fur strip
		Collar	Chartreuse saddle hackle
		Head	White thread
		Eyes	Painted, yellow outer rims with black centers

Step 1. Wrap the hook shank with thread up to the hook point.

Step 2. Tie in a chartreuse marabou blood feather ($^3/_4$ inch long) as the tail, and snip off the excess.

Step 3. Tie in a 12-inch-long piece of gold tinsel chenille, a 12-inch-long piece of chartreuse chenille, and a 12-inch-long piece of chartreuse floss in front of the tail.

Step 4. Tie a plastic nymph body form to the top of the hook shank (or form the underbody with art foam), bringing the thread forward to within $^1/_4$ inch of the hook eye.

Step 5. Select a 6-inch-long strip of chartreuse rabbit fur, and remove $^1/_8$ inch of the fur from the skin at one end of the strip.

Step 6. Starting at the tail end, wrap the underbody with the chartreuse floss by first capturing the $^1/_8$-inch area of the rabbit fur strip on top of the underbody. After the fur strip is secured, continue building up the remainder of the underbody forward to the thread. Secure the floss with the thread, and snip off the excess.

Step 7. Using the gold tinsel and chartreuse chenille, start weaving the overbody covering the floss. The gold chenille should be on the bottom of the body when you weave. After the entire body is covered, secure the chenille with the thread, and snip off the excess.

Step 8. Bring the rabbit fur strip forward over the top of the woven body to form the dorsal fin, securing the front end with the thread in front of the body, and snipping off the excess.

Step 9. Tie in a chartreuse saddle hackle in front of the body, and give it two to four wraps around the shank. Again secure it with the thread, and snip off the remaining excess. Using the thread, collar the hackle back over the body.

Step 10. Form a nice, tapered head with the white thread, and tie off with a whip finish. Give the head area three or four coats of pearlescent nail polish, and let it dry. After it dries, paint in the eyes.

Northern Pike Streamer

Origin: United States
Originator: Jacques Juneau
Used for: Northern pike

This pattern was submitted by Len Eckerly of the Chicago Fly Fishers. It's from the Federation of Fly Fishers' *Bugline*. The pattern is a variation of a typical saltwater tarpon fly that was modified by Jacques Juneau to use as a pike fly.

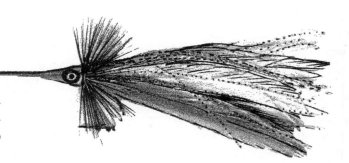

Thread	Red
Hook	Mustad 34007, size 1/0 to 2/0
Tail	White bucktail with 2 white saddles and 1 red saddle on each side (splayed), topped with red, silver, or pearl Krystal Flash
Collar	Red and white hackles

Head	Red thread tapered at the hook bend
Body	Red thread wrapped forward toward the eye of the hook and coated with Cellaire or epoxy cement
Eyes (optional)	Painted or Styrofoam, white with black centers

Step 1. Starting at the hook bend, tie in the red thread.

Step 2. Tie in a sparse bunch of long, white bucktail on top of the shank at the bend.

Step 3. Tie in one red saddle hackle on top of the bucktail with two white saddle hackles (splayed) on each side of the hook.

Step 4. Top the tail with four to six strands of Krystal Flash on each side of the tail.

Step 5. Tie in a red and a white saddle hackle.

Step 6. Wrap a red and white hackle around the shank to form a collar, securing them with the thread and snipping off the excess.

Step 7. Taper the thread to the hook shank, forming a neat head at the hook bend (over the area where the tail was tied in), then continue wrapping the entire shank with close wraps toward the eye of the hook. Tie off with a whip finish behind the eye, and coat the thread with head cement or clear epoxy.

Missionary

Origin: New Zealand
Originator: Captain J. J. Dunn
Demonstrator: Jerry Wasil 1986–87
Used for: Trout

An old New Zealand pattern first tied by Captain J. J. Dunn. The original pattern was tied with a white hackle, which was changed to orange by a Mr. C. G. Heywood when he was fishing the Tongariro River in New Zealand. The modern version of this pattern (tied with a red or orange hackle) was modified by Dick Shrive of the United Kingdom.

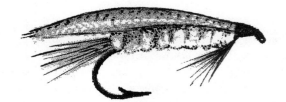

Thread	Black or white	**Body**	White chenille
Hook	Mustad 79580, size 6 to 10	**Wing**	Silver mallard duck flank feather
Tail	Scarlet red or orange hackle fibers	**Beard**	Orange or scarlet red cock hackle fibers
Rib	Oval silver tinsel	**Head**	Black or white thread

Step 1. Wrap the shank with thread up to the bend of the hook, and tie in a bunch of orange or scarlet red hackle fibers for the tail (tail length equal to body length).

Step 2. Tie in a short piece of oval silver tinsel at the tail tie-in point as the ribbing. Also tie in a short piece of white chenille at the same point, bringing the thread forward to about 1/8 inch behind the hook eye. Use the chenille to form the body, going forward with close, tight wraps. Secure the chenille with your thread, and remove any excess.

Step 3. Using the silver tinsel, rib the body with equally spaced wraps and secure the tinsel with the thread. Snip off excess materials.

Step 4. Select a silver mallard duck flank feather, and tie it in flat (tent style) on top of the shank as the wing. The length of the wing can be as long as the body plus the tail, just a little bit shorter than the tail, or just a little bit longer than the body. Snip off any excess material.

Step 5. Tie in a sparse bunch of orange or scarlet cock hackle fibers under the hook shank to form the beard (beard fibers about half the body length). Build a small, neat head with the thread, and tie off with a whip finish. Give the head a coat of head cement.

Appetiser

Origin: United Kingdom
Originator: Bob Church
Demonstrator: Jerry Wasil 1986–87
Used for: Trout

This pattern was designed by Bob Church in 1972 especially for large trout found at Grafham near Northampton, Britain. It was the first time a marabou wing was used for a streamer lure pattern in Britain. It has been a very successful pattern that works well on all waters.

Thread	Black (white optional)	**Wing**	White marabou
Hook	Mustad 79580, size 6 to 10	**Overwing**	Natural gray squirrel tail
Tail	Green, orange, and silver mallard duck hackle fibers, mixed	**Throat**	Green, orange, and silver mallard duck hackle fibers, mixed
Body	White chenille	**Head**	Black or white thread
Rib	Silver tinsel		

Step 1. Wrap the shank with thread up to the bend of the hook, and tie in a bunch of mixed green, orange, and silver mallard duck hackle fibers for the tail (tail length equal to body length).

Step 2. Tie in a short piece of silver tinsel at the tail tie-in point as the ribbing. Also tie in a short piece of white chenille at the same point, bringing the thread forward to about $1/8$ inch behind the hook eye. Use the chenille to form the body, going forward with close, tight wraps. Secure the chenille with your thread, and remove any excess.

Step 3. Using the silver tinsel, rib the body with equally spaced wraps and secure the tinsel with the thread. Snip off any excess materials.

Step 4. Select a white marabou feather, and tie it in on top of the shank as the wing. The length of the wing should be just a little bit longer than the hook length. Snip off any excess material.

Step 5. Add the natural gray squirrel tail fiber overwing on top of the marabou wing. Secure the squirrel fibers with your thread, and remove any excess material.

Step 6. Tie in a sparse bunch of mixed green, orange, and silver mallard duck hackle fibers under the hook shank to form the throat (throat fibers about half body length). Build a small, neat head with the thread, and tie off with a whip finish. Give the head a coat of head cement.

Skinner's Centennial

Origin: United States
Demonstrator: George Carcao 1988–89
Used for: Trout

A dark baitfish imitation pattern used for trout. The pattern probably originated in the United States, but the name of the originator (other than Skinner) is unknown. George Carcao, who demonstrated the pattern, has had great success using it.

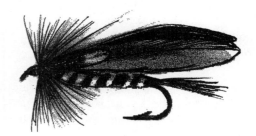

Thread	Black	**Wing**	2 scarlet red saddle hackles flanked by 2 black saddle hackles
Hook	Mustad 9672 or 38941, size 2 to 10	**Cheek** (optional)	Jungle cock
Tail	Scarlet red hackle fibers	**Collar**	Black hackle (collared back)
Rib	Flat silver tinsel	**Head**	Black thread
Body	Black dubbing		

Step 1. Wrap the shank with thread up to the bend of the hook, and tie in a bunch of scarlet red hackle fibers for the tail (tail length half of body length).

Step 2. Tie in a short piece of flat silver tinsel at the tail tie-in point as the ribbing, and let it hang.

Step 3. Use black dubbing such as wool or rabbit to dub the body, going forward to about an $1/8$ inch behind the hook eye.

Step 4. Using the silver tinsel, rib the body with equally spaced wraps, and secure the tinsel with the thread. Snip off any excess materials.

Step 5. Now add the wing. Select a pair of scarlet red saddle hackles and a pair of black saddle hackles. Sandwich the red hackles between the black hackles, and tie them in on top of the hook shank. The length of the wing should be as long as the body plus the tail. Snip off any excess material.

Step 6. Add the optional jungle cock cheeks on each side of the wing, if desired.

Step 7. Tie in a black hackle in front of the wing, and give it two or three wraps, securing it collar style with the thread. Build a small, neat head with the thread, and tie off with a whip finish. Give the head a coat of head cement.

Black Nosed Dace

Origin: United States
Originator: Art Flick
Demonstrator: George Cik 1995–96
Used for: Trout, bass

Designed to represent a member of the minnow family called a dace, this pattern was originated in the New York Catskills by Art Flick. It works well just beneath the surface of the water for trout or bass and is one of the most realistic dace imitations.

Thread	Black	**Wing**	White calf tail, over which is black bear or skunk, with natural brown bucktail on top (all half a shank length past the tail)	
Hook	Mustad 9575, size 4 to 12			
Tail	Red wool tied short			
Rib (optional)	Oval silver tinsel			
Body	Flat silver tinsel	**Head**	Black thread	

Step 1. Wrap the shank with thread up to the bend of the hook, and tie in a short piece of red wool for the tail (tail length half of body length).

Step 2. If desired, tie in a short piece of oval silver tinsel at the tail tie-in point as the ribbing, and let it hang. Also tie in a piece of flat silver tinsel at the same tie-in point for the body.

Step 3. Wrap the flat silver tinsel forward along the shank to form the body, to about $1/8$ inch behind the hook eye. Remove any excess material.

Step 4. If you're using the oval silver tinsel, rib the body with equally spaced wraps, and secure the tinsel with the thread. Snip off any excess materials.

Step 5. Now add the wing. Tie in a sparse bunch of white calf tail on top of the shank, followed by a sparse bunch of black bear or skunk hairs, topped with a sparse bunch of natural brown bucktail on top of the calf tail. The wing should extend about half a shank length beyond the tail. Snip off any excess material.

Step 6. Build a small, neat head with the thread, and tie off with a whip finish. Give the head a coat of head cement.

Joe's Smelt

Origin: United States
Originator: Joe Sterling
Demonstrator: Eric Heckman 1985–86
Used for: Trout, salmon

Another baitfish design, this one made to represent a member of the minnow family called a smelt. This pattern is often tied tandem and is highly recommended for landlocked salmon or trout.

Thread	Black and red		**Wing**	Narrow pintail flank feather tied flat on top
Hook	Mustad 9575, size 2 to 10		**Head**	Black thread
Tail	Red calf-tail fibers tied short		**Eyes**	Painted or Styrofoam, yellow with black centers
Body	Silver mylar tubing			
Beard	Red hackle fibers			

Step 1. Using the red thread, wrap the shank with thread up to the bend of the hook, and tie in the red calf-tail fibers for the tail (tail length half of the gap width).

Step 2. Remove the core from a piece of silver mylar tubing slightly shorter than the hook shank. Slip the tubing over the shank, and secure the rear end of the tubing with the red thread at the tail tie-in point, using close neat wraps. Tie off with a whip finish.

Step 3. Tie in the red thread at the front of the tubing, and secure the opposite end. *Note: Enough space should be allowed between the hook eye and the body for the wing and bulky head, which will be added later.*

Step 4. Tie in a bunch of red hackle fibers at the front of the body (under the shank) as the beard (beard length about one-third of body length). Tie off with a whip finish.

Step 5. Tie in the black thread. Select a narrow pintail flank feather (length should reach to the end of the tail), and tie it in flat on top of the shank.

Step 6. Using the black thread, build up a bulky head, and tie off with a whip finish.

Step 7. Give the head a coat of epoxy cement, and allow it to dry. After it dries, paint or add Styrofoam eyes, and cover them with a coat of cement.

Thunder Creek

Origin: United States
Originator: Keith C. Fulsher
Demonstrators: Jerry Wasil 1984–85
George Cik 1991–92
Used for: Trout

Originally designed as a series to represent members of the minnow family, such as the black-nose dace, golden shiner, red fin shiner, silver shiner, emerald minnow, spot-tailed minnow, and common smelt.

Thread	White		**Head**	Pulled-back bucktail (bullet head)
Hook	Mustad 79580, size 2 to 10		**Collar**	White thread
Body	Embossed silver tinsel		**Eyes**	Painted white with black centers or Styrofoam
Wing	Lateral stripe—black bucktail, with white bucktail under the shank and brown bucktail over the black			

Step 1. Wrap the shank with thread up to the bend of the hook, and tie in a short piece of embossed silver tinsel for the body, bringing the thread forward to about 1/4 inch or 3/8 inch behind the hook eye.

Step 2. Using the tinsel, wrap the shank forward with neat, close wraps, and secure it with the thread. Snip off any excess material.

Step 3. Tie in a sparse bunch of black bucktail on top of the shank in front of the body. The bucktail fibers should extend a little beyond the hook bend. Then bring your thread back behind the hook eye.

Step 4. Tie in a sparse bunch of brown bucktail on top of the shank (butt ends) in front of the body so that the tips extend beyond the eye of the hook. Again wrap the thread over the butt ends up to the hook eye, then return back to the tie-in point. *Note: These fibers should first be measured for length to make sure that when they are pulled back, the tips will align with the tips of the black bucktail.*

Step 5. Tie in a sparse bunch of white bucktail under the shank (butt ends) so that the tips extend beyond the eye of the hook. Wrap the thread over the butt ends up to the hook eye, then return back to the tie-in point. *Note: These fibers should be slightly shorter than the brown bucktail tips when pulled back.*

Step 6. Pull back the brown and white bucktail over the hook shank (while holding both tautly), and secure them about 1/4 to 3/8 inch behind the hook eye to form a bullet head with the thread. Form a neat thread collar behind the head using close wraps of the thread. Tie off with a whip finish, and coat the head and thread collar with epoxy cement.

Step 7. After the cement dries, paint or add Styrofoam eyes. Cover them with a coat of epoxy cement.

Little Brook Trout

Origin: United States
Demonstrator: Todd McCagg 1990–91
Used for: Trout, bass

One of the eastern bucktails designed to represent a small brook trout fry. This pattern was originated many years ago in the eastern United States and is a very popular pattern.

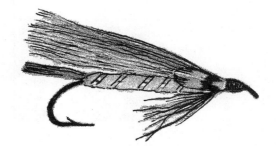

Thread	Black	**Wing**	Equal amounts of hair fibers tied in as follows: white bucktail, followed by orange bucktail, followed by bright green bucktail, topped with badger or gray squirrel hair
Hook	Mustad 9575, size 2 to 12		
Tail	Short section of bright red floss with bright green bucktail over it		
Rib	Narrow flat silver tinsel		
Body	Cream-colored fur dubbing	**Cheek** (optional)	Jungle cock
Throat	Small bunch of bright orange bucktail	**Head**	Black thread

Step 1. Wrap the shank with thread up to the bend of the hook, and tie in a short piece of bright red floss with a sparse bunch of bright green bucktail over it as the tail. The bright green bucktail should be half the length of the body, and the floss should be half the length of the bucktail.

Step 2. Tie in a short piece of narrow flat silver tinsel at the tail tie-in point as the ribbing, which will be used later.

Step 3. Use cream-colored fur dubbing to dub the body, going forward to within 1/4 inch of the hook eye.

Step 4. Wrap the flat silver tinsel forward along the shank with equally spaced wraps, and secure the tinsel with the thread. Snip off any excess materials.

Step 5. Tie in a sparse bunch of bright orange bucktail under the shank in front of the body for the beard (fibers about half of body length).

Step 6. Now add the wing, which consists of equal amounts of hair fibers tied in on top of the shank as follows: white bucktail, followed by orange bucktail, followed by bright green bucktail, topped with badger or gray squirrel hair. The wing length should be equal to the body plus the tail.

Step 7. If desired, you can tie in the jungle cock cheeks on each side of the wing. Build a small, neat head with the thread, and tie off with a whip finish. Give the head a coat of head cement.

Royal Coachman Trude

Origin: United Kingdom
Demonstrator: Jerry Wasil 1997–98
Used for: Trout

A very old pattern that was devised in England and is still one of the most popular patterns used for trout. This pattern can be tied as a dry fly, streamer, nymph, or wet fly.

Thread	Black	**Wing**	White calf tail
Hook	Mustad 94840 or Tiemco TMC 100, size 8 to 16	**Hackle**	Coachman brown
		Head	Black thread
Tail	Golden pheasant tippet fibers		
Body	Bronze peacock herl and red floss		

Step 1. Lay down a base of black thread, stopping just before the hook bend.

Step 2. Tie in a few golden pheasant tippet fibers as the tail.

Step 3. Tie in a couple of bronze peacock herls and a short piece of red floss. Starting with the peacock herl, form a ball (butt) at the tail tie-in point, and secure the herl with the thread, bringing the thread forward to within 1/4 inch of the hook eye.

Step 4. Wrap the red floss forward over the remaining herl, forming an even body from the rear butt to within 1/4 inch of the hook eye. Secure the floss with the thread, and remove any excess floss. *Note: Do not remove the peacock herl.*

Step 5. Using the remaining peacock herl, form another ball in front of the body, and secure it with the thread. Remove any excess material.

Step 6. Tie in a clump of stacked white calf tail on top of the shank in front of the body. Wing length should equal the length of the body up to the middle of the tail.

Step 7. Tie in a pair of Coachman brown hackles in front of the wing, and make a couple of close wraps with each hackle. Secure them with the thread, and snip off any excess material.

Step 8. Form a neat head with your thread, and tie off with a whip finish.

Llama

Origin: United States/Canada
Used for: Trout

A very nice-looking pattern that probably originated in the United States or Canada. Recently revived, the pattern enjoys growing popularity among many fly fishermen.

Thread	Black		**Body**	Red floss or wool
Hook	Mustad 9672 or 38941, size 6 to 12		**Wing**	Woodchuck body hair, both the guard hairs and the underfur
Tail	Soft grizzly hackle fibers		**Hackle**	Soft grizzly (collared back)
Rib	Oval gold tinsel		**Head**	Black thread

Step 1. Wrap the shank with thread up to the bend of the hook, and tie in a bunch of soft grizzly hackle fibers for the tail (tail length half of body length).

Step 2. Tie in a short piece of oval gold tinsel at the tail tie-in point as the ribbing, and let it hang.

Step 3. Use red floss or wool to form the body, going forward to about $1/8$ inch behind the hook eye.

Step 4. Using the gold tinsel, rib the body with equally spaced wraps, and secure the tinsel with the thread. Snip off any excess materials.

Step 5. Select a clump of woodchuck body hair, both the guard hairs and the underfur, and tie it in on top of the hook shank as the wing. The wing should be as long as the body plus the tail. Snip off any excess material.

Step 6. Tie in a soft grizzly hackle in front of the wing, and give it two or three wraps, securing it collar style (collared back) with the thread. Build a small, neat head with the thread, and tie off with a whip finish. Give the head a coat of head cement.

Nine-Three

Origin: United States/Canada
Demonstrator: Bill Somerville 1984–85

Excellent pattern for spring trout and fall salmon fishing.
A nice-looking pattern that's been around for a while and
is not too difficult to tie. The original pattern had the
green hackle tied flat over the shank with the black hackles tied on edge above the green. The pattern is often tied
tandem as a trolling streamer.

Thread	Black	**Wings**	2 green saddle hackles (back-to-back) inside, 2 black saddle hackles outside
Hook	Mustad 9575 or 9572, size 2 to 12		
Body	Flat silver tinsel	**Cheeks**	Jungle cock
Underwing	Small bunch of white bucktail fibers	**Head**	Black thread

Step 1. Wrap the shank with black thread up to the hook point. Tie in a 6-inch-long piece of flat silver tinsel.

Step 2. Form the body by wrapping the shank with the tinsel to within $^3/_{16}$ inch behind the hook eye. Secure the material with your thread, and snip off the excess.

Step 3. Tie in a small bunch of white bucktail fibers over the body as the underwing (fiber length equal to hook length).

Step 4. Tie in two green saddle hackles (back-to-back) inside and two black saddle hackles outside the wings over the white bucktail (hackles one and a half times body length).

Step 5. Tie in the jungle cock cheeks on each side of the wings. The cheeks should be about one-third of the body length with the second eye showing.

Step 6. Using the thread, build a neat head, and tie off with a whip finish. Coat the head with head cement or epoxy.

Harris Special

Origin: United States
Demonstrator: Roger Hetzke 1997–98
Used for: Trout

A nice-looking attractor pattern designed to represent a baitfish. It works well for both trout and salmon.

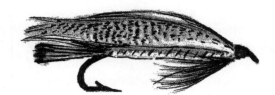

Thread	Black	**Throat**	Red hackle fibers or bucktail, two-thirds the length of the wing
Hook	Mustad 9575 or Tiemco TMC 300, size 6 to 12	**Underwing**	Sparse white bucktail to end of tail
Tail	Golden pheasant tippet fibers	**Wing**	Narrow symmetrical wood duck flank feather to end of tail and tied flat
Body	Flat gold mylar tinsel or gold diamond braid	**Head**	Black thread

Step 1. Wrap the shank with black thread up to the hook bend. Tie in a sparse bunch of golden pheasant tippet fibers as the tail, and a short piece of flat gold mylar tinsel or gold diamond braid at the same tie-in point.

Step 2. Wrap the shank, going forward with the flat gold mylar tinsel or gold diamond braid to within $1/4$ inch behind the hook eye to form the body.

Step 3. Tie in a sparse bunch of red hackle fibers or bucktail, two-thirds the length of the wing under the shank as the beard.

Step 4. Tie in a sparse bunch of white bucktail (extending to the end of tail) on top of the shank as the underwing.

Step 5. Select a narrow, symmetrical wood duck flank feather long enough to cover the underwing and reach the end of the tail, and tie it in flat on top of the shank.

Step 6. Using the thread, build a neat head, and tie off with a whip finish. Coat the head with head cement or epoxy.

Crappie Mickey

Origin: United States
Demonstrator: Jerry Wasil 1984–85
Used for: Crappie, trout

Excellent pattern for spring crappie or trout. A nice-looking attractor pattern that's not too difficult to tie.

Thread	Black	**Body**	Medium embossed or flat silver mylar tinsel
Hook	Mustad 79580, size 6	**Wings**	Yellow over red over yellow bucktail
Weight	.025 lead wire tied parallel to the shank	**Hackle**	Red saddle
Rib	Oval gold mylar tinsel	**Head**	Black thread

Step 1. Wrap the shank with black thread up to the hook bend.

Step 2. Lay two pieces of .025 lead wire (slightly shorter than the hook shank) parallel to the shank (on both sides), and secure them with the thread, then return the thread to the bend.

Step 3. Tie in a 6-inch-long piece of oval gold mylar tinsel and a 6-inch-long piece of medium embossed or flat silver mylar tinsel.

Step 4. Using the medium embossed or flat silver mylar tinsel, form a tapered body to within ³/₁₆ inch behind the hook eye. Secure the material with your thread, and snip off the excess.

Step 5. Rib the body with the oval gold mylar tinsel, using equally spaced wraps, and remove the excess.

Step 6. Tie in a sparse bunch of yellow bucktail as the wings on top of the hook shank, followed by a sparse bunch of red bucktail on top of the yellow, followed by another sparse bunch of yellow bucktail over the red. The wing length should be twice the body length.

Step 7. Tie in red saddle hackle, and give it two to three wraps in front of the body. Secure it with the thread, and snip off the excess.

Step 8. Using the thread, build a neat head, and tie off with a whip finish. Coat the head with head cement or epoxy.

Marabou Muddler

Origin: United States
Demonstrator: Bob Dulian 1986–87
Used for: Trout

An Alaskan trout and salmon pattern that utilizes deer hair for the head and collar. Designed to represent a muddler minnow, which is a favorite food of both trout and salmon.

Thread	Black	**Underwing**	Brown marabou feather or gray squirrel tail fibers
Hook	Mustad 9672, size 4 to 10	**Overwing**	Black marabou feather
Weight	.025 lead wire	**Collar**	Spun natural brown deer-hair fibers
Tail	Red marabou feather or red hackle fibers	**Head**	Spun natural brown deer-hair fibers trimmed to shape
Body	Silver mylar tinsel chenille		

Step 1. Wrap the shank with black thread up to the hook bend.

Step 2. Wrap about two-thirds or half of the shank with the lead wire to weight the pattern. Secure the wire with your thread at the front and back, and return the thread to the bend.

Step 3. Tie in a red marabou feather or red hackle fibers, extending slightly beyond the back of the hook as the tail.

Step 4. Tie in a 6-inch-long piece of silver mylar tinsel chenille, and bring your thread forward to within ³⁄₈ inch behind the hook eye.

Step 5. Going forward, wrap the shank with the silver mylar tinsel chenille, using close wraps. Secure it with the thread, and snip off any excess material.

Step 6. Tie in a brown marabou feather or gray squirrel tail fibers on top of the shank as the underwing, and top with a black marabou feather as the overwing.

Step 7. Select a stacked bunch of deer-hair fibers, and spin them around the shank in front of the body and wing as the collar. *Note: The tips of the deer-hair fibers should be to the back of the hook. In addition, at this point, the tips can be tied to a piece of thread to simplify trimming the head so that you don't cut off the collar fibers.*

Step 8. Tie in (spin) a couple bunches of natural brown deer hair in front of the collar, until you fill the shank up to the hook eye. Tie off with a whip finish. *Note: Make sure the bunches are tight by pushing back with your fingers one each bunch you add.*

Step 9. Using scissors and a pair of forceps, trim the head to shape, being careful not to cut off the collar fibers. Then release the collar by removing the thread used to hold it out of the way.

Cardinelle

Origin: United States
Demonstrator: Len Eckerly 1986–87
Used for: Trout, salmon, several other species

An excellent pattern for spring trout and fall salmon fishing. A nice-looking pattern that's been around for a while and is not too difficult to tie. It is very popular in southern New England, where it is used for smallmouth and largemouth bass, walleye, pike, stripers, and muskie.

Thread	Fluorescent red or orange	**Wing**	Cerise marabou feather
Hook	Mustad 9575 or 79580, size 2 to 10	**Collar**	Yellow saddle hackle collared and tied back
Body	Fluorescent red or orange wool	**Head**	Fluorescent red or orange thread
Underwing	Fluorescent red or orange synthetic FishHair		

Step 1. Wrap the shank with thread up to the hook bend. Tie in a 6-inch-long piece of fluorescent red or orange wool, and wrap the shank going forward to within $1/4$ inch of the hook eye.

Step 2. Tie in a sparse bunch of fluorescent red or orange synthetic FisHair fibers over the body as the underwing (fiber length twice the body length).

Step 3. Tie in a cerise marabou feather as the wing over the fluorescent red or orange synthetic FisHair. The wing should be slightly shorter than the underwing.

Step 4. Tie in a yellow saddle hackle in front of the wing, and give it a couple of close wraps. Secure it with the thread. Use the thread to collar back the fibers, and snip off any excess material.

Step 5. Using the thread, build a neat head, and tie off with a whip finish. Coat the head with head cement or epoxy.

Hamill's Killer

Origin: New Zealand
Demonstrator: George Carcao 1988–89
Used for: Trout

This pattern is very similar to the Mrs. Simpson and Walker's Killer. It is a possible imitation of a bullhead or one of many other small baitfish.

Thread	Black	**Wings**	8 gray partridge feathers dyed pale green, with 4 tied midway along the body (2 on each side) and 4 tied at the head (2 on each side)
Hook	Mustad 3906, size 2 to 6		
Tail	Black squirrel tail fibers with 2 small pale green partridge feathers (1 on each side)		
Body	Red wool or chenille	**Head**	Black thread

Step 1. Wrap the shank with black thread up to the hook bend.

Step 2. Tie in a sparse bunch of black squirrel tail fibers (length equal to the shank), with two small pale green partridge feathers (one on each side) as the tail. The partridge feathers should cover about half the black squirrel tail fibers.

Step 3. Tie in a piece of red wool or chenille at the tail tie-in point, and wrap the shank midway with tight, close wraps as part of the body.

Step 4. Tie in four pale green partridge feathers (two on each side) at the shank midway point, and using the red wool or chenille, continue wrapping the shank forward, using close wraps to within $1/8$ inch of the hook eye to finish the body. The partridge feathers should be slightly shorter than the feathers covering the tail.

Step 5. Tie in four more pale green partridge feathers (two on each side) in front of the body. These feathers should be slightly shorter than those tied in at the midway point.

Step 6. Using the thread, build a neat head, and tie off with a whip finish. Coat the head with head cement or epoxy.

Spruce Fly

Origin: United States
Originators: Bert and Clarence Milo Godfrey
Demonstrators: George Cik 1985–86,
Ray Podkowa 1992–93,
Roger Hetzke 1994–95
Used for: Trout

This pattern was originated in the state of Oregon by Bert and Clarence Milo Godfrey in 1918 or 1919. It's an excellent pattern that is used very successfully on western rivers. The pattern can be tied either as a Light Spruce or a Dark Spruce.

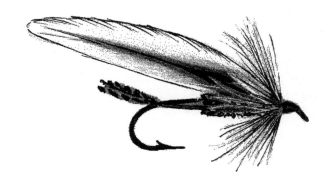

Thread	Black	**Wings**	Light Spruce: 2 light badger saddle hackles
Hook	Mustad 9672 or 9575, size 4 to 10		Dark Spruce: 2 furnace saddle hackles
Tail	Four peacock sword fibers	**Hackle**	Light Spruce: Badger saddle
Body	Rear third: Red floss		Dark Spruce: Furnace saddle
	Front two-thirds: Peacock herl	**Head**	Black thread

Step 1. Wrap the shank with black thread up to the hook bend. Tie in four peacock sword fibers as the tail, with the length beyond the hook bend equal to the hook gap.

Step 2. Tie in a short piece of red floss at the same tie-in point, and wrap the first third of the shank with the floss to form a tapered body. Secure the floss with the thread, and remove any excess material.

Step 3. Tie in a couple of peacock herls in front of the floss, and bring your thread forward to ¼ inch behind the hook eye.

Step 4. Wrap the herl forward using close wraps to cover the remaining two-thirds of the body. Secure the herl with your thread, and remove any excess material.

Step 5. Add the hackle wings on top of the shank (wing length twice the body length).

Step 6. Tie in the hackle, and give it two to three wraps in front of the body. Collar the hackle back using the thread, and remove any excess material.

Step 7. Using the thread, build a neat head, and tie off with a whip finish. Coat the head with head cement or epoxy.

Sculpin-n-Egg

Origin: United States
Demonstrator: Len Eckerly 1987–88
Used for: Trout

Excellent pattern for fall salmon or steelhead fishing. Designed to represent a sculpin feeding on an egg during the fall salmon or steelhead runs.

Thread	Black	**Wing**	Matched pair (left and right) of grouse feathers or 2 brown or dark olive webby grizzly hackles with one side of the barbules stripped away
Hook	Mustad 9578 or 9674, size 1/0 to 2		
Rib	Thin gold wire or small oval gold mylar tinsel	**Head**	Spun deer hair or muddler-shaped head
Body	Tan, brown, or olive chenille or dubbing	**Egg**	Pink or red fluorescent yarn

Step 1. Wrap the shank with black thread up to the hook bend. Tie in a 6-inch-long piece of thin gold wire or small oval gold mylar tinsel.

Step 2. Tie in tan, brown, or olive chenille at the same point, or if you're using dubbing, prepare the dubbing on the thread. Wrap or dub in a tapered body, going forward, covering two-thirds of the shank. *Note: If using chenille, secure it with the thread, and remove any excess material.*

Step 3. Tie in a pair of grouse feathers or two brown or dark olive webby grizzly hackles in front of the body on top of the shank as the wing (wing length twice the body length).

Step 4. Pull the wing tips back over the shank using one hand, and secure them with a single wrap of thin gold wire or small oval gold mylar tinsel by working it through the feather barbules at the bend of the hook.

Step 5. Rib the remaining body and wing with the wire or tinsel, using equally spaced wraps. Remove any excess material.

Step 6. Using a few bunches of spun deer hair or wool, tie in the head in front of the body. *Note: Leave enough space behind the eye for the egg.*

Step 7. Tie in a short piece of pink or red fluorescent yarn, and give it a couple of close wraps to form the egg. Tie off with a whip finish.

Step 8. Using a pair of forceps to hold the pattern, shape the head, muddler style, with a pair of scissors.

Olive Matuka

Origin: United States
Demonstrator: Warren Wormann 1987–88
Used for: Trout

Matuka-style patterns have had a surprising amount of success in recent years. All Matukas are dressed in the same way, with the distinguishing feature being the wing tied down on the body using ribbing material.

Thread	Black	**Wing**	4 dyed olive grizzly saddle hackles (half the shank length past the bend)
Hook	Mustad 9575, size 2 to 10		
Rib	Medium oval gold tinsel	**Collar**	Dyed olive grizzly saddle hackle (collared down)
Body	Olive chenille or wool, or black dubbing	**Head**	Black thread

Step 1. Lay down a thread base to the hook point, and tie in a piece of medium oval gold tinsel.

Step 2. Tie in a piece of olive chenille or wool, or use black dubbing. Form the body by wrapping the chenille or dubbing forward to about ³/₁₆ inch behind the hook eye. Remove any excess material.

Step 3. Select four dyed olive grizzly saddle hackles (half the shank length past the bend), and strip off the fluff at the base.

Step 4. Tie them in on top of the shank in front of the body, and pull the feathers down over the top. While holding them in position, make a wrap through the feather barbules at the bend with the tinsel ribbing. Repeat, wrapping down the feathers on top of the shank with the tinsel, using equally spaced wraps. When your reach the front end of the body, secure the tinsel with the thread, and remove any excess.

Step 5. Tie in a dyed olive grizzly saddle hackle in front of the wing, and give it a couple of close wraps. Secure it with the thread, collaring it back and removing any excess material.

Step 6. Form a neat head with the thread, and tie off with a whip finish. Coat the head with head cement or epoxy.

Mickey Finn

Origin: United States
Demonstrator: Ed Kopecky 1998–99
Used for: Trout

Old standby pattern for spring trout and fall salmon fishing. A nice-looking pattern that's been around for a while and is not too difficult to tie.

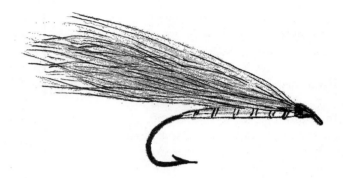

Thread	Black	**Wings**	Yellow, then red, then yellow calf tail or bucktail half a shank length past the bend
Hook	Mustad 9575, size 2 to 12		
Rib	Oval silver tinsel	**Head**	Black thread
Body	Flat silver tinsel		

Step 1. Wrap the shank with black thread up to the hook bend. Tie in a 6-inch-long piece of oval silver tinsel and a 6-inch-long piece of flat silver tinsel, and bring your thread forward to behind the hook eye.

Step 2. Wrap the shank with the flat silver tinsel, going forward to within $3/16$ inch of the hook eye. Secure the tinsel with the thread, and remove any excess material.

Step 3. Rib the body with the oval silver tinsel, using equally spaced wraps. Secure it with the thread, and remove the excess.

Step 4. Tie in a sparse bunch of stacked yellow, then red, then yellow calf tail or bucktail (half a shank length past the bend) on top of the shank in front of the body as the wings.

Step 5. Using the thread, build a neat head, and tie off with a whip finish. Coat the head with head cement or epoxy.

Hornberg

Origin: United States
Originator: Frank Hornberg
Demonstrators: Scott Hodlmair 1986–87
Steve Almgreen 1998–99
Used for: Trout

In addition to being a streamer pattern representing a baitfish, the Hornberg is also considered a dry or wet fly imitating some of the adult caddis and stoneflies found in many lakes and streams. The pattern was devised by Frank Hornberg in the early 1950s and can be tied in a variety of colors.

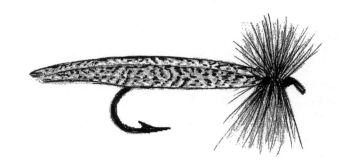

Thread	Black	**Wing**	2 silver mallard duck flank feathers
Hook	Mustad 38941 or 9671, size 6 to 10	**Cheeks** (optional)	Jungle cock, second eye showing
Body	Flat silver tinsel	**Collar**	Grizzly and brown hackle, mixed
Underwing	Dyed yellow calf-tail fibers	**Head**	Black thread

Step 1. Wrap the shank with black thread up to the hook bend. Tie in a 6-inch-long piece of flat silver tinsel, bringing the thread forward to ¼ inch from the hook eye.

Step 2. Wrap the shank with the flat silver tinsel, going forward. Secure it with the thread, and remove any excess material.

Step 3. Tie in a sparse bunch of dyed yellow calf-tail fibers on top of the shank as the underwing. The fibers should be tilted at a slightly upward angle and should be half a shank length past the bend.

Step 4. Tie in a silver mallard duck flank feather on each side of the calf tail as a wing. The flank feathers should also be half a shank length past the bend.

Step 5. (Optional) Tie in the jungle cock eye feathers on each side of the wing, with the second eye showing.

Step 6. Tie in a grizzly and a brown hackle in front of the wing. Starting with the grizzly hackle, give it three or four close wraps, secure it with the thread, and remove any excess material. Next, give the brown hackle three or four wraps through the grizzly hackle, secure it with the thread, and remove any excess material.

Step 7. Using the thread, build a neat head, and tie off with a whip finish. Coat the head with head cement or epoxy.

CHAPTER 5

Lure Patterns

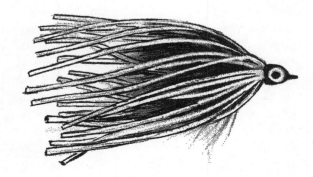

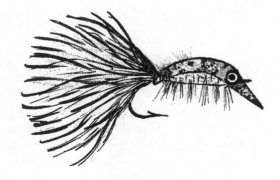

Muskie Lure

Origin: United States
Originator: John Betts
Modified by: Bill Sherer
Demonstrator: Eric Heckman 1995–96
Used for: Muskie, northern pike

John Betts developed the Bull-It-Perch pattern as a bass fly on a #2 hook in a frog and black pattern. Bill Sherer, who is a muskie guide, fly shop owner, and writer, modified that pattern for both muskie and northern pike. When fished, the Muskie Lure has a tight side-to-side wiggle like a crankbait and stays at a constant level for skimming over weed beds. The pattern should be fished with a heavy sink-tip 9- or 10-weight line.

Thread	White 3/0 or 0 Monocord	**Head**	White Evasote foam, $^3/_8$ inch wide by $^3/_8$ inch high by 3 $^1/_2$ inches long
Hook	Mustad 9082S, size 2/0		
Lip	.016-thick clear plastic (see pattern)		
Tail/body	In the following order: 3 $^1/_2$-inch orange marabou blood feather under shank, 3-inch yellow marabou blood feather on top of shank, 3 strands of gold Krystal Flash on each side, a 4 $^1/_2$-inch olive saddle hackle on each side, and a 1 $^1/_2$-inch olive marabou feather on top of shank	**Head markings**	Pantone permanent markers: orange (bottom), yellow (sides), black (side stripes), dark olive (top)
		Eyes	Movable doll eyes (7mm)

Step 1. Tie in your thread about midway on the hook shank. Then tie in the tail and body in the sequence specified above.

Step 2. Cut out the plastic lip using the actual-size template below. Fold the rear half of the lip in half down the center as indicated by the dotted line for fold #1.

Lip Template

fold #2

fold #3   fold #1

Step 3. Attach the lip to the bottom of the hook shank, starting at the rear, using tight wraps and going forward to cover the forward kink in the hook (about $^3/_8$ inch behind the hook eye). Bring your thread forward to the hook eye by going between the lip and the hook shank, and secure it with a whip finish. Bend the lip down, putting a crease perpendicular to the hook shank right behind the hook eye.

Step 4. Tie in the foam strip at the middle with very tight wraps right behind the hook eye. Use figure-eight wraps to secure it, and then bring your thread back to the middle of the hook shank. Fold back both sides of the foam, and at the back end, round the foam with a pair of scissors.

Step 5. Apply some gel superglue on top of the lip over the thread, and pull the foam back on both sides to slightly past the middle of the hook shank. Secure it with a few very tight wraps, one on top of the other, and tie off with a whip finish.

Step 6. Color the foam with the Pantone markers in the sequence listed in the recipe.

Step 7. Glue on the doll eyes using epoxy cement or Goop.

Step 8. Crease the lip as indicated in the template along the dotted lines for folds #2 and #3, so that it flares up on both sides. Trim the lip to fine-tune the desired action.

Wobbler Fly

Origin: United States
Originator: John B. Cave
Modified by: George Cik
Demonstrator: George Cik 1995–96
Used for: Bass and saltwater fishing

John B. Cave, a guide in southern Florida, developed the Wobbler pattern as a saltwater fly for redfish. George Cik, who is a member of the Chicago Fly Fishers and an expert tier, modified the pattern to simplify the tying procedure by using a plastic insert to form the spoon shape. When fished, the pattern has a tight, side-to-side wobbling action and stays at a constant level for skimming over weed beds.

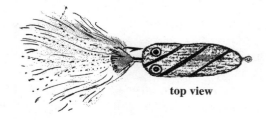

top view

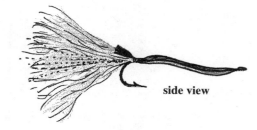

side view

Thread	White or red, 3/0 or 0 Monocord	**Body**	$^3/_8$-inch-diameter mylar tubing for hook sizes 1/0 to 3/0, or $^1/_4$-inch-diameter tubing for hook sizes 1 to 4, slipped over and glued to the underbody with clear epoxy
Hook	Mustad 3407 or Tiemco TMC 800S, size 4 to 3/0		
Tail	White marabou blood feather with 4 to 6 strands of silver Krystal Flash (each side), topped with a red marabou blood feather cut very short	**Body markings**	Flashabou strips glued in place
		Eyes	Yellow or white Styrofoam with black centers
Underbody	.016-thick clear plastic sheet material approximately as long as the hook shank and as wide as the mylar tubing when flattened		

Step 1. Tie in your thread about midway on the hook shank. Then tie in the tail and body as specified above.

Step 2. Cut out the plastic underbody to the shape shown in the template below.

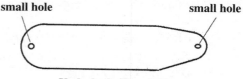

small hole   small hole

Underbody Template

Step 3. Attach the underbody to the shank by slipping the hook eye through the holes, keeping it on top of the shank, and then gluing the underside to the shank with epoxy cement. *Note: At this point, the hook shank can be bent slightly as shown in the side view above to give the lure more action.*

Step 4. After the cement is dry, tie in one end of the mylar tubing body behind the hook eye, and tie off. Give the underbody a complete coat of epoxy cement, top and bottom, and slip the mylar tubing body over it (turning the tubing inside out) to the back of the hook. While pulling on the back end of the tubing to make it tight over the underbody, secure the tubing at the tail tie-in point with your thread, using neat wraps, and tie off. Using your fingers, press the tubing to flatten it so that it adheres to the underbody.

Step 5. After the cement is dry, apply another light coat of epoxy cement to both sides of the body, and add the Flashabou stripes and the Styrofoam eyes as shown in the top view above. Cover the eyes and stripes with the epoxy cement.

Wiggle Tail Lure

Origin: United States
Originator: George Cik
Used for: All species

Developed as a bass fly, this pattern can be also used for most any game fish. It's a surface-type lure that works very well over weed beds and is almost weedless because of its construction.

Thread	White 3/0 or 0 Monocord	**Body**	$^3/_8$-inch-diameter by $^3/_4$-inch-long white Evasote foam, formed to a bullet-head shape (see pattern example)
Hook	Mustad 3366, size 4 to 8		
Tail	Fluorescent pink chenille wrapped over the hook shank to the bend, with white, red, and black Krystal Flash tied in as a beard over the hook barb (see pattern example)	**Body markings**	Olive green Pantone permanent marker
		Eyes	Yellow Styrofoam with black centers
Body wire	.006 to .010 diameter, looped at both ends and as long as the body		

Step 1. Lay down a thread base up to the hook bend. Tie in a piece of chenille at the bend, and wrap forward to behind the hook eye.

Step 2. Tie in a small bunch of white Krystal Flash as a beard extending beyond the hook bend, with a shorter bunch of red Krystal Flash over the white, followed by a shorter bunch of black Krystal Flash over the red. Form a neat head and tie off. Give the head a coat of head cement.

Step 3. Pass a piece of wire through the hook eye of the tail assembly. Using a pair of long-nose pliers, form a loop eye securing the tail assembly to the wire (see pattern example above). Form a second loop eye at the opposite end of the wire with approximately $^3/_4$ inch between both eyes. Using the pliers, bend the wire in the center to form a small kink or bump (see sketch below).

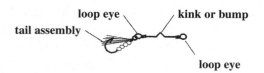

Step 4. Form a neat bullet-head body from a piece of white ($^3/_8$-inch-diameter) Evasote foam.

Step 5. Check to see that the body fits between the two loop eyes on the wire, then cut a slit down the bottom as shown in the sketch below.

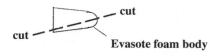

Evasote foam body

Step 6. Apply some epoxy cement inside the slit, and slip the body onto the wire. *Note: Using an X-acto knife, make a slightly deeper cut at the center of the body to allow for the kink in the wire. The kink would prevent the body from rotating around the wire.*

Step 7. Color the foam as desired with a Pantone marker.

Step 8. Glue on the Styrofoam eyes using epoxy cement, and also give the entire body a light coat of cement.

Transparent Minnow

Origin: United States
Demonstrator: George Cik 1995–96
Used for: All species

Developed as a baitfish imitation, the pattern works well for all types of fish species in both fresh and salt water. The shape and coloring can be varied to imitate a variety of baitfish, making the pattern adaptable for all types of fishing.

Thread	Black 3/0 or 0 Monocord	**Body**	Hook shank wrapped with Krystal Flash, with a fine mylar piping outer shape, filled with epoxy
Hook	Mustad 9082S, size 2/0		
Beard	Magenta FisHair		
Tail	1-inch-long black marabou blood feather with 6 to 8 strands of gold Krystal Flash	**Body markings**	Black Pantone permanent marker with gold Sparkle Dust as the lateral line
		Eyes	Red Styrofoam eyes with black centers

Step 1. Lay down a thread base, and tie in the magenta FisHair beard about one-third of the hook shank behind the eye. *Note: The beard should be sparse and extend to the point of the hook.*

Step 2. Tie in the tail at the bend of the hook, as well as a few strands of gold Krystal Flash. Going forward, wrap the entire shank with the Krystal Flash. Remove any excess material and tie off. *Note: Allow about 1/16 inch of bare shank behind the hook eye.*

Step 3. Remove the center core from a 4-inch-long piece of fine mylar piping. Fold the piping in half, and force the hook eye through the piping at the center of the fold.

Step 4. Bring the loose ends of the piping back over the top and bottom of the hook shank, and secure the ends at the tail tie-in point with your thread. *Note: At this point, the shape of the body is determined by how much you pull back on the piping when you tie it down at the tail.*

Step 5. Tie off with a whip finish, and unravel the ends of the piping behind the thread.

Step 6. Separate the beard into equal parts on each side of the bottom piping. Mix a liberal amount of five-minute epoxy cement, and fill the center area between the top and bottom piping. Once the cement starts to set, sprinkle the gold Sparkle Dust down the center of the body on both sides.

Step 7. Add the Styrofoam eyes on each side, and give the entire body a coat of epoxy cement.

Step 8. After the glue is dry, color the top of the body area with the black Pantone permanent marker.

The Widowmaker

Origin: United States
Demonstrator: Bob Dulian 1989–90
Used for: Largemouth bass

Developed basically as a bass pattern to imitate baitfish, but it also works well for all types of fish species. The material colors can be varied to imitate a variety of baitfish, making the pattern adaptable for all types of fishing.

Thread	Black 3/0 or 0 Monocord	**Body**	Black rabbit fur or equivalent
Hook	Bob John's class ten streamer hook, 6X long, 4X wire, size 1 to 6	**Pectoral fins**	White rabbit fur or calf tail
		Wing topping	White rabbit fur or calf tail
Wing	Black dyed rabbit fur strip	**Head**	Black wool
Rib	Gold expandable Japan braid or oval gold mylar tinsel	**Eyes**	Amber-colored plastic doll eyes with black centers

Step 1. Lay down a thread base from behind the eye back to about $1/8$ inch forward of the point, and form a small thread hall.

Step 2. Tie in the black dyed rabbit fur strip on top of the shank at the ball, with the end hairs extending approximately $1\,1/4$ inch beyond the rear of the hook. Give it two wraps on top, then lift the forward end and make a wrap under the strip, then another two wraps on top to secure it.

Step 3. Bring the thread back under the strip, and tie in the gold expandable Japan braid or oval gold mylar tinsel ribbing.

Step 4. Form a dubbing loop with the thread, and using black rabbit fur dubbing or an equivalent, dub the body to within $3/4$ inch of the hook eye. Rib it with the gold expandable Japan braid or oval gold mylar tinsel. Remove any excess materials.

Step 5. Secure the forward end of the black dyed rabbit fur strip wing with the thread, and cut off any excess material.

Step 6. Tie in a $1/8$-inch-diameter bunch of white rabbit fur or calf tail on top of the shank for the pectoral fin. Divide the bunch into two equal parts, and figure-eight each part to lock it in the divided position on each side of the body. *Note: The fin material should extend from the tie-in point to the hook point.*

Step 7. Add the wing topping (white rabbit fur or calf tail) between the pectoral fins at the same tie-in point on top of the shank. *Note: The hairs of the wing topping should be as long as or slightly longer than the hair of the rabbit fur strip wing.*

Step 8. Tie in the head, using bunches of tightly packed black wool. Start at the bottom, and add bunches to the sides and top until the entire area from the wing topping to the hook eye is completely covered. Tie off with a whip finish, and remove the pattern from the vise.

Step 9. Using serrated scissors, trim the head to a rough shape, starting on the bottom and making a flat cut close to the shank. Then cut the top and sides, starting at the eye, with a curved slant cut toward the back. Complete the trimming with fine-point scissors to the desired shape.

Step 10. Glue the plastic doll eyes on each side of the head.

Edge Water Wiggle Bug

Origin: United States
Originator: Larry Tullis
Demonstrator: George Cik 1994–95
Used for: All species

This pattern adds a new dimension in fly tying by utilizing modern materials such as Evasote foam, while it builds traditional fish-catching action into the design. The action and design make it a great leech, damselfly, minnow, crayfish, or shrimp imitation, giving the fisherman a number of options when pursuing various fish species.

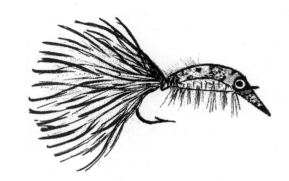

Thread	Size A (color tier's choice)	**Body**	1 ½-inch-long by ¼-inch-wide by ³⁄₁₆-inch thick piece of white Evasote foam or multicolored beach sandal foam
Hook	Tiemco TMC 200R or TMC 9395-4X long or Mustad 3366 or 9674-4X long, size 1, 2, or 4		
Underbody	Chenille (color tier's choice)	**Tail**	Marabou blood feather (color tier's choice) and a few strands of Krystal Flash
Underbody rib	Saddle hackle (color tier's choice)		
		Eyes	Styrofoam eyes (color tier's choice, with black centers)
		Body markings	Pantone permanent markers (color tier's choice)

Step 1. Lay down a thread base from behind the eye back to the bend, and return to behind the eye.

Step 2. Tie in a piece of chenille followed by webby saddle hackle behind the eye (don't crowd the eye), and bring your thread back to the bend.

Step 3. Wrap the shank with the chenille, and secure it with the thread. Remove any excess. Palmer the chenille underbody with the webby saddle hackle, securing it with the thread and removing any excess.

Step 4. Take a piece of Evasote foam or beach sandal, and cut it to the shape shown below.

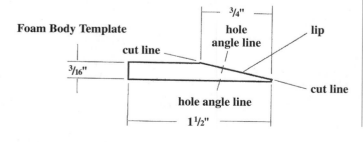

Foam Body Template

Then, with your bodkin or a large needle, punch a hole through the top center of the cut (lip) at the angle shown.

Step 5. Put some five-minute epoxy cement on top of the chenille underbody, and quickly insert the hook eye through the hole you made in the body lip. Bend the foam down at the back end, and firmly secure it at the hook bend with your thread. *Note: The foam or sandal material will compress about 50 to 75 percent. Center the body on the shank; before the cement sets.*

Step 6. Tie in the marabou tail with a few strands of Krystal Flash over the body tie-down point, using neat, close wraps. Tie off with a whip finish. *Note: The marabou tail and the Krystal Flash should be about 1 ½ inches long.*

Step 7. If you used white Evasote foam, color the body with the Pantone markers.

Step 8. Cement the Styrofoam eyes on each side of the head.

Skip Morris Panfish "SMP" Fly

Origin: United States
Originator: Skip Morris
Demonstrator: Walter Story 1997–98
Used for: All panfish species

Developed as a bluegill fly, this pattern can be also used for most any type of panfish. The most effective way to use it is to let it sink to whatever depth is appropriate, and then draw it slowly and steadily back with your rod tip only an inch or two above the water.

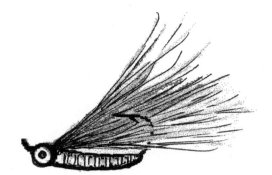

Thread	Orange flat waxed nylon		**Eyes**	Gold bead chain
Hook	Dai-Riki 300 or any light wire 1X long dry-fly hook, size 8 to 14		**Wing**	Orange marabou over yellow marabou
Body	Orange flat waxed nylon		**Head**	Orange flat waxed nylon
Rib	Fine gold oval tinsel			

Step 1. Tie in the orange thread, and lay down a neat, close-wrapped thread base slightly past the hook bend.

Step 2. Tie in a piece of fine gold oval tinsel at the bend, securing it with the orange thread. Then bring the thread forward, using close, neat wraps, to approximately $1/8$ inch behind the hook eye.

Step 3. Rib the orange thread body with the fine gold oval tinsel, and secure it with the thread. Remove any excess tinsel material.

Step 4. Cut a pair of eyes from a bead chain, using tin snips or a wire cutter, and tie them in using crisscross (figure-eight) wraps on top of the shank midway between the body and the hook eye.

Step 5. Invert the hook in the vise, bringing the thread behind the eyes, and tie in the wing, using an orange marabou plume over a yellow marabou plume. Remove any excess material. *Note: The marabou wing should extend about a body length beyond the hook bend.*

Step 6. Use the thread to build a neat head over the wing tie-in point and between the bead chain eyes, and tie off with a whip finish.

Step 7. Give the head and body a coat of five-minute epoxy cement.

Calcasien Pig Boat

Origin: United States
Demonstrator: George Cik 1997–98
Used for: Bass

Developed as a bass fly on the Calcasien River in southwest Louisiana, this pattern can be also used for most any type of game fish. It can be tied in assorted color combinations, such as green and white, red and white, or black and yellow. This pattern is for the original color combination. The most effective way to use this fly is to keep the rubber hackles moving with short twitches and jerks and to change its speed when it is retrieved.

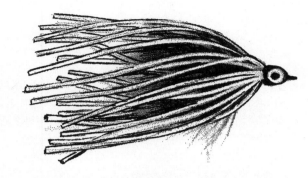

It can also be tied weedless by adding a mono or wire weed guard.

Thread	Black		**Rib**	Black saddle hackle palmered over body
Hook	Mustad 3366 or VMC 9145, size 1/0		**Collar**	36 strands of black rubber hackle
Weed guard (optional)	Mono or wire		**Head**	Black thread (oversize)
Body	Heavy black chenille		**Eyes**	Styrofoam or painted yellow with red centers

Step 1. Lay down a thread base to the bend of the hook. *Note: If you elect to make the pattern weedless, add the weed guard at this point.*

Step 2. Tie in a piece of heavy black chenille and a black saddle hackle (butt end) at the bend, securing them with the thread, then bring the thread forward to approximately 1/8 inch behind the hook eye.

Step 3. Use the heavy black chenille to form the body, going forward with tight, close wraps. Secure it with the thread, and remove any excess material.

Step 4. Rib the body with the black saddle hackle, using evenly spaced wraps. Secure it with the thread, and remove any excess material.

Step 5. Add the collar in front of the body, taking about a dozen strands at a time of black rubber hackle material and tying them in by doubling them over and spreading them evenly around the hook shank. Use about three bunches, until you have a full collar. *Note: The rubber hackle material should extend about an inch beyond the hook bend. If it's too long, trim the hackles with a pair of scissors.*

Step 6. Form a neat, oversize head with the thread, and tie off with a whip finish. Give the head a coat of five-minute epoxy cement. If you're using Styrofoam eyes, put them in position as the cement is starting to set. Give the head another coat of cement over the Styrofoam eyes. If you're going to paint the eyes, wait until the cement dries.

Big Eyed Fingerling

Origin: United States
Originator: Gene Kugach
Used for: All game fish species

This pattern was designed to represent any young trout, perch, or other species in the fingerling stages of its life. The species it's supposed to represent is determined by the color markings applied to the pattern.

Thread	Bright red or black	**Body**	Pearlescent mylar tubing (medium)
Hook	Mustad 3191 or Partridge CS17, size 1/0 to 2	**Throat**	Red hackle barbules
Tail	Marabou ½ inch to ¾ inch long (color tier's choice)	**Head**	Bright red or black thread
		Eyes	Movable plastic doll eyes (7mm)
Underbody	Aluminum Zonker Tape or equivalent, ¾ inch × 1 ½ inch)	**Color markings**	Pantone permanent markers (colors tier's choice)

Step 1. Tie in and lay down a thread base to the hook point. *Note: At this point, a fine lead weight can be applied to the shank if desired.*

Step 2. Tie in the marabou tail, and tie off your thread with a whip finish.

Step 3. Form the underbody using a ¾-inch-wide by 1 ½-inch-long strip of aluminum Zonker Tape or piece of aluminum cut from a pop can. Fold it in half over the hook shank, with the wide part on top of the hook, leaving about ³/₁₆ inch open behind the hook eye, and secure it to the shank by crimping it at the fold along the shank with a pair of pliers.

Step 4. Cut the underbody to the proper shape, rounded at the end and tapered to the back, as shown in the pattern illustration.

Step 5. Remove the core from a 2 ½-inch-long piece of mylar tubing. Slip the tubing over the hook eye and the underbody toward the back of the hook. *Note: If you have difficulty sliding it over the underbody, trim the underbody a little more.*

Step 6. Tie in your thread behind the hook eye, and secure the front end of the tubing with your thread. Also tie in the red hackle barbule beard on top of the hook shank. Form a neat head behind the eye with the thread, and tie off with a whip finish.

Step 7. Tie in at the point where you tied in the tail, and pull back on the mylar tubing, using your bodkin to unravel the mylar from the tie-in point to the end. Work the thread through the mylar until you can secure it to the shank at the tie-in point. Use three to four neat wraps, one in front of the other, when securing the tubing. Tie off with a whip finish.

Step 8. Glue in the plastic doll eyes, as shown in the pattern illustration, using some five-minute epoxy cement.

Step 9. Color the mylar tubing using the permanent markers to match the fish species you want the pattern to represent. *Note: After you finish coloring the body, give it a light coat of epoxy cement to make it more durable.*

Gene's Minnow

Origin: United States
Originator: Gene Kugach
Used for: Trout, panfish

This pattern, like the previous one, was designed to represent a fingerling. The color markings can be varied to imitate a particular species.

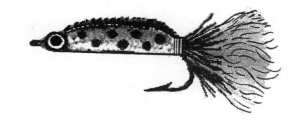

Thread	Black	**Throat** (optional)	Red hackle barbules
Hook	Mustad 3371, size 4 or 8	**Topping**	Peacock herl
Tail	Marabou $^1/_2$ inch to $^3/_4$ inch long (color tier's choice)	**Head**	Black thread
		Eyes	Painted yellow with black centers
Underbody	Yarn, wool, or mylar tubing core	**Color markings**	Pantone permanent markers (colors tier's choice)
Body	Pearlescent mylar tubing		

Step 1. Tie in and lay down a thread base to the hook bend. *Note: At this point, a fine lead weight can be applied to the shank if desired.*

Step 2. Tie in the marabou tail.

Step 3. Form the underbody using yarn, wool, or the core from a piece of mylar tubing. *Note: The body should taper from the back forward and should be no thicker than the core diameter.*

Step 4. Bring your thread back to the tail tie-in point, and tie in two peacock herls on top of the shank.

Step 5. Remove the core from a 1 $^1/_2$-inch-long piece of mylar tubing. Also unravel about a $^1/_2$-inch area at one end, and slip this end of the tubing over the hook eye and the underbody toward the back of the hook.

Step 6. Secure the back end of the tubing with three to four neat wraps, one in front of the other, at the tail tie-in point, bringing the peacock herl forward as you wrap.

Step 7. Tie in the optional red hackle barbule beard in front of the body if you desire. Use your thread to create a neat head, and tie off with a whip finish.

Step 8. Apply a coat of five-minute epoxy to the head and the thread area at the tail tie-in point. Allow the glue to dry, and then paint the eyes on each side of the head.

Step 9. After the painted eyes are dry, color the mylar tubing using the permanent markers to match the fish species you want the pattern to represent. *Note: After you finish coloring the body, give it and the eyes a light coat of epoxy cement to make them more durable.*

Mini Mylar Minnow

Origin: Unites States
Originator: Gene Kugach
Used for: All game fish species

This pattern was designed to represent trout, perch, or other species in the fingerling stages. The color markings can be varied to imitate a particular species.

Thread	Bright red or black	**Body**	Pearlescent mylar tubing
Hook	Mustad 3261, size 8 to 12	**Eyes**	White Styrofoam with black centers
Tail	Marabou ½ inch to ¾ inch long, with 6 to 8 strands of Flashabou (color tier's choice)	**Color markings**	Pantone permanent markers (color tier's choice)
Underbody	Aluminum Zonker Tape or equivalent		

Step 1. Tie in and lay down a thread base to the hook point. *Note: At this point, a fine lead weight can be applied to the shank if desired.*

Step 2. Tie in the marabou and Flashabou for the tail, and tie off your thread with a whip finish.

Step 3. Form the underbody using a strip of aluminum Zonker Tape or a piece of aluminum cut from a pop can. Fold it in half over the hook shank, with the wide part on top of the hook, leaving about ¹/₁₆ inch open behind the hook eye, and secure it to the shank by crimping it at the fold along the shank with a pair of pliers.

Step 4. Cut the underbody to the proper shape, rounded at the front and tapered to the back, as shown in the pattern illustration.

Step 5. Tie in behind the hook eye. Remove the core from a piece of mylar tubing. Slip the tubing over the hook eye, and secure it with your thread behind the eye. Tie off with a whip finish.

Step 6. Pull and slide the tubing over the underbody toward the hook bend. *Note: If you have difficulty sliding it over the underbody, trim the underbody a little more.* Using three to four neat, close wraps of your thread, one in front of the other, tie in over the tubing at the tail tie-in point. Secure the back end of the tubing at the hook bend as shown in the pattern illustration, and tie off with a whip finish.

Step 7. Using your bodkin, unravel the mylar from the tie-in point at the bend to the end.

Step 8. Glue on the Styrofoam eyes, as shown in the pattern illustration, using some five-minute epoxy cement.

Step 9. Color the mylar tubing using the permanent markers to match the fish species you want the pattern to represent. *Note: After you finish coloring the body, give the entire body (including the eyes) a light coat of epoxy cement to make it more durable.*

Water Sneaker

Origin: United States
Originator: Gene Kugach
Used for: All game fish species

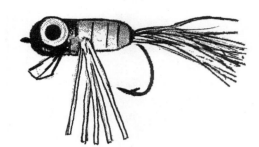

This pattern was designed as a surface lure for large-mouth bass. The color combinations can vary depending on the color of the material (sandal plug) used for the body in the pattern construction.

Thread	Black	**Body**	³/₈-inch-diameter sandal plug as long as the hook shank length, rounded at the front and back, with a slight taper to the back
Hook	Mustad 37187, size 6 or 10		
Tail	8 strands each of silver and blue Flashabou over 6 strands of white Living Rubber hackle and 1 green Living Rubber hackle	**Legs**	4 strands of white Living Rubber hackle
		Lip (optional)	.016-thick clear plastic
		Eyes	Movable plastic doll eyes (7mm)

Step 1. From a beach sandal, cut out a ³/₈-inch-diameter plug. Round the front end using sandpaper, taper the plug slightly to the back, and round the opposite end. After you finish shaping the plug, cut a slit using a knife or razor blade halfway to the center of the plug to slip over the hook shank. *Note: At this point, you can also cut a slit about one-third of the body length across the front end of the body for the optional lip.*

Step 2. Using a thin needle, double-thread a strand of white Living Rubber hackle through the needle eye, and push the needle through the sides at the center of the sandal plug body. *Note: Make sure that the rubber hackle protrudes evenly on both sides of the body, then cut it off at the needle eye.*

Step 3. Lay down a base of thread up to the start of the hook bend. Tie in the tail of Living Rubber hackle and Flashabou, and tie off your thread with a whip finish.

Step 4. Apply some five-minute epoxy cement to the threaded area of the hook shank and into the slit in the body plug. Slip the sandal body plug over and onto the hook shank. Check the body position to see that it sits right on the shank, and allow the cement to dry.

Step 5. (Optional) After the cement is dry, mix another small batch of cement, and glue in the lip plate, if desired (see the lip plate pattern template below).

Lip Plate Template

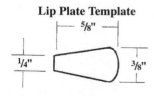

Step 6. Glue on the plastic doll eyes (as shown in the pattern illustration) using the five-minute epoxy cement.

Step 7. Trim the tail and legs to the desired length.

Mylar Fingerling

Origin: United States
Originator: Gene Kugach
Used for: All game fish species

This pattern was designed to represent trout, perch, or other species in the fingerling stages. The color markings can be varied to imitate a particular species.

Thread	Bright red or black	**Body**	Pearlescent mylar tubing
Hook	Mustad 3193, size 1	**Eyes**	White Styrofoam with black centers
Tail	Marabou ½ inch to ¾ inch long (color tier's choice)	**Color markings**	Pantone permanent markers (colors tier's choice)
Underbody	Aluminum Zonker Tape or equivalent		

Step 1. Tie in and lay down a thread base to the hook point. *Note: At this point, a fine lead weight can be applied to the shank if desired.*

Step 2. Tie in the marabou tail, and tie off your thread with a whip finish.

Step 3. Form the underbody using a strip of aluminum Zonker Tape or a piece of aluminum cut from a pop can. Fold it in half over the hook shank, with the wide part on top of the hook, leaving about ¹⁄₁₆ inch open behind the hook eye, and secure it to the shank by crimping it at the fold along the shank with a pair of pliers.

Step 4. Cut the underbody to the proper shape, rounded at the front and tapered to the back, as shown in the pattern illustration.

Step 5. Tie in behind the hook eye. Remove the core from a piece of mylar tubing. Slip the tubing over the hook eye, and secure it with your thread behind the eye. Tie off with a whip finish.

Step 6. Pull and slide the tubing over the underbody toward the hook bend. *Note: If you have difficulty sliding it over the underbody, trim the underbody a little more.* Using three to four neat, close wraps of your thread, one in front of the other, tie in over the tubing at the tail tie-in point. Secure the back end of the tubing at the hook bend as shown in the pattern illustration, and tie off with a whip finish.

Step 7. Using your bodkin, unravel the mylar from the tie-in point at the bend to the end.

Step 8. Glue in the Styrofoam eyes, as shown in the pattern illustration, using some five-minute epoxy cement.

Step 9. Color the mylar tubing using the permanent markers to match the fish species you want the pattern to represent. *Note: After you finish coloring the body, give the entire body (including the eyes) a light coat of epoxy cement to make it more durable.*

Royce Dam's Little Silver Minnow

Origin: United States
Originator: Royce Dam
Used for: Walleye, panfish

This pattern was designed by Royce Dam of Wauwatosa, Wisconsin. It's one of his own creations, which he developed to simulate a minnow when he fishes for panfish or walleye. It can also be used for most any game fish and is a simple pattern to tie. It should be fished deep with a slow, jerking motion.

Thread	White	**Body**	Pearlescent mylar tubing, topped with Sparkle Yarn and overwrapped with flat, medium Pearlescent mylar tinsel (kind that comes on a spool)
Hook	Mustad 9671 2XL, size 6 to 8		
Underbody	Round toothpick cut at both ends at a 30-degree angle from the horizontal on the same side (toothpick length of the shank from eye to hook point)		
		Head	White thread
		Eyes	Tiny dots of black paint

Step 1. Wrap the hook shank with a thread base. Tie on the cut piece of toothpick with the cuts sloping down toward the hook shank, then tie off.

Step 2. Cut a piece of mylar tubing long enough to extend about ¼ inch past the bend of the hook.

Step 3. Remove the core from the mylar tubing. Slide the tubing over the toothpick, and tie it in above the barb, allowing ¼-inch overhang at the back of the hook. (Royce says that he sometimes uses red thread for a little extra color when tying in the tubing).

Step 4. At the same point, tie in the pearlescent mylar tinsel and the Sparkle Yarn topping, allowing the yarn to extend to the end of the tubing at the back of the hook. Tie off with a whip finish, and coat the area with a drop of head cement. Using a bodkin, pick out the yarn and tubing at the back of the hook to form the tail.

Step 5. Tie in the white thread behind the hook eye, and let it hang.

Step 6. Bring the topping straight over the top of the mylar tubing body, securing both the tubing and the yarn where the toothpick ends at the front end of the hook shank.

Step 7. Wrap the pearlescent mylar tinsel forward in tight wraps, covering the body and topping, and secure it with the thread.

Step 8. Build up a tapered head from the hook eye to where you can feel the top of the angle on the toothpick.

Step 9. Add the eyes, using pinpoints of black paint. Finish the body with a coat of glaze or epoxy cement.

Big Eye

Origin: United States
Demonstrator: George Cik 1985–86
Used for: Bass, panfish

This pattern was in the 1986 issue of *Scientific Angler,* vol. 2, no. 3, in an article regarding fly fishing for bass and panfish. It can be tied in an assortment of colors and is a simple pattern to tie.

Thread	Color of body and tail (color tier's choice)	**Tail**	Rabbit fur strip tied matuka style (color tier's choice)
Hook	Mustad 37187, size 6 to 10	**Head**	Thread
Rib	Silver oval tinsel or copper wire	**Eyes**	Black-and-yellow doll eyes
Body	Dubbed rabbit fur, bottom brushed (color tier's choice)		

Step 1. Wrap the hook shank with a thread base to the hook point, and tie in a 6-inch-long piece of silver oval tinsel or copper wire as ribbing, which will be used later in the pattern construction.

Step 2. Using rabbit fur dubbing (color tier's choice), dub the shank going forward to within $1/8$ inch of the hook eye.

Step 3. From a $3\,1/2$-inch-long rabbit fur strip (color tier's choice), remove about $1/16$ inch of the fur at the end that you are going to tie in. Tie in the strip on top of the shank behind the hook eye.

Step 4. Pull the strip back over the dubbed body, and secure it at the hook point using the silver oval tinsel or copper wire. Continue securing the fur strip (matuka style), going forward, using equally spaced wraps up to the thread. Secure the wire or tinsel with the thread, and remove any excess material.

Step 5. Form a small, neat head with the thread, and tie off with a whip finish.

Step 6. Using a toothbrush, brush out the bottom of the dubbed body.

Step 7. Give the head a coat of cement, and glue in the black-and-yellow doll eyes just behind the hook eye using epoxy cement.

George's Minnow

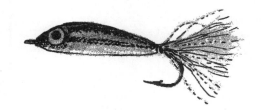

Origin: United States
Originator: George Cik
Used for: Bass, panfish

This pattern was created by George Cik of the Chicago Fly Fishers. It's a baitfish imitation that works well for most game fish.

Thread	White	**Body**	Silver or gold mylar tubing
Hook	Mustad 36620, size 2 to 4	**Coloring**	Blue and red permanent color markers
Tail	White and light blue calf tail topped with light blue Krystal Flash	**Eyes**	Yellow Styrofoam with black centers
Underbody	Shaped Styrofoam		

Step 1. Wrap the hook shank with a thread base to the hook point.

Step 2. Tie in a sparse bunch of white calf tail (about $^3/_4$ inch long) at the hook bend, followed by a sparse bunch of light blue calf tail, and topped with a few strands of light blue Krystal Flash as the tail.

Step 3. Make an underbody from a Styrofoam cup or egg carton shaped as shown below. Use a fairly thick piece of Styrofoam, and cut a slot along the bottom for the hook shank.

Step 4. Apply a little cement to the shank, and slip on the Styrofoam piece. Allow the glue to dry, then tie in your thread behind the hook eye. *Note: Allow about $^1/_{16}$ inch behind the hook eye when you glue in the Styrofoam piece.*

Step 5. Slip one end of a $1 ^3/_4$-inch-long piece of silver or gold mylar tubing over the hook eye, and tie it in with the thread. Make sure you tie it in as close to the hook eye as possible, then tie off with a whip finish.

Step 6. Tie in the thread at the hook bend. Slip the silver or gold mylar tubing over the Styrofoam underbody by pushing it back over the hook shank, turning it inside out. *Note: You may need to trim the Styrofoam if you have difficulty slipping the tubing over it.*

Step 7. Pull the back end of the tubing tight, and secure it with the thread, using close wraps. Tie off with a whip finish. Cut away or unravel any of the tubing at the back end, and give the thread wraps a coat of cement.

Step 8. Color the mylar tubing body with permanent color markers as follows: top area, blue; side stripes, blue; gills, red. After the colors are dry, glue the Styrofoam eyes on each side of the head, and give the entire body a coat of epoxy cement.

Brooks Bouldin's Crappie Fly

Origin: United States
Originator: Brooks Bouldin
Demonstrator: Len Eckerly 1994–95
Used for: Crappie, panfish

This pattern was submitted by Len Eckerly from *Sunfishes,* by Jack Ellis (Lyons Press, 1995). It's a baitfish imitation that works well for most panfish.

Thread	Black	**Tail**	White calf tail
Hook	Mustad 3906B, size 4	**Body**	Pearlescent Sparkle Braid
Eyes	$1/50$-ounce lead eyes painted black		

Step 1. Wrap the hook shank with a thread base to the hook point, and return the thread to $1/8$ inch behind the hook eye.

Step 2. Tie on the lead eyes on top of the shank, using figure-eight wraps, and return the thread to the hook bend.

Step 3. Tie in a sparse bunch of white calf-tail fibers (length should extend just past the bend, curving downward a bit) as the tail. *Note: Wrap the butt ends along the shank to build up the body.*

Step 4. Tie in a 6-inch-long piece of pearlescent Sparkle Braid on top of the shank, wrapping back to the tail windings and returning back in front of the lead eyes with the thread.

Step 5. Wind the pearlescent Sparkle Braid forward in close wraps, crisscrossing the lead eyes with figure-eight wraps to a point forward of the eyes.

Step 6. Secure the pearlescent Sparkle Braid with the thread, and remove any excess material. Form a neat head with the thread, and tie off with a whip finish. Give the thread a coat of head cement.

Grindle Bugger

Origin: United States
Demonstrator: Len Eckerly 1985–86
Used for: Bass, panfish

This pattern was submitted by Len Eckerly from the 1985 *Scientific Angler,* vol. 2, no. 3. It's a pattern that works well for both bass and panfish. The pattern is very similar to a Woolly Bugger, with the addition of the rubber hackle legs. It can be tied in a variety of color combinations and sizes.

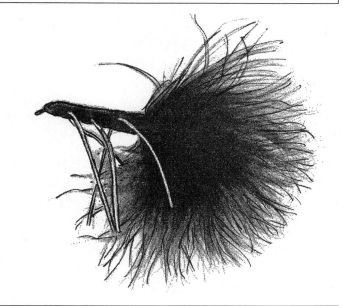

Thread	Color of body (tier's choice)	**Body**	Chenille (color tier's choice)
Hook	Mustad 79580, size 2 to 6	**Legs**	White rubber hackle
Tail	Marabou feather (color tier's choice) 1 ⅓ times the shank length	**Head**	Thread, color of body (tier's choice)

Step 1. Lay down a thread base to the hook bend, and tie in a marabou feather one and a third times the shank length as the tail.

Step 2. Tie in a 6-inch-long piece of chenille, and wrap one-quarter of the shank, going forward with close wraps.

Step 3. Tie in a 2-inch-long single strand of white rubber hackle in front of the last chenille wrap, centered on top of the shank, and secure it with a couple of figure-eight wraps. Continue wrapping another quarter of the shank with the chenille, and add another 2-inch-long single strand of white rubber hackle. Repeat the close wraps with the chenille, covering another quarter, and add another rubber hackle. Wrap the chenille forward to within 1/16 inch of the hook eye. Secure the chenille with your thread, and snip off any excess material.

Step 4. Form a neat head with the thread, and tie off with a whip finish. Give the head a coat of head cement.

Quill Bodied Mylar Minnow

Origin: United States
Originator: Whygin Argus
Demonstrator: Chuck Stoops 1988–89
Used for: Bass, panfish

This pattern was submitted by Chuck Stoops from the *Fly-Tyer's Almanac,* by Robert H. Boyle and Dave Whitlock (Winchester Press). It's a simple baitfish pattern that works well for both bass and other surface-feeding fish.

Thread	Red or black	**Outer body**	Silver or gold mylar tubing
Hook	Mustad 9575, size 8	**Shoulders** (optional)	Fur hair fibers or hackle fibers
Tail	White saddle hackle tips or bucktail, with (optional) a few strands of silver or gold mylar tinsel equal to the shank length	**Head**	Red or black thread
		Eyes	Styrofoam or painted, yellow or white with black centers
Body	Quill shaft from a large bird (such as peacock or goose)		

Step 1. Cut off a segment of a quill shaft slightly shorter than the length of the hook shank. Cut a slit halfway through the rough underside along the entire length of the quill.

Step 2. Lay down a thread base to the hook bend. For the tail, tie in a pair of white saddle hackle tips or bucktail fibers, with a few strands of silver or gold mylar tinsel, if desired, equal to the shank length.

Step 3. Place the quill shaft (centered) on top of the shank, and gently press down along the slit. Secure it with the thread along the entire length, bringing the thread to the back of the quill shaft.

Step 4. Cut a piece of silver or gold mylar tubing slightly longer than the quill body, and remove the core. Slide the mylar tubing over the quill, and secure it at the tail tie-in point, using a few close wraps. Tie off with a whip finish.

Step 5. Tie in the thread at the front of the quill body, and secure the silver or gold mylar tubing with the thread. At this point, if desired, add the optional fur hair fibers or hackle fibers on each side of the shank as the shoulders.

Step 6. Use the thread to build a neat, bulky head behind the hook eye and slightly over the body, and tie off with a whip finish.

Step 7. Glue on or paint the eyes on each side of the head. Also unravel the mylar tubing after the threads at the rear of the body. *Note: Give the head and the thread at the back of the body a coat of epoxy cement after the eyes are glued in place or are painted in and have dried.*

Foam Head Popper

Origin: United States
Originator: Clay Rawn
Demonstrator: Clay Rawn 1998–99
Used for: All species

This pattern is one of Clay Rawn's creations. It uses a Betts-style bullet head made of foam material. The pattern was designed as a surface bass lure that can be tied in various color combinations. It can also be used for other species.

Thread	Black	**Body**	Fluorescent orange cactus chenille or ice chenille
Hook	Mustad 37187 or Tiemco TMC 8089, size 6	**Collar**	Fluorescent orange hackle (collared and tied down)
Tail	In the following order: 10 strands of pearl Flashabou, with 1 strand of yellow or orange Living Rubber hackle (folded twice to form 4 strands), followed by 4 fluorescent orange saddle hackles, with 4 furnace saddle hackles on top	**Head**	Brown Fly Foam strips
		Eyes	Doll eyes (7mm), orange with black centers

Step 1. Lay down a thread base to the hook bend, and tie in ten strands of pearl Flashabou about 3 inches long.

Step 2. Take a single strand of Living Rubber, double it over twice to make four strands, and tie it in on top of the Flashabou. The rubber strands should be as long as the Flashabou.

Step 3. Tie in four fluorescent orange saddle hackles (same length as the Flashabou), splayed out on top of the rubber.

Step 4. Tie in four furnace saddle hackles on top of the orange hackles.

Step 5. Tie in another fluorescent saddle hackle at the same tie-in point, and make a couple of close wraps to form the collar. Secure the hackle with the thread, collaring it back and down, and remove any excess material.

Step 6. Tie in a short piece of orange cactus or ice chenille, and wrap it forward along the shank to within one and a half to two times the diameter of the hook eye. Secure it with the thread, and remove any excess.

Step 7. Take a couple of $1/4$-inch- to $3/8$-inch-wide by 2-inch-long strips of brown Fly Foam, and tie one end of each strip behind the eye, with the opposite end protruding beyond the hook eye. *Note: Tie in the strips one at a time at an angle (tent style) at the top.* After they are securely in place, return the thread over the chenille body to the tail tie-in point.

Step 8. Pull the strips back toward the tail, and secure them with the thread, using close, neat wraps. Tie off with a whip finish.

Step 9. Trim the back ends (flaps) of the strips close to the tie-down point, and glue the eyes on each side of the head with Zap-A-Gap. Also give the threads at the collar a coat of cement.

Prismatic Shad

Origin: United States
Originator: Dave Whitlock
Demonstrator: Bob Dulian 1985–86
Used for: All species

This pattern utilizes prismatic tape in its construction, which gives it a flashing effect when retrieved in the water. The pattern was designed to represent any number of small baitfish found in most lakes, rivers, and streams.

Thread	Fluorescent white floss	**Body**	Silver pearl prismatic mylar tape
Hook	Mustad 9575, size 3/0 to 8	**Gills**	Red hackle or marabou fibers or red mylar tape
Weight (optional)	Lead wire		
Wing	White marabou feather topped with 3 or 4 gray emu or ostrich herls, with 3 peacock herls over the emu or ostrich	**Cheeks**	Mallard breast or flank feathers
		Eyes	Doll eyes (7mm), white or yellow with black centers

Step 1. Lay down a thread base to the hook bend. If desired, wrap in a lead wire around the shank for weight. Secure the wire with the thread, bringing the thread forward to ¼ inch behind the hook eye.

Step 2. Tie in the wing behind the eye in the following order: one white marabou feather, topped with three or four gray emu or ostrich herls, with three peacock herls over the emu or ostrich (wing length about twice the hook shank length).

Step 3. Take a ³/₄-inch by 1 ½-inch piece of silver pearl prismatic mylar tape, and fold it in half to form a ³/₈-inch by 1 ½-inch piece. Using scissors, cut the tape to the shape shown below.

Step 4. Remove the protective backing from the tape, and slip it from under the body up over the lead wire and the lower part of the wing. Pinch both sides of the tape together.

Step 5. Tie in a few red hackle or marabou fibers or apply red mylar tape under the shank in front of the body as the gills.

Step 6. Take a couple of mallard breast or flank feathers, and using just the tips, tie them in on each side of the body as the cheeks.

Step 7. Form a neat head with the thread, and tie off with a whip finish.

Step 8. Give the head a coat of cement, and glue the eyes on each side midway between the head and the part of the body just above the gills, using epoxy cement or Zap-A-Gap.

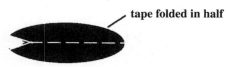

tape folded in half

Prismatic Spoon

Origin: United States
Originator: Gene Kugach
Used for: All species

The Prismatic Spoon was developed by Gene Kugach as a fly-rod spoon made from a lightweight material. The construction utilizes a piece of prismatic-colored aluminum cut from an empty beer or pop can and covered with prismatic tape.

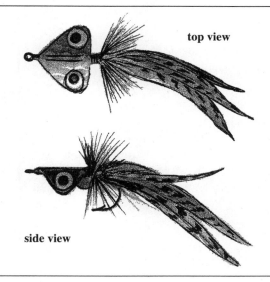

top view

side view

Thread	Black	**Collar**	Red saddle hackles, collared back
Hook	Eagle Claw 214, size 2/0	**Body**	2 pieces orange prismatic aluminum foil cut to shape
Tail	2 red hackles (3 inches long) sandwiched by 2 grizzly hackles (2 inches long)	**Eyes**	Doll eyes (7mm), white with black centers

Step 1. Lay down a thread base to the hook bend, and tie in two red hackles (3 inches long) sandwiched by two grizzly hackles (2 inches long) as the tail.

Step 2. Tie in another red saddle hackle at the same tie-in point, make a couple of close wraps, and secure the hackle with the thread. Collar the hackle back with the thread, and remove any excess material.

Step 3. Take a piece of prismatic aluminum foil or a piece of aluminum from an empty pop or beer can, and cut out the body shape using the template below. Make two identical pieces.

Step 4. Position one of the body pieces (bottom piece) on the underside of the shank, and crimp the back and front tabs around the shank with a pair of long-nose pliers.

Step 5. Apply a coat of five-minute epoxy to the bottom piece surface, place the top piece on top of it, and crimp the front and rear tabs.

Step 6. Secure the rear tab with the thread, and tie off with a whip finish.

Step 7. Tie in the thread at the front tab, and form a neat head. Tie off again with a whip finish.

Step 8. Give the head and the thread at the rear tab a coat of cement. Glue the eyes on each side of the top piece, and slightly bend the head downward on each side of the shank.

Prismatic Minnow

Origin: United States
Originator: Gene Kugach
Used for: All species

The Prismatic Minnow was developed by
Gene Kugach of the Chicago Fly Fishers. The
construction utilizes aluminum foil or (if the foil
can't be obtained) a piece of aluminum cut from an empty
beer or pop can and covered with prismatic tape. It can be
tied in a variety of color combinations and sizes. A red
and white version works very well for northern pike.

Thread	Black	**Collar**	Red saddle hackles, collared back
Hook	Eagle Claw 218, size 2/0	**Body**	Silver prismatic aluminum foil cut to shape
Tail	2 grizzly hackles (3 inches long) sandwiched by 2 short white body feathers (1 ½ inches long)	**Eyes**	Doll eyes (7mm), white with black centers

Step 1. Lay down a thread base to the hook bend, and
tie in two grizzly hackles (3 inches long) sandwiched by two white body feathers (1 ½ inches
long) as the tail.

Step 2. Tie in another red saddle hackle at the same tie-
in point, make a couple of close wraps, and
secure the hackle with the thread. Collar the
hackle back with the thread, and remove any
excess material.

Step 3. Take a piece of prismatic aluminum foil or a
piece of aluminum from an empty pop or beer
can, and cut out the body shape using the template below.

Step 4. Fold the body piece in half, and position it on
the shank, with the wide side upward. Crimp
the back and front tabs around the shank with a
pair of long-nose pliers.

Step 5. Apply a coat of five-minute epoxy to the inside
surface of the folded foil, pinch both sides
together, and allow to dry.

Step 6. Secure the rear tab with the thread, and tie off
with a whip finish.

Step 7. Tie in the thread at the front tab, and form a
neat head. Tie off with a whip finish.

Step 8. Give the head and the thread at the rear tab a
coat of cement. Glue the eyes on each side of
the body.

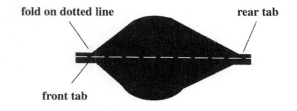

fold on dotted line · rear tab · front tab

Poly Frog

Origin: United States
Demonstrator: Jeff Norberte 1997–98
Used for: Bass

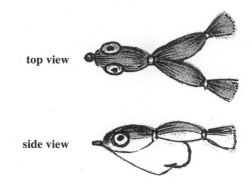

top view

side view

This frog pattern can be tied as a floater or a sinker. It can also be tied using cream or white polypropylene yarn for the underside of the body and legs.

Thread	Olive	**Body/head**	Thick strand of polypropylene yarn, olive green over yellow
Hook	Mustad 37187 or Tiemco TMC 8089, size 6	**Legs**	Polypropylene yarn divided into equal bunches at rear of the body
Weed guard	.012 to .018 stainless steel wire	**Eyes**	Doll eyes (7mm), orange with black centers
Weight (optional)	Lead wire		
Underbody	Polypropylene dubbing or foam		

Step 1. Using a small pair of pliers, cut and shape a wire weed guard to fit the hook as shown below. Secure the weed guard on the hook with thread, and bend the guard wires forward to clear the thread for tying.

Weed Guard

Step 2. If you choose to weight the pattern, wrap the shank with some lead wire, and secure it with the thread. Dub the shank with polypropylene dubbing or tie in a piece of foam to form an underbody, and return the thread behind the hook eye.

Step 3. Tie in a thick strand of yellow polypropylene yarn (about 6 inches long) under the shank behind the eye, with the ends protruding forward beyond the hook eye. *Note: Secure the yarn as close to the eye as possible.*

Step 4. Tie in a thick strand of olive green polypropylene yarn (about 6 inches long) on top of the shank behind the eye, with the ends protruding forward beyond the hook eye, and return the thread to the hook bend. *Note: Secure the yarn as close to the weed guard tie-in as possible.*

Step 5. Pull both strands back over the shank, keeping the yellow under the shank and the green on top. Secure both strands at the hook bend with a couple close wraps of thread to form the body and head, and tie off with a whip finish.

Step 6. Divide the olive green and yellow polypropylene yarn into equal bunches, keeping the green on top of the yellow, to form the legs.

Step 7. Using the olive thread, tie in the leg joint (a couple of close wraps) on each bunch of yarn at a point equal to the body length, and tie off with a whip finish.

Step 8. Trim the back ends of the legs. Glue the eyes on each side of the head with Zap-A-Gap, and give the leg threads a coat of cement. Bend the weed guard wire back over the hook point.

Floating Minnow

Origin: United States
Demonstrator: Jim Lucchesi 1998–99
Used for: All species

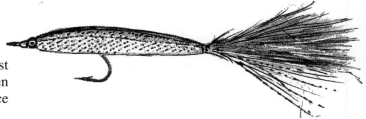

The Floating Minnow, when tied correctly, floats just under the water surface or barely creasing it. When jerked, it should dive and then bob back up to the surface to create the effect of an injured minnow.

Thread	White
Hook	Mustad 34007 or 34011 or Eagle Claw 254N, size 4 to 3/0
Body	$\frac{1}{2}$-inch-diameter silver Corsair tubing (closed body)
Insert	$\frac{1}{4}$-inch or $\frac{5}{16}$-inch by 2- to 3-inch-long closed-cell foam strip
Tail	4-inch-long white marabou plume with blue Flashabou strands
Eyes (optional)	Doll eyes (7mm), yellow with black centers

Step 1. Cut a 2- to 3-inch-long piece of silver Corsair tubing, and insert the hook into the tubing until $\frac{1}{4}$ inch of the shank remains exposed behind the hook eye, pushing the point through the bottom wall. *Note: Make sure the thread lines are on each side of the hook shank.*

Step 2. Attach your thread just behind the hook eye.

Step 3. Take a $\frac{1}{4}$-inch or $\frac{5}{16}$-inch by 2- to 3-inch-long strip of closed-cell foam, and insert it through the rear of the tubing and along the shank until it meets a point just in back of the hook eye.

Step 4. Strip away about 2 inches of base fibers from the butt of a 4-inch-long white marabou feather, and thread the butt end through the tubing beneath the foam on top of the shank until a 1- to 2-inch tail is attained at the opposite end of the tubing. Tie down the marabou just behind the eye, and snip off any excess.

Step 5. Take about ten strands of blue Flashabou, and fold them in half. Using a crochet needle, insert them into the tubing on top of the marabou feather. Tie down the Flashabou just behind the eye, and snip off any excess.

Step 6. Pinch the tubing with your fingers, forcing it to stretch forward, and tie down the front end with the thread just behind the hook eye. Snip off any excess material, form a neat head with the thread, and tie off with a whip finish.

Step 7. Push the rear portion of the tubing forward to reveal the foam, and trim the foam to the desired body length. Push the tubing back with your fingers over the remaining foam, and using the thread, tie down the tubing just behind the foam with close, neat wraps. Tie off with a whip finish.

Step 8. Unravel the rear tubing behind the threads, and give the threads and the head a coat of cement.

Step 9. (Optional) If desired, glue the eyes on each side of the head with Zap-A-Gap.

CHAPTER 6

Terrestrial Patterns

Peach Tree Borer

Origin: United States
Originator: Gene Kugach
Used for: Trout, panfish

The Peach Tree Borer pattern represents a small fly-type insect found in the southern parts of the United States. It's a simple pattern that can be used for both trout and panfish.

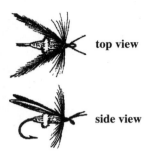

top view

side view

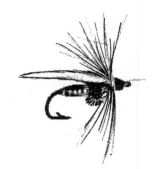

Thread	Black	**Wings**	Tips of black saddle hackles
Hook	Mustad 7957B, size 8 to 10	**Collar**	Black saddle hackle
Body	Rear half: ⅛-inch-thick strip of black art foam	**Antennae**	Hackle stems
	Center joint: Red ostrich herl	**Head**	Black thread
	Front half: ⅛-inch-thick strip of black art foam		

Step 1. Wrap the shank with thread up to the bend of the hook, and tie in a strip of black art foam. Bring your thread back on the shank to the hook point.

Step 2. Start forming a tapered body with the art foam, covering half of the hook shank, and securing the foam with your thread. *Note: When securing the foam, make three to four wraps (one in front of the other and then back to where you started). This will allow an area for the tie in of the center joint.*

Step 3. Tie in a red ostrich herl, and form the center joint with three or four wraps. Secure the herl with your thread, and snip off the excess.

Step 4. With the remaining piece of art foam, continue forming the body in front of the center joint to within ⅛ inch of the hook eye. Secure the foam with your thread, and snip off the excess.

Step 5. Now add the wings and antennae. The wings are made from the tips of a pair of black saddle hackles, and the stripped stems are used for the antennae. Strip the saddle hackles back until the remaining tips are the approximate length of the hook shank. Tie in the tips in a spent position angled toward the back of the fly, allowing the stems to extend beyond the hook eye. Bring the thread forward with a few close wraps over the stems, creating a small flat area. Secure the antennae (stems) with a figure eight (flaring them out), bringing the thread back behind the figure eight.

Step 6. Tie in a black saddle hackle for the collar between the wings and the antennae. Make three or four wraps of the hackle around the shank, securing the wraps with your thread and then cutting off the excess. Use the thread to build a small head between the hackle collar and the antennae, and tie off with a whip finish.

Step 7. Coat the head with cement, then trim back the antennae until they are approximately ⅛ inch long.

Tussock Caterpillar

Origin: United States
Originator: Gene Kugach
Used for: All species

The Tussock Caterpillar is a terrestrial pattern designed to represent a common caterpillar found in the northern parts of the United States. It can be fished for panfish as a surface fly or submerged just below the water surface.

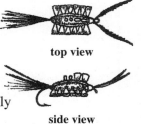

top view

side view

Thread	White or yellow	**Body tufts**	7 2 $\frac{1}{2}$ -inch-long pieces of 3-strand, white acrylic yarn; 2 $\frac{1}{2}$ -inch-long piece of bright red floss
Hook	Mustad 94831, size 6 to 10		
Tail	Small bunch of fine, white deer hair, topped with a small bunch of black hackle fibers	**Body**	Yellow or gold floss (12 inches long)
		Antennae	Black turkey feather segments
Body stripes	2 peacock herls	**Head**	Bright red thread

Step 1. Wrap the shank with thread to the bend of the hook. Tie in the tail, using a small bunch (as long as the shank) of fine, white deer hair topped with a few black hackle fibers.

Step 2. Tie in two peacock herls and the 12-inch-long floss. These will be used later in the pattern.

Step 3. Starting just before the bend, tie in six evenly spaced 2 $\frac{1}{2}$ -inch-long (three-strand) white acrylic yarn. When you come to the third piece, add the 2 $\frac{1}{2}$ -inch piece of red floss on top of the yarn. Also add another piece of acrylic yarn on top of the fourth piece, with the opposite end on top of the fifth piece. Figure-eight each piece of yarn when you add them onto the hook. The side pieces could be cut shorter to make the next step easier.

Step 4. Take the floss, and form the body by wrapping the shank between the yarn to the front of the hook (figure-eight each piece of yarn). *Note: Be sure that the top pieces of floss and yarn stand straight up and the side pieces are in the same horizontal position on each side.* Snip off the excess piece of floss after you secure it at the front of the hook.

Step 5. Bring the two peacock herls forward, with one on each side of the red floss and the white yarn, and secure them at the front. Snip off the excess herl and trim the red floss and the white yarn as shown in the pattern illustration.

Step 6. Tie in a pair of segments from a black turkey feather just behind the eye of the hook. Make a figure eight between the segments to separate them so they represent antennae. Tie off your thread behind the antennae, and add a drop of cement.

Step 7. Using bright red thread, form a nice head behind the antennae, and tie off with a whip finish. Coat the head with epoxy or head cement.

Step 8. Remove the hook from your vise, and using your bodkin needle, unravel all the pieces of white yarn on the top and sides to form the tufts (see pattern illustration). *Note: You may need to even up the tufts with your scissors after you unravel the yarn.* Your caterpillar is now complete.

Skunk Woolly Worm

Origin: United States
Originator: L. Stoner
Demonstrator: Jerry Wasil 1984–1985
Used for: All species

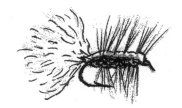

Another variation of the famous Woolly Worm pattern, whose origin is lost in time, but which simulates a land-dwelling insect or an aquatic nymph found in or around freshwater lakes, ponds, or streams.

Thread	Black	**Hackle (legs)**	Black or dark brown neck hackle, tied in at the hook bend and palmered over the under- and overbody
Hook	Mustad 3906B, size 10 to 14		
Weight	4 to 6 wraps of .18-inch-diameter lead wire	**Tail/overbody**	White marabou tied in behind the hook eye and pulled over the top of the underbody
Underbody	Black chenille tied in at the hook bend		

Step 1. Lay down a thread base, and wrap in the lead wire about midshank with four to six wraps. Secure the lead wire with the thread, and bring the thread back to the hook bend.

Step 2. Tie in the black or dark brown neck hackle at the bend of the hook, along with a 2- to 3-inch-long piece of black chenille, then bring your thread forward to behind the hook eye.

Step 3. Tie in behind the eye a bunch of white marabou at the butt ends, with the tips extending about twice the body length beyond the hook eye. *Note: When tying in the marabou, leave ample space (about ¹/₈ inch) behind the hook eye for the head.*

Step 4. Using tight wraps, wrap the black chenille forward over the shank, covering the lead wire and the marabou butts to the marabou tie-in point forming the underbody. Snip off the excess chenille, and tie off with a whip finish.

Step 5. Tie in your thread at the hook bend, then bring the white marabou over the top of the underbody while holding it taut, and secure it at the bend with the thread to form the tail.

Step 6. Using the thread, rib the body forward over the chenille and marabou with evenly spaced cross-hatched wraps to behind the hook eye.

Step 7. Palmer the neck hackle forward over the thread rib to behind the hook eye, secure it with the thread, and remove any excess material.

Step 8. Use the thread to build a small, neat head, and tie off with a whip finish. Give the head a coat of cement.

Bear Creek Cricket

Origin: United States
Originator: C. B. Nance
Demonstrator: Len Eckerly 1988–89
Used for: Panfish

A simple cricket pattern submitted by Len Eckerly, used for bluegill or other panfish. This pattern appeared in the winter 1988 *Bugline*.

Thread	Black	**Body**	Tan chenille
Hook	Mustad 3399A, size 8 to 10	**Rib**	Brown hackle
Tail	Goose biots, white or gold	**Legs**	2 sets of 4 or 5 pheasant tail fibers tied together with an overhand knot
Overbody	Turkey wing quill segment	**Head**	Gray ostrich herl

Step 1. Lay down a thread base, and tie in a pair of white or gold goose biots at the hook bend as the tail. The biots should form a V.

Step 2. Tie in a turkey wing quill segment about ¼ inch wide (that has been coated with head cement) at the same tie-in point. Also tie in a short piece of tan chenille and a brown hackle to be used to rib the body.

Step 3. Form the body by wrapping the tan chenille forward to within ⅛ inch of the hook eye. Secure it with the thread, and remove any excess material.

Step 4. Palmer the brown hackle forward, using equally spaced wraps over the body. Secure it with the thread, and remove any excess material.

Step 5. Bring the turkey wing quill segment over the top of the body, secure it with the thread, and remove any excess.

Step 6. Take four to five pheasant tail fibers, and tie an overhand knot in the center to form a leg. Repeat the process for the second leg.

Step 7. Tie in the legs on each side of the shank in front of the body.

Step 8. Tie in a single gray ostrich herl, and using close wraps, form the head up to the hook eye. Secure the herl with the thread, remove any excess material, and tie off with a whip finish.

Crowe Beetle

Origin: United States
Demonstrators: Bill Somerville 1985–86
Jerry Wasil 1992–93
Used for: Panfish, trout

Beetles are terrestrial insects which at times fall into the water and are eaten by fish. The following is a simple pattern imitating a Crowe Beetle that can be used for panfish or trout.

top view

side view

Thread	Black		**Body**	Peacock herl
Hook	Mustad 34640 or 94842, size 10 to 14		**Head**	Hair fiber butts
Shell	Black deer- or elk-hair fibers		**Adhesive**	Pliobond or vinyl cement
Legs	Black rubber hackle			

Step 1. Lay down a thread base, returning the thread to within 1/8 inch of the hook eye. Next, tie in a bunch of black deer or elk hair fibers on top of the shank up to the hook bend. *Note: Even up the tips by cutting them, and clean out the underfur from the black deer or elk hair fibers.*

Step 2. Tie in three short pieces of black rubber hackle on the underside and at the midpoint of the shank, forming six legs. Adjust the legs to the desired position and secure them in place using figure-eight wraps.

Step 3. Return the thread back to the hook bend, form a dubbing loop with the thread, and tie in some peacock herls at the bend. Bring the thread forward to behind the hook eye.

Step 4. Using the loop, wind the peacock herl in the loop to strengthen the herl strands.

Step 5. Apply a coat of Pliobond or vinyl cement over the top of the shank and wrap the herl forward to the hook eye.

Step 6. After the body is completed, take deer or elk hair fibers, pull them forward over the body to form the shell, and secure them with three or more close wraps of the thread just behind the hook eye.

Step 7. Tie off with a whip finish and trim the hairs at the hook eye, leaving short hair butts as the head.

Step 8. Coat the shell with Pliobond or vinyl cement and allow it to dry.

Black Cricket

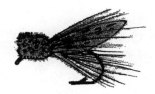

Origin: United States
Demonstrator: George Cik 1990–91
Used for: Trout, panfish

This simple pattern is very effective for trout and panfish.

Thread	Black	**Overwing**	Black deer-hair fiber tips
Hook	Mustad 94840, size 10 to 14	**Head**	Black deer-hair fibers, spun and trimmed to shape
Body	Black deer-hair fibers		
Underwing	Faust Fly Sheet		

Step 1. Starting midshank, tie in a sparse bunch of black deer-hair fibers under the shank with the tips extending beyond the hook bend.

Step 2. Pull the tip ends back over the top of the shank and secure them, using evenly spaced wraps back to the midpoint. Snip off any excess material forward of the midpoint.

Step 3. Make an underwing from a Faust Fly Sheet using the following template.

Faust Fly Sheet
Underwing

Step 4. Tie in the Faust Fly Sheet underwing on top of the shank at the midpoint.

Step 5. Stack and tie in a sparse bunch of black deer-hair fibers on top of the underwing with the tips over and as long as the underwing. *Note: Hold the hairs with your fingers to prevent them from spinning when tying them in.*

Step 6. Fill the remaining half of the shank by spinning tightly packed bunches of black deer hair up to the hook eye. Tie off with a whip finish.

Step 7. Remove the hook from the vise and, while holding it with a pair of forceps, trim the deer hair to form the head. *Note: The head should be cylindrical with a flat bottom. Be careful not to trim off the overwing.*

George Heinz Hopper

Origin: United States
Demonstrator: George Heinz
Demonstrator: George Cik 1990–91
Used for: Trout, panfish

This pattern uses a synthetic winging material. The pattern is a simple imitation of a grasshopper that can be used for trout, panfish, or any other species.

Thread	Yellow Nymo Plus	**Underwing**	Faust Fly Sheet
Hook	Mustad 94831, size 6 to 10	**Legs**	Trimmed large stem red hackle
Tail	Red bucktail fibers	**Overwing**	Natural deer-hair fiber tips
Rib	Brown hackle (palmered)	**Head**	Natural deer-hair fibers, spun and trimmed to shape
Body	Yellow deer-hair fibers		

Step 1. Starting midshank, lay down a thread base to the hook bend and tie in a sparse bunch of red bucktail fibers about a hook shank-long as the tail.

Step 2. After the tail is in place, also tie in a brown hackle for the rib, which will be used later in the pattern construction, then return the thread to midshank.

Step 3. Take a sparse bunch of yellow deer-hair fibers and tie them in under the shank up to the tail tie-in point with the tip ends extending beyond the bend.

Step 4. Fold the tip ends of the yellow deer hair forward on top of the shank and secure them with evenly spaced wraps up to the midshank point.

Step 5. Rib the body with the brown hackle using equally spaced wraps to the midpoint of the shank and secure it with the thread and remove any excess materials.

Step 6. Make an underwing from a Faust Fly Sheet using the following template.

Faust Fly Sheet Underwing

Step 7. Tie in the Faust Fly Sheet underwing on top of the shank at the midpoint.

Step 8. After the underwing is in place, take a couple of red hackles with thick stems and trim off the barbules on each side. Cut the stems to the proper length (hook shank plus the tail) and bend them as shown below to form the legs. *Note: Put a drop of cement at each bend and allow it to dry.* After the cement dries, tie in the legs on each side of the body at the midshank point.

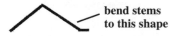

bend stems to this shape

Step 9. Tie in stacked bunches of natural deer-hair fibers (tips to the rear and as long as the underwing) in front of the underwing on top of the shank as the overwing. Hold the fibers with your fingers to prevent them from spinning.

Step 10. Fill the remaining half of the shank with tightly packed bunches of natural deer-hair fibers up to the hook eye and tie off with a whip finish.

Step 11. Remove the hook from the vise, and, while holding it with a pair of forceps, trim the deer hair to form the head. *Note: The head should be cylindrical with a flat bottom.*

George's Sandal Body Bee

Origin: United States
Originator: George Cik
Demonstrator: George Cik 1997–98
Used for: All species

One of George Cik's innovative creations, designed to represent a bee. This pattern can be used for trout as well as most other species.

Thread	White	**Wing**	Dyed yellow elk hair tied on top of the body
Hook	Mustad 3906B, size 12	**Head**	Spun yellow elk hair trimmed to shape
Body	¼-inch-diameter by ¹/₁₆-inch-thick yellow and black sandal plug material, laminated together using Emviretex Lite epoxy and tapered to shape		

Step 1. Using yellow and black ¼-inch-diameter sandal plugs, cut the plugs into ¹/₁₆-inch-thick slices, and use Emviretex Lite epoxy to laminate the slices together, alternating colors, until you have a plug approximately ³/₈ inch long. After the cement dries, taper one end of the plug to ¹/₈-inch diameter, and round off the edges at the opposite end using an X-acto knife and sandpaper. After you finish shaping the plug, cut a ¹/₁₈-inch-deep slit along the length of the plug so that it can be slipped over the hook shank.

Step 2. Put your hook into the vise, and tie in your thread. Lay down a thread base covering two-thirds of the hook shank. *Note: Leave about one-third of the hook shank bare behind the hook eye.* Apply epoxy cement over the thread base, and slip the body, using the slit, onto the top of the shank (tapered end toward the hook eye). Allow the cement to dry.

Step 3. Tie in the elk-hair wing in front of the body on top of the shank. Pull the butt ends back, and secure the wing with a half hitch and a drop of head cement. *Note: The wing hair tips should extend as far back as the rear of the body.*

Step 4. Cover the remaining open area between the body and the hook eye with tightly packed bunches of spun elk hair for the head. *Note: Again, add a half hitch after each bunch with a drop of cement.* After the bunches are secured, tie off and remove the hook from the vise.

Step 5. Trim the elk hair to the desired head shape (see pattern illustration). *Note: Be careful not to cut away any of the wing tip ends when trimming the head; trim only the butt ends of the hair fibers used for the wing.*

Walter's Bee

Origin: United States
Originator: Walter Brewer
Demonstrator: Walter Brewer 1986–87
Used for: Trout, panfish

This pattern was developed by Walter Brewer of the Chicago Fly Fishers. The pattern represents a small bee, similar to the McGinty pattern. It's a simple pattern that can be used for both trout and panfish.

Thread	Black	**Wing**	Woodchuck hair fibers
Hook	Mustad 3906, size 8 to 12	**Hackle**	Brown hen
Tail	Scarlet hackle fibers	**Head**	Black thread
Body	Black and yellow chenille		

Step 1. Wrap the shank with thread up to the bend of the hook, and tie in a sparse bunch of scarlet hackle fibers as the tail.

Step 2. Tie in a short piece of black chenille, followed by a yellow piece, at the same tie-in point as the tail. Bring the thread forward to just behind the hook eye.

Step 3. Starting with the black chenille, make one wrap around the shank at the tie-in point.

Step 4. Make a single wrap in front of the black chenille with the yellow chenille.

Step 5. Repeat the process of black chenille followed by the yellow chenille, until the hook shank is covered. Secure the chenille with your thread, and cut off any excess materials.

Step 6. Tie in a sparse bunch of stacked woodchuck hair fibers in front of the body on top of the shank as the wing. The length of the fibers should be as long as the body plus half the tail length.

Step 7. Tie in a brown hen hackle in front of the wing, make a few close wraps, and secure it with the thread. Remove any excess material, and collar it back.

Step 8. Form a neat head, and tie off with a whip finish. Give the head a coat of cement.

Gill Getter

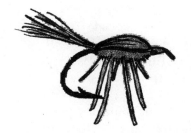

Origin: United States
Demonstrators: George Cik 1989–90
Len Eckerly 1992–93
Used for: Trout, panfish

An excellent pattern for both trout and panfish. The pattern was originally in the August 1989 issue of *Fly Tyer* (vol. 5, no. 2).

Thread	Chartreuse or bright green	**Legs**	Fine white rubber hackle
Hook	Mustad 94840, size 8 to 12	**Body**	Bright green or chartreuse chenille
Tail	Dark moose mane fibers	**Head**	Chartreuse or bright green thread
Shellback	Dark moose mane fiber (lacquered)		

Step 1. Wrap the shank with thread up to the bend of the hook, and tie in a bunch (about twenty) of stacked dark moose mane fibers (length equal to the hook shank) as the tail. *Note: Secure the fibers at the bend with a couple of wraps; do not wrap over the butt ends.*

Step 2. Lift the butt ends, and bring the thread forward. Tie in a short piece of bright green or chartreuse chenille in front of the butt ends, and advance the thread to about midshank.

Step 3. Take a single strand of white rubber hackle, and fold it in half twice. Center the folded hackle on your thread, and tie it in on top of the shank at the midpoint with a couple of close wraps.

Step 4. Using scissors, cut the folded rubber hackle at each loop to form eight individual legs. Figure-eight each strand until you have four strands going forward (two per side) and four strands going backward (two per side), like the legs of a spider.

Step 5. Bring the thread forward to within $1/16$ inch of the hook eye. Wrap the entire shank with the bright green or chartreuse chenille, going forward with tight, close wraps, and secure it with the thread. Snip off any excess material.

Step 6. Use head cement to coat the butt ends of the dark moose mane fibers used to tie in the tail, and allow them to dry. Pull the fibers over the top of the body to form the shellback. Secure the fibers with the thread, and remove any excess material.

Step 7. Form a neat head with the thread, and tie off with a whip finish. Give the head a coat of cement, and if necessary, trim the rubber hackle legs to the desired lengths.

Gartside Pheasant Hopper

Origin: United States
Originator: Jack Gartside
Demonstrators: George Cik 1990–91
Bob Dulian 1994–95
Used for: Trout, panfish

This pattern is a simple imitation of a grasshopper that can be used when fishing for trout, panfish, or any other species.

Thread	Yellow or body color	**Underwing**	Deer-hair fibers (body color)
Hook	Mustad 94831, size 8 to 14	**Legs**	Natural deer-hair fibers (half a shank long) tied alongside the body
Tail	Dark moose-hair fibers		
Body	Light gray, olive, tan, or yellow poly yarn, tapered front to back	**Overwing**	Mottled pheasant fiber from the back of the bird
Rib	Stiff badger or furnace hackle trimmed on top and cut at a tapered angle on the bottom so that the fibers are half a gap width at the tip and a full gap at the base	**Head**	Natural deer-hair fibers, spun and trimmed to shape

Step 1. Starting midshank, lay down a thread base to the hook bend, and tie in a sparse bunch of dark moose-hair fibers about a hook gap long as the tail.

Step 2. Tie in a short piece of poly yarn and a stiff badger or furnace hackle for the rib, which will be used later in the pattern construction. Then return the thread to midshank.

Step 3. Using the poly yarn, wrap in a slightly tapered body, going forward to the midshank point. Secure the yarn with the thread, and remove any excess material.

Step 4. Using the stiff badger or furnace hackle, palmer the body with equally spaced wraps to midshank, securing the hackle with the thread and removing any excess material. *Note: The hackle should be a gap width at the front and half a gap width at the hook point area.*

Step 5. Tie in a sparse stacked bunch of deer-hair fibers (tips to the rear up to the midpoint of the tail) in front of the body on top of the shank as the underwing. Hold the fibers with your fingers to prevent them from spinning.

Step 6. Tie in the legs using about a half dozen natural deer-hair fibers on each side of the body.

Step 7. Tie in a mottled ring-necked pheasant back feather on top of the underwing in front of the body, extending to the center of the tail as the overwing. *Note: Coat the feather with head cement before tying it in, and allow it to dry. Then cut a V-notch in the tip by folding the feather.*

Step 8. Fill the remaining half of the shank with tightly packed bunches of spun deer-hair fibers up to the hook eye, and tie off with a whip finish.

Step 9. Remove the hook from the vise, and while holding it with a pair of forceps, trim the deer hair to form the head. *Note: The head should be cylindrical with a flat bottom.*

Gene's Field Cricket

Origin: United States
Originator: Gene Kugach
Used for: All species

Developed by Gene Kugach of the Chicago Fly Fishers, this pattern was designed to represent a common field cricket found throughout the United States. It's a simple pattern to tie and can be used for all species.

Thread	Black	**Wing**	3/8-inch-wide black goose feather segment folded in half and cut at an angle to form a V shape at the back end and tied in front of the rear body
Hook	Mustad 94831, size 10 to 12		
Tail	Goose quill biots		
Rear body	1/8-inch-wide by 12-inch-long strip of black art foam wrapped to form a tapered body about half the shank length	**Front body**	Remaining strip of black art foam wrapped to form a ball from the point where the wing and legs were tied in to within 1/8 inch of the hook eye
Legs	Black hackle tips trimmed with scissors to shape, bent and creased in the center and at the tips, and then tied in on the sides of the rear body. *Note: Bend and crease the hackle stems at the tie-in point so the legs angle toward the back (see pattern illustration)*	**Collar**	Two black saddle hackles, tied in in front of the ball and given a few wraps
		Antennae	Stems of the black saddle hackle used for the collar
		Head	Black thread

Step 1. Lay down a thread base, and build a small ball of thread at the bend.

Step 2. Tie in two black goose biots parallel to the shank as the tail behind the ball. *Note: The biots should lie flat and slightly angled out.*

Step 3. Tie in a strip of black art foam, and form a tapered body covering half of the hook shank. *Note: Don't cut off the excess foam.*

Step 4. Select a pair of black saddle hackles, and using scissors, trim the hackles to form the legs as shown below. After you finish trimming them, tie them in in front of the tapered body.

hackle barbules cut to shape

bend and crease

bend and crease

hackle stem

Note: Trim barbules in this area as close to the stem as possible.

Step 5. Tie in the wing flat over the tapered body between the legs.

Step 6. With the remaining art foam, form a ball from the point where the wing and legs were tied in to within 1/8 inch of the hook eye. Secure the foam with your thread, and snip off the excess.

Step 7. Now add the collar and antennae. The collar is made from the tips of a pair of black saddle hackles, with the stripped stems as antennae. Tie in the hackle stems on top of the shank, using a figure eight to spread them as the antennae in front of the hook eye. Give each hackle tip a few wraps to form the collar. Snip excess materials and trim antennae to the desired lengths.

Step 8. Using the thread, build a small, neat head, and tie off with a whip finish. Coat with cement.

George's Moth

Origin: United States
Originator: George Cik
Demonstrator: George Cik 1986–87, 1988–89, 1991–92
Used for: All species

One of George Cik's creations, this pattern simulates a large moth. A notable feature in the pattern construction is the use of a sandal plug for the body.

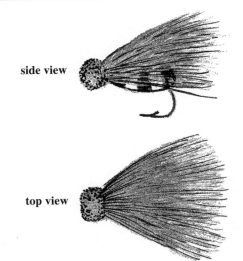

side view

top view

Thread	Tan	**Wing**	Deer-hair fibers
Hook	Mustad 94840 or 3366, size 2 to 10	**Head**	Deer-hair fibers trimmed to shape
Body	Shaped sandal plug		

Step 1. Form a sandal plug body from a yellow or white beach sandal to fit the size of the hook. The body should be egg shaped and about the length of the hook shank. Use a black permanent marker to color the plug with a couple of black stripes (bee style).

Step 2. Cut a slit in the plug bottom, and glue the plug onto the hook shank with five-minute epoxy cement. *Note: The front of the plug should be about one-third of the shank behind the hook eye.*

Step 3. Take a good-size stacked bunch of natural color deer-hair fibers, and tie them in on top of the shank. *Note: Hold the hairs with your fingers to prevent them from spinning when tying them in.* After securing them with a few wraps, spread them evenly over the top of the body to form the wing.

Step 4. Fill the remaining half of the shank with tightly packed bunches of spun deer-hair fibers up to the hook eye, and tie off with a whip finish.

Step 5. Remove the hook from the vise, and while holding it with a pair of forceps, trim the deer hair to form the head. *Note: The head should be cylindrical with a flat bottom.*

CHAPTER 7

Nymph Patterns

Gill Killer (Gilly)

Origin: United States
Originator: Gene Kugach
Demonstrator: Gene Kugach 1990–91
Used for: Panfish, trout

The Gilly pattern was developed by Gene Kugach of the
Chicago Fly Fishers. It's a simple nymph pattern that
works very well for bluegill, other panfish, or trout.

Thread	Black	**Thorax**	Bright red yard or dubbing
Hook	Mustad 3906B, size 10 to 14	**Legs**	Brown hackle
Tail	Light green mallard flank feather fibers	**Wing case**	Dark blue mallard quill section
		Head	Black thread
Abdomen	Gold or yellow floss		

Step 1. Wrap the shank with thread up to the bend of the hook, and tie in four to six flank feather fibers (length equal to the hook shank) as the tail.

Step 2. Tie in a 6-inch piece of yellow or gold floss, and form a tapered abdomen about half the length of the hook shank.

Step 3. Snip out a $^3/_{16}$-inch-wide piece of the blue-black part of a mallard duck secondary wing feather for the wing case, and tie it in with the dull side up in front of the abdomen on top of the hook shank.

Step 4. Strip back the fluff from the end of a narrow brown hackle (which will be used for the legs), and tie it in with the shiny side out at the same location as the wing case material.

Step 5. Using bright red dubbing or by tying in a piece of bright red yarn, form the thorax (which should be wider than the abdomen) in front of the abdomen. *Note: Allow $^1/_{16}$ inch behind the hook eye for the remaining three steps.*

Step 6. Palmer (wind) the brown hackle around the thorax, giving it two or three wraps. Secure the hackle with the thread, and snip off the excess.

Step 7. Bring the wing case material over the top of the thorax, and secure it with your thread, snipping off the excess material.

Step 8. Form a neat head with your thread, and tie off with a whip finish. Give the head a couple of coats of head cement, and allow it to dry.

Jenni's Caddis Nymph

Origin: United States
Originator: Steve Almgreen
Used for: Trout

A simple nymph pattern developed by Steve Almgreen of the Chicago Fly Fishers to represent a caddis nymph in a larval stage.

Thread	Light brown 6/0 Danville	**Body**	Fine bronze or black Larva Lace
Hook	Mustad 80050BR, size 16 to 18	**Collar**	Peacock herl
Head	Bright green seed bead		

Step 1. With a pair of flat pliers, smash the small barb down to make the hook barbless.

Step 2. Thread the seed bead onto the hook against the hook eye, and place the hook into the vise.

Step 3. Attach the thread about midshank, and wrap back to the hook point.

Step 4. Tie in the Larva Lace, wrapping over it to the hook barb and then bringing the thread forward to behind the seed bead.

Step 5. Wrap the shank forward with the Larva Lace, using tight close wraps. Secure it with the thread behind the seed bead, and remove any excess material.

Step 6. Tie in one or two peacock herls by the tips behind the bead, and form the collar with a couple of tight wraps, securing the herls with the thread.

Step 7. Snip off any excess material, and tie off with a whip finish.

Black Knight

Origin: United States
Demonstrator: Gene Kugach 1995–96
Used for: Panfish, trout

The Black Knight is a simple nymph pattern that works very well for bluegill, other panfish, or trout.

Thread	Black	**Abdomen**	Black thread tapered to the tail
Hook	Tiemco TMC 9300, size 10 to 14	**Thorax**	Peacock herl
Weight	.010 to .020 lead wire	**Head**	Black thread
Tail	Moose mane fibers		

Step 1. Wrap the shank with thread up to the bend of the hook, and tie in four to six moose mane fibers (length equal to the hook shank) as the tail.

Step 2. Form a tapered abdomen (about two-thirds of the hook shank) with the black thread.

Step 3. Tie in a peacock herl, and use tight, close wraps to create the thorax. Secure the herl with your thread, and snip off the excess.

Step 4. Form a neat head with the thread, and tie off with a whip finish.

Step 5. Coat the abdomen and the head with a couple coats of head cement, and allow it to dry.

Slate/Brown Wiggle Nymph

Origin: United States
Demonstrator: Bill Somerville 1984–85
Used for: Trout

One of the many nymph patterns found in the Doug Swisher and Carl Richards book *Tying the Swisher/Richards Flies (P. J. Dylan, 1977).*

Thread	Olive	**Wing case**	Gray-black mallard duck quill section	
Hook (abdomen)	Mustad 37360 fine wire, ring eye, cut to length, size 2	**Thorax**	Reddish brown fur dubbing	
Hook (thorax)	Mustad 3906, size 16	**Legs**	Merganser flank feather or partridge feather fibers	
Tail	Merganser flank feather or partridge feather fibers	**Head**	Olive thread	
Rib	Fine copper wire			
Abdomen	Reddish brown fur dubbing			

Step 1. Starting with the abdomen hook, wrap the shank with thread almost to the bend of the hook, and tie in four merganser flank feather or partridge feather fibers (length equal to the thorax hook shank) as the tail.

Step 2. Using sparse amounts of reddish brown fur dubbing, dub the entire hook shank to the eye, and rib it with the fine copper wire. Tie off with a whip finish, remove the hook from the vise, and snip off the hook at the bend, removing the point and barb.

Step 3. Now take the thorax hook, and wrap the shank with thread up to the bend of the hook. Tie in the modified abdomen hook (using the eye) on top of the thorax hook shank.

Step 4. Tie in the gray-black mallard duck quill section for the wing case.

Step 5. Form the thorax with the reddish brown fur dubbing. Pull the wing case material over the top of the dubbed thorax, secure it with your thread, and remove any excess material.

Step 6. Add the legs (merganser flank feather or partridge feather fibers) in front of the thorax under the hook shank, and remove any excess materials.

Step 7. Form a neat, small head with the thread, and tie off with a whip finish.

Peeking Caddis Larva

Origin: United States
Demonstrator: George Cik 1987–88
Used for: Trout, panfish

Young caddisflies (order Trichoptera) are called larvae rather than nymphs. Many fishermen also call them caddis worms rather than larvae because of their appearance. They are a very popular food for brown trout and are found in many streams during the early part of the trout season. The Peeking Caddis Larva is an excellent nymph pattern that works very well for trout and can also be used for panfish.

Thread	Black		**Thorax**	Spectrum #5 green or #31 tan dubbing
Hook	Mustad 9671, size 10 to 14		**Legs**	Brown Hungarian partridge body feather
Rib	Fine gold tinsel		**Head**	Black ostrich herl
Abdomen	Hare's mask blend			

Step 1. Wrap the shank with thread up to the bend of the hook, and tie in a 6-inch piece of fine gold tinsel under the shank for the ribbing, which will be used later in the pattern.

Step 2. Form a tapered abdomen (about half of the hook shank) with the hare's mask blend dubbing.

Step 3. Using the fine gold tinsel, rib the abdomen using equally spaced wraps, and snip off any remaining excess material.

Step 4. Dub another quarter of the shank with either Spectrum #5 green or Spectrum #31 tan dubbing as the thorax.

Step 5. Tie in a brown Hungarian partridge body feather for the legs in front of the thorax, give it a couple of wraps, and secure it collar style with your thread. Snip off any excess material.

Step 6. Tie in a black ostrich herl, and form the head using close wraps, one in front of the other. Secure the herl with your thread, removing any excess material, and tie off with a whip finish.

Wiggling Damsel

Origin: United States
Demonstrator: Eric Heckman 1985–86
Used for: Trout, panfish

One of the many extended body patterns designed to imitate a damselfly nymph, with additional action given to the pattern by adding a plastic scoop.

Thread	Olive		**Wing case**	Gray quill section
Hook	Mustad 94838, size 12		**Thorax**	Olive ostrich herl
Weight (optional)	Lead wire		**Legs** (optional)	Olive grizzly hackle
Tail	Grizzly hackle tip dyed olive		**Scoop**	Plastic cut from a six-pack retainer
Abdomen	Olive ostrich herl wrapped around the grizzly hackle		**Head**	Olive thread

Step 1. Wrap the shank with thread up to the bend of the hook. If you want the pattern weighted, wrap the optional lead wire on the shank, secure the wire with the thread, and return to the bend.

Step 2. Select a grizzly hackle tip about three times the length of the hook shank, and tie it in at the bend on top of the shank.

Step 3. Tie in a single strand of olive ostrich herl, and going along the grizzly hackle extending beyond the bend, wrap the herl about halfway up around the tail feather and then back toward the tie-in point, using close wraps to form the abdomen. Secure the herl with your thread, and remove any excess material.

Step 4. Tie in another ostrich herl, an olive grizzly hackle (optional), and a gray quill section (on top of the shank). Wrap the shank with the ostrich herl, using close wraps to a hook eye width behind the eye, followed by the grizzly hackle, using equally spaced wraps. Secure them with your thread, and snip off any excess materials.

Step 5. Pull the quill section over the top of the ostrich herl thorax, and secure it with your thread, forming the wing case. Remove any excess material.

Step 6. Using a piece of plastic from a six-pack, cut out a thin scoop about 3/16 inch long and about 1/8 inch wide, with a slight taper to the back. Tie it in on top of the shank behind the eye, then lift it up and add some further wraps under the front. Form a neat head, and tie off with a whip finish.

Bitch Creek

Origin: United States
Demonstrators: Len Eckerly 1987–88, 1991–92
Walter Story 1997–98
Used for: Trout, panfish

The Bitch Creek pattern can be tied in several ways to achieve the two-color effect for the abdomen. It can be woven, or it may be formed by using black chenille for the top of the shank and yellow or orange under the shank.

Thread	Black	**Abdomen**	Fine orange or yellow chenille on the bottom, black chenille on top
Hook	Mustad 79580, size 4 to 8		
Weight	Lead wire on each side of the shank	**Legs**	Brown hackle
Tail	2 strands of white rubber hackle	**Thorax**	Medium black chenille
Antennae	2 strands of white rubber hackle same length as tail	**Head**	Black thread

Step 1. Wrap the shank with thread up to the hook point, and tie in a single strand of white rubber hackle about 1 ¼ inches long and folded in half as the tail. Use a couple of figure-eight wraps to separate the strands, forming a V.

Step 2. Tie in a strip of lead wire on each side of the shank to weight the pattern. Secure the lead with the thread, and return to the tail tie-in point.

Step 3. Tie in a 6-inch piece of fine black and orange or yellow chenille at the tail tie-in point, and tie off with whip finish. Turn the vise so that the hook eye points directly at you.

Step 4. Grasp the orange or yellow and black chenille, and make an overhand knot. Slip the black chenille over the top of the shank and the orange or yellow underneath. Bring the unclosed knot to the rear of the shank (at the tail tie-in point), and pull the chenille tight, making sure that the black stays on top and the orange or yellow on the bottom. Repeat the process with the chenille until you cover the shank slightly forward of center.

Step 5. Tie on the thread in front of the chenille. Secure the chenille with the thread, and remove any excess materials. Also at the same point, tie in a brown hackle and a short piece of medium black chenille, and bring the thread forward behind the hook eye.

Step 6. Tie in a single strand of white rubber hackle (folded in half) as the antennae just behind the hook eye (same length as tail). Use a couple of figure-eight wraps to separate the strands, forming a V.

Step 7. Take the black chenille, and wrap it forward using tight, close wraps to form the thorax up to the antennae. Secure the chenille with the thread, and remove any excess.

Step 8. Palmer (wind) the brown hackle around the thorax, giving it two or three wraps to form the legs. Secure the hackle with the thread, and snip off the excess.

Step 9. Bring the thread forward of the antennae, and form a neat head with your thread. Tie off with a whip finish. Give the head a couple coats of head cement, and allow it to dry.

Olive Sedge

Origin: United States
Demonstrator: Bob Dulian 1987–88
Used for: Trout

One of the many sedge patterns that are often considered wet-fly patterns as well as nymphs. Bob Dulian obtained this pattern from the *American Fly Tying Manual* by Randall Kaufmann (Frank Amato Publications, 1975).

Thread	Brown		**Legs**	Brown partridge fibers tied beard style
Hook	Mustad 3906, size 14 to 18		**Thorax**	Hare's ear fur dubbing
Abdomen	Olive fur or dubbing		**Head**	Brown thread
Wing slats	Gray mallard duck wing quill sections			

Step 1. Wrap the shank with thread up to the bend of the hook, and dub in the abdomen using olive fur or olive dubbing covering two-thirds of the hook shank.

Step 2. Take a matched pair (left and right) of gray mallard duck wing quills, and cut out matching sections about ⅛ inch wide. Tie in the sections on each side of the abdomen, and remove any excess material.

Step 3. Tie in a few brown partridge fibers under the shank (beard style) as the legs.

Step 4. Using hare's ear fur dubbing, dub in the thorax up to the hook eye.

Step 5. Form a neat, small head with your thread, and tie off with a whip finish. Give the head a couple coats of head cement, and allow it to dry.

Royal Nymph

Origin: United Kingdom
Demonstrator: Warren Wormann 1987–88
Used for: Trout

The Royal Nymph is supposed to be the nymphal stage of the Royal Coachman, but neither the Royal Nymph or the Royal Coachman represents any known insect. The Royal Coachman originated in the United Kingdom, and it was just a matter of time before someone created a nymph pattern.

Thread	Black	**Wing case**	Dark blue mallard quill section or dark mottled turkey
Hook	Mustad 3906, size 12 to 16	**Legs** (optional)	Brown hackle
Tail	Golden pheasant tippets	**Thorax**	Chocolate brown rabbit fur dubbing
Weight (optional)	Lead wire		
Butt	Peacock herl	**Head**	Black thread
Abdomen	Scarlet floss		

Step 1. Wrap the shank with thread up to the bend of the hook, and tie in a few golden pheasant tippets (length equal to the hook shank) as the tail. Bring the thread forward to the hook eye.

Step 2. If you want the pattern weighted, wrap a piece of lead wire around the shank (three or four wraps) behind the eye, secure the wire with the thread, and return to the tail tie-in point.

Step 3. Tie in a strand of peacock herl, and form the butt at the tail tie-in by making a couple of close wraps. Secure the herl with the thread, and remove any excess material.

Step 4. Tie in a short piece of scarlet floss in front of the butt, and build a neat abdomen, going forward to about $3/16$ inch from the hook eye. Secure the floss with the thread, and remove any excess material.

Step 5. Cut out a $1/8$-inch-thick section of a dark blue mallard quill feather or dark mottled turkey feather, and coat it with some head cement. After the glue is dry, tie in the feather section at the front of the abdomen, and also tie in a brown hackle if you choose to add the optional legs.

Step 6. Using chocolate brown rabbit fur dubbing, dub in the thorax up to the hook eye. After the thorax is finished, palmer the brown hackle through it, and secure it with the thread. Remove any excess material.

Step 7. Bring the wing case material over the top of the thorax, and secure it with your thread, snipping off the excess material.

Step 8. Form a neat head with your thread, and tie off with a whip finish. Give the head a couple coats of head cement, and allow it to dry.

Carrot Nymph

Origin: United States
Demonstrator: Jerry Wasil 1985–86
Used for: Panfish, trout

A great pattern for both trout and panfish. Very simple to tie, using few special materials.

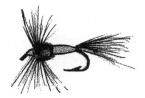

Thread	Orange	**Thorax**	Black chenille or fur dubbing
Hook	Mustad 3906B, size 10 to 16	**Legs**	Black hackle
Tail	Black hackle barbules	**Head**	Orange thread
Abdomen	Orange thread or acetate floss		

Step 1. Wrap the shank with thread up to the bend of the hook, and tie in four to six black hackle barbules (length equal to the hook shank) as the tail.

Step 2. Tie in a 6-inch piece of acetate floss or use the orange thread to form a tapered abdomen, going forward to about three-fourths of the shank length.

Step 3. Tie in a short piece of black chenille in front of the abdomen, give it a couple of wraps, secure it with the thread, and remove any excess material. Alternatively, dub in the thorax in front of the abdomen using black rabbit, beaver, or any other fur dubbing.

Step 4. Tie in a black hackle in front of the thorax, and give it a couple of wraps. Secure it with the thread, and remove any excess material.

Step 5. Form a neat head with your thread, and tie off with a whip finish. Give the head a couple coats of head cement, and allow it to dry.

Giant Stonefly Nymph

Origin: United States
Originator: George Cik
Demonstrator: George Cik 1984–85
Used for: Trout, panfish

This Giant Stonefly Nymph pattern was developed by George Cik of the Chicago Fly Fishers. It works very well for most trout species in western rivers and streams.

Thread	Black		**Legs**	Black goose biots
Hook	Mustad 3665A or 94720, size 4		**Thorax**	Orange dubbing
Tail	Black goose biots		**Wing case**	Black latex or Swiss straw
Weight	Fine lead wire		**Antennae**	Black goose biots
Underbody	1/16-inch-thick orange foam strip		**Head**	Black thread
Abdomen	#22 clear or #23 amber Swannundaze			

Step 1. Wrap the shank with thread up to the bend of the hook, making a small ball of orange dubbing at the bend, and tie in a pair of black goose biots behind the ball as the tail. The ball should spread out the biots to a V shape beyond the bend.

Step 2. Tie in a piece of fine lead wire, and wrap it around the shank (from 1/4 inch behind the eye to the hook point), securing it with the thread. Flatten it along the shank with a pair of pliers, and return the thread to the tail tie-in point.

Step 3. Tie in the thin foam strip and tightly wrap it over the lead, covering the entire shank as the underbody. Secure it with the thread, and remove any excess material. *Note: Using a black permanent marker, color the top of the foam black.*

Step 4. Tie in a 6-inch-long piece of Swannundaze, and advance the thread to midshank. Wrap the Swannundaze forward with tight, close wraps over half the hook shank to form the abdomen, secure it with the thread, and remove any excess material. Advance the thread to the front of the underbody.

Step 5. Tie in a pair of black goose biots on each side of the shank at the front of the underbody (with the tips pointing back) to represent the legs.

Step 6. Tie in a second pair of biots about halfway between the first pair and the abdomen, then tie in a third pair in front of the abdomen.

Step 7. Using orange dubbing, make a close wrap behind and two close wraps in front of the last pair of biots.

Giant Stonefly Nymph continued

Step 8. Take a 6-inch-long by $^3/_{16}$-inch-wide strip of black latex or Swiss straw, and tie it in with the opposite end toward the back of the hook. Using your bodkin, fold the strip over until about $^5/_{16}$ inch protrudes behind the tie-in point, and secure it with the thread to form the first part of the wing case. Then cover it with a wrap of dubbed thread.

Step 9. Repeat Steps 7 and 8 until you have added two more sections to the wing case between the remaining pairs of biots, and continue dubbing in the thorax to behind the hook eye.

Step 10. Form a small ball of dubbing behind the hook eye, and tie in the last pair of goose biots protruding over the hook eye to form the antennae. The ball should spread out the biots to a V shape beyond the eye. Cover the tie-in point with dubbing, returning the thread forward under the antennae biots, and tie off with a whip finish.

Torpedo

Origin: United States
Demonstrator: Jerry Wasil 1985–86
Used for: Panfish, trout

The source of the Torpedo pattern was the *American Nymph Tying Manual* by Randall Kaufmann (Frank Amato Publications, 1995). It's a simple nymph pattern that works very well for bluegill, other panfish, or trout.

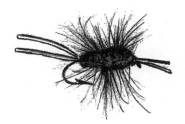

Thread	Black	**Legs**	Black hackle
Hook	Mustad 9672, size 6 to 10	**Thorax**	Black chenille
Tail	2 white rubber hackles	**Antennae**	2 white rubber hackles
Abdomen	Black chenille	**Head**	Black thread

Step 1. Wrap the shank with thread up to the bend of the hook, and tie in a 1-inch piece of white rubber hackle, folded in half, using a couple of figure-eight wraps to spread the ends out into a V shape as the tail.

Step 2. Tie in a 6-inch piece of black chenille, and form an abdomen about half the length of the hook shank.

Step 3. Tie in a black hackle, and continue wrapping the black chenille forward to within $^1/_{16}$ inch of the hook eye as the thorax. *Note: Make the thorax thicker than the abdomen by doubling the chenille wraps.* Secure it with the thread, and remove any excess material.

Step 4. Palmer the black hackle over the thorax, secure it with the thread, and remove any excess material.

Step 5. Take another 1-inch piece of white rubber hackle, and tie it in at the front of the thorax, using a couple of figure-eight wraps to spread them out into a V shape as the antennae.

Step 6. Form a neat head with your thread, and tie off with a whip finish. Give the head a couple coats of head cement, and allow it to dry.

Ron's Swannundaze Damsel

Origin: United States
Demonstrator: Len Eckerly 1986–87
Used for: Trout

The source of this pattern was the Alaska Flyfishers' pattern book, *Fly Patterns of Alaska* (Frank Amato Publications, 1993). It was submitted by Len Eckerly.

Thread	Olive	**Wing case**	Ring-necked pheasant tail fibers
Hook	Mustad 9672, size 6 to 10	**Legs**	Brown hackle
Tail	2 brown hackle tips	**Thorax**	Dark olive rabbit dubbing
Rib	#18 olive Swannundaze	**Head**	Olive thread
Abdomen	Olive chenille		

Step 1. Wrap the shank with thread up to the bend of the hook, and tie in two brown hackle tips as the tail.

Step 2. Tie in a 6-inch piece of olive Swannundaze (#18) as the ribbing to be used later in the pattern construction.

Step 3. Tie in a 6-inch piece of olive chenille, and wrap about two-thirds of the shank, going forward with close, tight wraps to form the abdomen. Secure the chenille with the thread, and remove any excess material.

Step 4. Rib the abdomen with the olive Swannundaze, using equally spaced wraps, and secure it with the thread. Remove any excess material.

Step 5. Tie in a section of ring-necked pheasant tail fibers (about 1/8 inch wide) that have been coated with head cement in front of the abdomen as the wing case, plus a brown hackle, which will be used for the legs.

Step 6. Using dark olive rabbit dubbing, dub in the thorax in front of the abdomen, making it slightly thicker than the abdomen.

Step 7. Palmer (wind) the brown hackle around the thorax, giving it two or three wraps. Secure the hackle with the thread, and snip off the excess.

Step 8. Bring the wing case material over the top of the thorax, and secure it with your thread, snipping off the excess material.

Step 9. Form a neat head with your thread, and tie off with a whip finish. Give the head a couple coats of head cement, and allow it to dry.

Steve's Emerger

Origin: United States
Originator: Steve Almgreen
Used for: All species

Created by Steve Almgreen, a member of the Chicago Fly Fishers, as a nymph pattern that can be used for most species.

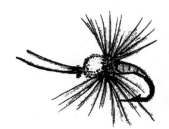

Thread	Black	**Tag**	Gold mylar
Hook	Dai-Riki 070, size 10	**Body**	Rear $\frac{1}{4}$ inch chartreuse floss, front $\frac{1}{8}$ inch peacock herl
Antennae	2 stripped hackle stems		
Head	White closed-cell foam	**Hackle**	2 or 3 wraps of a badger or ginger hackle

Step 1. Tie in the two stripped hackle stems as the antennae behind and on each side of the hook eye, splayed out using figure-eight wraps.

Step 2. Tie in a narrow strip of white closed-cell foam at the same tie-in point, with a few wraps going back securing it on top of the hook shank. Return the thread behind the hook eye, and pull the foam over the wraps to form the head. Secure it with the thread behind the hook eye, then tie off with a whip finish.

Step 3. Retie in the thread behind the head and wrap back, forming a thread base to the hook barb.

Step 4. Tie in a short piece of gold mylar and form the tag, going back with three or four wraps beyond the bend and returning to the tie-in point. Secure the mylar with the thread, and remove any excess material.

Step 5. Tie in a short piece of chartreuse floss and wrap forward, creating a tapered body covering about one-quarter of the hook shank. Secure the floss with the thread, and remove any excess material.

Step 6. Just in front of the floss, tie in a peacock herl, and wrap it forward using close wraps up to the foam head. Secure it with the thread, and remove any excess material.

Step 7. Tie in a badger or ginger hackle in front of the peacock herl, and make two or three close wraps, securing it with the thread behind the head. Remove any excess material, and tie off with a whip finish.

Marabou Nymph

Origin: United States
Originator: Bob Long
Demonstrator: Don Reinhardt 1998–99
Used for: Panfish, trout

The Marabou Nymph pattern is a simple tie, requiring no dubbing and only a bit of marabou. It should be fished slow on the bottom with a quick, short, darting movement or with smooth strips to make it swim.

Thread	Color to match body	**Tail**	Tip of a marabou plume
Hook	Mustad 3906B or Tiemco TMC 200, size 8 to 12	**Body**	Remaining part of marabou plume, twisted and wrapped forward
Weight	.025 to .035 lead wire (8 wraps)	**Wing pad**	Philoplume feather (small aftershaft feather)
Eyes	Small bead chain, darkened with a felt-tip marker	**Head**	Thread, color to match body

Step 1. Wrap the shank with thread up to the bend of the hook, and return to the hook eye. Attach the bead chain eyes a little behind the hook eye with a couple of figure-eight wraps.

Step 2. Wrap the lead wire just behind the eyes, and secure it with the thread, bringing the thread back to the hook bend.

Step 3. Lay the marabou plume on top of the shank, and tie in the tips as the tail at the hook bend, extending about a hook shank beyond the bend. Return the thread to the hook eye.

Step 4. Gently twist the remaining end of the marabou plume to form a marabou rope. Wrap the rope forward to the space in front of the hook eye, tie it down under the eyes, and remove any excess material.

Step 5. Tie in a small Philoplume feather over the top for the wing pad (length equal to the body).

Step 6. Remove any excess material, and then form a neat head with the thread. Tie off with a whip finish.

George's Damsel Nymph

Origin: United States
Originator: George Cik
Used for: Trout

The following pattern is one of George Cik's creations, designed to represent a damselfly nymph. It can be tied in assorted colors and is an excellent trout pattern.

Thread	Color of body	**Wing case**	Orlon or wool strands
Hook	Mustad 3906B, size 8 to 10	**Head**	Thread, body color
Eyes	Bead chain or burnt mono	**Extended abdomen/tail**	Orlon or wool strands (color tier's choice: olive, green, brown, or yellow)
Thorax	Dubbing, color to match body		

Step 1. Lay down a thread base to about midshank, returning the thread to about $1/16$ inch behind the hook eye. Starting about $1/16$ inch behind the hook eye, tie in a pair of bead chain or mono eyes on top of the shank, using figure-eight wraps. Return the thread to midshank.

Step 2. Using olive, green, brown, or yellow dubbing, dub in the thorax, going forward to the hook eye. *Note: The thorax should be ball shaped.*

Step 3. Tie in a couple of orlon or wool strands (about 2 inches long, color to match the dubbing) on top of the shank in front of the eyes for the wing case. Secure it over and between the eyes with figure-eight wraps, and then form a neat head in front of the eyes. Return the thread behind the eyes.

Step 4. Lift the orlon or wool strands behind the eyes, and advance the thread back to the midshank point.

Step 5. Pull the orlon or wool strands back over the thorax, forming the wing case, and secure them at the midshank point with the thread and a whip finish.

Step 6. Make the extended abdomen and tail by lifting and wrapping back over the orlon or wool strands, using equally spaced wraps (two close wraps per segment) to create a four-segmented abdomen. Tie off with a whip finish, and trim the remaining ends of the orlon or wool strands to about $1/4$ inch to form the tail.

SS (Slow Sink) Damsel

Origin: United States
Originator: Jeff Hines
Demonstrator: Jerry Wasil 1994–95
Used for: Trout, panfish

The SS Damsel pattern was developed by Jeff Hines of Dallas. It works incredibly well for taking big bluegill and redear sunfish.

Thread	Black	**Thorax**	Dark olive or olive gray Antron dubbing with 2 strands of pearl or light green Krystal Flash on each side
Hook	Tiemco TMC 200, size 10 to 12		
Tail	Olive marabou fibers	**Hackle**	Hungarian partridge
Rib	Pearl or light green Krystal Flash	**Head**	Black thread
Underbody	Polycelon foam or Fly Foam		
Abdomen	Dark olive or olive gray Antron dubbing		

Step 1. Wrap the shank with thread up to the bend of the hook, and tie in the olive marabou feather fibers (length equal to one-third of the hook shank) as the tail.

Step 2. Tie in a single strand of pearl or light green Krystal Flash as ribbing material to be used later in the pattern construction.

Step 3. Cut a piece of Polycelon foam or Fly Foam sheeting, approximately 10cm long and 3cm wide, and tie it in at the tail tie-in point. Going forward, wrap the entire shank to form the underbody for the abdomen (about two-thirds of the shank) and a fatter thorax (the remaining one-third of the shank). Secure the foam behind the eye, leaving enough room for the hackle and head, and remove any excess material.

Step 4. Bring the thread back to the tail tie-in point, and using dark olive or gray Antron dubbing, dub the entire abdomen (about two-thirds of the shank).

Step 5. Rib the abdomen with the pearl or light green Krystal Flash strand, using equally spaced wraps. Secure it with the thread, and remove any excess material.

Step 6. Continue dubbing the thorax with the dark olive or olive gray Antron dubbing. Then tie in a couple strands of pearl or light green Krystal Flash (length equal to the shank) on each side of the thorax.

Step 7. Tie in a Hungarian partridge body feather in front of the thorax, and give it a couple of wraps. Secure it with the thread (collar style), and remove any excess material.

Step 8. Form a neat head with your thread, and tie off with a whip finish. Give the head a couple coats of head cement, and allow it to dry.

Ugly Helgy

Origin: United States
Originator: Dick Stewart
Demonstrator: Len Eckerly 1991–92
Used for: Trout

One of Dick Stewart's patterns, designed to represent a hellgrammite. It is easy to tie using two common materials, ostrich and chenille.

Thread	Black or brown	**Body**	Brown chenille
Hook	Mustad 79580, size 2 to 8	**Legs**	Sections of black ostrich herl, (2 per side)
Weight	Lead wire, full shank		
Tail	4 pieces of black ostrich herl	**Head**	Black or brown thread
Rib	Black ostrich herl		

Step 1. Lay down a thread base, and then wrap in the lead wire (full length of the shank) to weight the pattern. Secure the wire with the thread, returning it to the hook bend.

Step 2. Tie in four pieces of black ostrich herl (about two-thirds body length) as the tail.

Step 3. Tie in a single strand of black ostrich herl and a 6-inch piece of brown chenille at the tail tie-in point. Form the body with the brown chenille, using close, neat wraps, going forward to within $1/16$ inch of the hook eye. Secure the chenille with the thread, and remove any excess material.

Step 4. Palmer (wind) the single strand of black ostrich herl around the body, using equally spaced wraps. Secure the hackle with the thread, and snip off the excess.

Step 5. Take four sections of black ostrich herl about half the body length, and tie in two on each side of the body.

Step 6. Form a neat head with your thread, and tie off with a whip finish. Give the head a couple coats of head cement, and allow it to dry.

Tellico Nymph

Origin: United States
Demonstrator: Jerry Wasil 1985–86, 1998–99
Used for: Trout

Excellent nymph pattern used for trout throughout the United States. Often used as a last resort, because it represents a wide range of food that most all trout species are attracted to.

Thread	Black	**Rib**	Peacock or ostrich herl
Hook	Mustad 3906B or 9671 or Tiemco TMC 3761, size 8 to 14	**Body**	Yellow floss
		Hackle	Furnace or brown hackle
Tail	Guinea hen feather fibers	**Head**	Black thread
Wing case	Peacock herl or pheasant tail segment		

Step 1. Wrap the shank with thread up to the bend of the hook, and tie in a few (six to eight) guinea hen feather fibers (length equal to one and a half the gap) as the tail.

Step 2. Tie in about three or four peacock herls or a $1/8$-inch-wide pheasant tail segment (coated with head cement) at the tail tie-in point as the wing case, which will be used later in the pattern construction.

Step 3. Tie in a single peacock or ostrich herl at the same tie-in point as ribbing, which will be used later in the construction.

Step 4. Tie in a 6-inch piece of yellow floss at the same point, and form a tapered body, going forward to about one eye length behind the hook eye. Secure the floss with the thread, and remove any excess material.

Step 5. Palmer (wind) the single peacock or ostrich herl around the entire body, using equally spaced wraps. Secure the herl with the thread, and snip off the excess.

Step 6. Tie in the furnace or brown hackle in front of the body, and make about two wraps with the hackle. Then use your fingers to pull down the fibers under the shank, and secure them with the thread (collar style). Remove any excess.

Step 7. Bring the wing case material (peacock herl or pheasant tail segment) over the top of the body, and secure it with your thread, snipping off the excess material.

Step 8. Form a neat head with your thread, and tie off with a whip finish. Give the head a couple coats of head cement, and allow it to dry.

Beadhead Prince

Origin: United States
Originator: Doug Prince
Demonstrator: Len Eckerly 1996–97
Used for: Trout, panfish

The Beadhead Prince pattern is a variation of the original Prince Nymph developed by Doug Prince. The addition of the bead makes this pattern sink faster than the original and allows it to be fished closer to the bottom.

Thread	Black	**Rib**	Fine gold or silver tinsel
Hook	Mustad 9671, size 8 to 12	**Body**	Peacock or black ostrich herl
Headb	Gold or brass-colored bead	**Hackle**	Brown hackle, beard style
Tail	2 black goose biots	**Wings**	2 white goose biots

Step 1. Slip a gold or brass-colored bead over the hook point, and slide it up to the hook eye. Starting behind the bead, wrap the shank with thread up to the bend of the hook, and tie in a pair of black goose biots (length equal to the hook gap, tied forked) as the tail.

Step 2. Tie in a 6-inch piece of fine gold or silver tinsel as the ribbing and a couple of strands of peacock herl or a black ostrich herl, and form the body going forward by wrapping the herl around the shank to the bead head. Secure the herl with the thread, and remove any excess material.

Step 3. Rib the body with equally spaced wraps up to the bead head, using the fine gold or silver tinsel. Secure the tinsel with the thread, and remove any excess material.

Step 4. Tie in a brown hackle in front of the body, and make about two wraps. Then use your fingers to pull down the fibers under the shank, and secure them with the thread (beard style). Remove any excess.

Step 5. Take a pair of white goose biots, and tie them in on each side of the body in the form of a V, so that they flare slightly upward and extend to the bend of the hook.

Step 6. Cover up the tie-in area behind the bead head with neat wraps, and tie off with a whip finish. Give the thread a coat of cement.

Gas Bubble Pupa

Origin: United States
Originator: John Ciulla
Demonstrator: George Cik 1993–94
Used for: Trout, panfish

This pattern was developed on the East Coast by John Ciulla of Park Ridge, New Jersey, to represent a caddis. John added the beads to imitate the expanding adult wings about to emerge from the nymphal shuck.

Thread	Black	**Wings**	Ostrich herl
Hook	Partridge K2B, size 10 to 14	**Collar**	Partridge, grouse, or duck flank feather
Body	Gas-Bubble-Beads (glass beads) and Australian opossum or rabbit dubbing	**Head**	Black thread

Step 1. Wrap the shank with thread just beyond the bend of the hook, and tie in a 4-inch piece of 7X clear monofilament at a point just ahead of the last thread wrap. Thread the Gas-Bubble-Beads (glass beads) onto the monofilament. Tie a few loose overhand knots at the end so the beads don't slide off. *Note: Five small beads are appropriate for a #10 hook; for larger hooks, use larger beads.*

Step 2. Bring the beaded mono forward, and secure one bead at a time to the shank with the thread. Position the beads around the shank so they are evenly distributed; avoid placing them on the bottom of the shank at either end.

Step 3. Bring the thread back to the rear of the hook. Dub the body with Australian opossum or rabbit dubbing, weaving the dubbed thread between the beads.

Step 4. Tie in an appropriate-sized clump of ostrich herl tips below and on each side of the shank just ahead of the body, and cover the thread wraps with a little more dubbing.

Step 5. Tie in the partridge, grouse, or duck flank feather, make a few wraps, and collar back the fibers. Secure the hackle with the thread, and remove any excess material.

Step 6. Form a neat head with your thread, and tie off with a whip finish. Give the head a couple coats of head cement, and allow it to dry.

Hexagenia Nymph

Origin: United States
Demonstrator: Roger Hetzke 1998–99
Used for: Trout

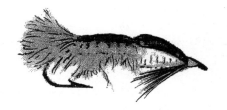

The Hexagenia Nymph is a mayfly pattern that, for all practical purposes, is half nymph and half dun (which is the first stage of an adult mayfly).

Thread	Primrose or yellow	**Gills**	Gray pheasant Philoplume feather
Hook	Tiemco TMC 200R, size 4 to 6	**Abdomen**	Yellow yarn
Tail	Natural gray marabou	**Wing case**	Dark turkey quill segment
Weight	Lead wire	**Thorax**	Yellow yarn
Rib	Copper wire	**Legs**	Mottled brown hen hackle
Back	Dark turkey quill segment	**Head**	Primrose or yellow thread

Step 1. Wrap the shank with thread up to the bend of the hook, and tie in the tip of a natural gray marabou plume about half the shank length as the tail.

Step 2. Weight the body with the lead wire, giving it eight wraps midshank. Secure it with the thread, and return the thread to the tail tie-in point.

Step 3. Tie in an 8-inch-long piece of copper wire, and form a dubbing loop in front of the wire with the thread.

Step 4. Tie in a long segment about 1/8 inch wide (that was coated with head cement) from a dark turkey quill in front of the dubbing loop. The turkey quill segment will be used as the back and wing case later in the pattern construction.

Step 5. Tie in a 6-inch-long piece of yellow yarn, and wrap it forward to about midshank. Secure the yarn with the thread.

Step 6. Select a long gray pheasant Philoplume feather, and center it in the dubbing loop. Spin the loop with a loop spinner, and then wrap the abdomen with the Philoplume rope while pulling the fibers back and down. Secure it with the thread, and remove any excess material.

Step 7. Bring the wing case material over the top of the abdomen, and secure it with your thread. Rib the abdomen up to the hook eye with the copper wire, avoiding tying down the Philoplume. Secure the wire with the thread, and remove any excess material.

Step 8. Wrap in the thorax (fuller than the abdomen) using the yellow yarn up to one hook eye behind the eye. Secure it with the thread, and remove any excess material.

Step 9. Pull the remaining dark turkey quill segment over the top of the thorax. Secure it with the thread, and remove any excess material.

Step 10. Strip the barbules off a mottled brown hen hackle to within 1/4 inch of the tip. Then cut away about 1/16 inch of the tip, leaving a few fibers on each side of the stem. Tie it in at the stem under the shank as the legs, secure it with the thread, and remove any excess material.

Step 11. Form a neat head with the thread, and tie off with a whip finish.

Crappie/Bluegill Damsel

Origin: United States
Demonstrator: Jerry Wasil 1987–88
Used for: Panfish, trout

The Crappie/Bluegill Damsel is considered a wet fly as well as a nymph pattern. It can be tied in a variety of colors and sizes and used for trout as well as other panfish. It should be fished near the bottom using a short, jerking motion for the best results.

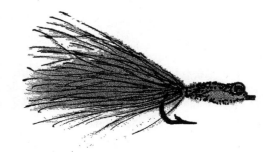

Thread	Body color	**Body**	Olive, brown, or black rabbit fur dubbing
Hook	Mustad 3406, size 8	**Head**	Body color thread
Eyes	Small bead chain		
Tail	Olive, brown, or black marabou plume tip		

Step 1. Lay down a thread base, and return the thread to the hook eye. Just behind the hook eye, tie in the bead chain eyes on top of the shank, using a couple of figure-eight wraps, and return the thread to the hook bend.

Step 2. Tie in an olive, brown, or black marabou plume tip as the tail, and remove any excess material.

Step 3. Using olive, brown, or black rabbit fur dubbing, dub in a slightly tapered body, going forward to the bead chain eyes.

Step 4. Wrap the dubbing around and through the eyes with figure-eight wraps, and build a neat head in front of the eyes. Tie off with a whip finish.

Montana Nymph

Origin: United States
Demonstrator: Warren Wormann 1988–89
Used for: Trout

The Montana Nymph is an excellent western pattern that is one of the most popular nymphs used today. It was designed to represent a stonefly nymph and is a common sight in most Montana fly fishermen's fly boxes.

Thread	Black	**Thorax**	Yellow chenille
Hook	Mustad 9672 or 38941, size 2 to 12	**Legs**	Moderately long-fibered soft black hackle
Tail	A few strands of short black crow feather fibers	**Wing case**	2 strands of black chenille
Abdomen	2 strands of black chenille	**Head**	Black thread

Step 1. Wrap the shank with thread up to the bend of the hook, and tie in a few fibers of short black crow feather (length equal to the hook shank) as the tail.

Step 2. Tie in two 6-inch pieces of black chenille, and form the abdomen about half the length of the hook shank. Secure the chenille on top of the shank with the thread.

Step 3. Tie in a moderately long-fibered soft black hackle in front of the abdomen. At the same point, also tie in a short piece of yellow chenille.

Step 4. Bring the thread forward close to the hook eye, and use the yellow chenille to form the thorax, which should be thicker than the abdomen. Secure the chenille with the thread, and remove any excess material.

Step 5. Palmer (wind) the black hackle around the thorax, giving it two or three wraps. Secure the hackle with the thread, and snip off the excess.

Step 6. Bring the two strands of black chenille (wing case material) over the top of the thorax, and secure it with your thread, snipping off the excess material.

Step 7. Form a neat head with your thread, and tie off with a whip finish. Give the head a couple coats of head cement, and allow it to dry.

Clouser's Swimming Nymph

Origin: United States
Originator: Bob Clouser
Demonstrator: Jerry Wasil 1990–91
Used for: Trout

The Clouser's Swimming Nymph pattern was in the May 1990 issue of *Fly Fisherman*. It's a simple pattern to tie and works well for most trout fishing.

Thread	Body color		**Wing case**	Peacock herl
Hook	Mustad 3906B, size 8		**Legs**	Hen back feather
Weight	.020-inch lead wire		**Thorax**	Ligas dark rust, dirty yellow, or natural hare's ear dubbing
Tail	Tip of a marabou plume (body color)		**Head**	Thread, body color
Abdomen	Ligas dark rust, dirty yellow, or natural hare's ear dubbing			

Step 1. Lay down a thread base, and wrap in the lead wire (about six wraps) to weight the pattern. Secure the wire with the thread, and return to the hook bend.

Step 2. Tie in the tip (length equal to the hook shank) of a marabou plume (body color) as the tail, and bring the thread to about the midpoint of the shank.

Step 3. Using Ligas dark rust, dirty yellow, or natural hare's ear dubbing, dub in a slightly tapered body to about the midshank point. Tie in two or three peacock herls for the wing case and a hen back feather for the legs.

Step 4. Dub in the thorax using the Ligas dark rust, dirty yellow, or natural hare's ear dubbing, making the thorax thicker than the abdomen.

Step 5. Palmer (wind) the hen back feather around the thorax, giving it two or three wraps. Secure the hackle with the thread, and snip off the excess.

Step 6. Bring the wing case peacock herl material over the top of the thorax, and secure it with your thread, snipping off the excess material.

Step 7. Form a neat head with your thread, and tie off with a whip finish. Give the head a couple coats of head cement, and allow it to dry.

CHAPTER 8

Dry-Fly Patterns

Gill Killer (Gilly)

Origin: United States
Originator: Gene Kugach
Used for: Panfish, trout

The Gilly pattern was developed by Gene Kugach of the Chicago Fly Fishers. It's a simple dry-fly pattern that works very well for bluegill, other panfish, or trout.

Threads	Black and bright red		**Body**	Gold or yellow floss (tapered)
Hook	Mustad 94840, size 10 to 20		**Hackle**	Brown
Wings	Blue-black mallard quill sections tied upright and divided		**Head**	Bright red thread
Tail	Light green mallard flank feather fibers			

Step 1. Snip out two segments (as wide as the hook gape) from the blue-black parts of a matched pair of mallard duck secondary wing feathers for the wings. Match up the segments with the dark sides facing out, and tie them in on top of the hook shank approximately a hook eye length behind the eye of the hook, extending forward over the hook eye (length of segments from tie-in point to tips equal to hook shank).

Step 2. Lift the wings up until they are perpendicular to the shank, and make a few wraps in front of them to keep them in the upright position. Then, using your thread, divide the wings by making a couple of figure-eight wraps between them.

Step 3. Bring the black thread up to the bend of the hook, and tie in four to six flank feather fibers (length equal to hook shank) as the tail.

Step 4. Tie in a 6-inch piece of yellow or gold floss, and form a tapered body, going forward up to the wings.

Step 5. Tie in the brown hackle at the stem behind and under the wing (brown hackle fibers equal to body length). Give the hackle a couple of wraps behind and in front of the wing, secure it with your thread, and remove any excess material. Tie off the black thread with a whip finish.

Step 6. Tie in the bright red thread in front of the wing,s form a neat head, and tie off with a whip finish. Give the head a couple coats of head cement, and allow it to dry.

Black Reaper

Thread	Black		**Body**	Rear third: bright red single-strand floss
Hook	Mustad 94840, size 10 to 20			Front two-thirds: black single-strand floss ribbed with a single strand of fine flat silver Flashabou
Wings	Blue-black mallard duck secondary wing feather sections or matched black goose quill section		**Hackle**	Black hackle
Tail	Yellow hackle fibers		**Head**	Black thread

Origin: United States
Originator: Gene Kugach
Used for: Trout, panfish

This pattern was designed to represent any small, black insect. It's an excellent pattern for evening-feeding panfish or trout.

Step 1. Snip out two segments (width of hook gape) from the blue-black parts of a matched pair of mallard duck secondary wing feathers or matched black goose quill sections for the wings. Match up the segments with the dark sides facing out, and tie them in on top of the hook shank approximately a hook eye length behind the hook eye, extending forward over the hook eye (length of segments from tie-in point to tips equal to hook shank).

Step 2. Lift the wings up until they are perpendicular to the shank, and make a few wraps in front of them to keep them in the upright position. Then, using your thread, divide the wings by making a couple of figure-eight wraps between them.

Step 3. Bring the black thread up to the bend of the hook, and tie in four to six yellow hackle fibers (length equal to hook shank) as the tail.

Step 4. Tie in a short piece of bright red single-strand floss at the bend, and bring your thread forward about one-third of the hook shank. Wrap the red floss forward (forming a slight taper) with neat wraps covering one-third of the hook shank, and secure it with your thread. Snip off any excess floss.

Step 5. Tie in a single strand of both silver Flashabou and a short piece of black floss under the shank in front of the red floss, bringing your thread just behind the wings.

Step 6. Wrap the black floss forward, continuing the taper in front of the red floss, covering the shank. Secure it with your thread.

Step 7. Rib the black segment of the body with the silver Flashabou strand, using equally spaced wraps, and secure it with the thread. Snip off any excess material from both the black floss and the Flashabou.

Step 8. Tie in the black hackle at the stem behind and under the wing (black hackle fibers equal to body length). Give the hackle a couple of wraps behind and in front of the wing, secure it with your thread, and remove any excess material.

Step 9. Form a neat head with the thread, and tie off with a whip finish. Give the head a couple coats of head cement, and allow it to dry.

Adams

Origin:	United States
Originator:	Len Halladay
Demonstrator:	Bob Dulian 1986–87
Used for:	Trout, panfish

The Adams pattern was originated by Len Halladay back in 1922 and was named in honor of his good friend Mr. C. F. Adams. It was first fished on the river Boardman in Michigan, and the original pattern was tied with spent wings.

Thread	Gray	**Body**	Muskrat or medium gray poly dubbing
Hook	Mustad 94840, size 10 to 20	**Hackle**	Brown and grizzly hackle mixed
Wings	Grizzly hackle tips, upright and divided	**Head**	Gray thread
Tail	Mixed brown and grizzly hackle fibers		

Step 1. Select a pair of grizzly hackles for the wings, and strip back the fibers until the tips are equal to the shank of the hook. Pair up the tips with the shiny sides facing out, and place them over the shank approximately a hook eye behind the eye, with the stems toward the rear and the tips extending forward in front of the hook.

Step 2. Secure the stems on top of the shank to the hook bend with your thread, and return to the tie-in point. Lift the tips until they are perpendicular to the shank, and make a few wraps in front to keep them in the upright position. Using your thread, divide the tips with a couple of figure-eight wraps, and return the thread to the hook bend. Remove any excess stem material.

Step 3. Tie in a mixed bunch of brown and grizzly hackle fibers (length equal to hook shank) as the tail at the bend on top of the shank. Snip off any remaining excess.

Step 4. Going forward, dub in a tapered body using muskrat or medium gray poly dubbing up to the wings.

Step 5. Tie in a brown and a grizzly hackle (fibers equal to body length) at the stems just behind the wings. Secure the stems with a little more dubbing, and then use your hackle pliers to give each hackle a couple of wraps behind and in front of the wings. After securing the hackles, snip off any excess material.

Step 6. Form a neat head with your thread, and tie off with a whip finish. Give the head a couple coats of head cement, and allow it to dry.

Gray Wulff

Origin: United States
Originator: Lee Wulff
Demonstrators: Bob Dulian 1984–85
Roger Hetzke 1992–93
Used for: Trout, steelhead, salmon

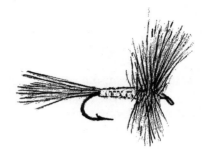

The Gray Wulff pattern was designed to represent an adult mayfly *(Ephemera guttulata)*. The materials used in its construction make it an excellent floater and give it good visibility in fast, rough currents. When tied in larger sized, it's an excellent pattern for both steelhead and salmon.

Thread	Black	**Body**	Muskrat or medium gray poly dubbing
Hook	Mustad 94840, size 8 to 14	**Hackle**	Medium dun
Wings	Natural deer body hair, upright and divided	**Head**	Black thread
Tail	Natural deer body hair tips or moose body hair		

Step 1. Lay down a thread base up to the bend of the hook, and bring the thread forward to within 1/4 inch behind the hook eye.

Step 2. Select a modest-size bunch (diameter of a pencil) of deer body hair fibers for the wings, and even the tips using a hair stacker. Tie in the stacked bunch of hair on top of the shank, with the tips facing forward (over the hook eye), while holding them in position to prevent them from spinning (wing length equal to length of hook).

Step 3. Lift the tips until they are perpendicular to the shank, and make a few tight wraps in front to keep them in the upright position. Using your thread, divide the tips into two equal parts with a couple of figure-eight wraps through the wings and a couple of turns around the base of each wing, and return the thread to the hook bend. Remove any excess material.

Step 4. Tie in a stacked sparse bunch of natural deer body hair tips or moose body hair as the tail at the bend on top of the shank. Snip off any excess.

Step 5. Dub in a tapered body using muskrat or medium gray poly dubbing, going forward up to the wings.

Step 6. Tie in medium dun hackle (fibers equal to body length) at the stem just behind the wings. Secure the stem with a little more dubbing, and then use your hackle pliers to give the hackle two to three wraps behind and in front of the wings. After securing the hackles, snip off any excess material.

Step 7. Form a neat head with your thread, and tie off with a whip finish. Give the head a couple coats of head cement, and allow it to dry.

Grizzly Wulff

Origin: United States
Originator: Lee Wulff
Demonstrator: Walter Story 1996–97
Used for: Trout, steelhead, salmon

The Grizzly Wulff represents an adult mayfly *(Ephemera guttulata)*. It is an excellent floater and quite visible in fast, rough currents. In larger sizes, it makes an excellent pattern for steelhead and salmon.

Thread	Black	**Tail**	Natural deer body hair tips or moose body hair	
Hook	Mustad 94831 or 9671, Tiemco TMC 5212, or Partridge H1A, size 8 to 16	**Body**	Yellow floss	
Wings	Natural deer body hair, upright and divided	**Hackles**	Grizzly and brown	
		Head	Black thread	

Step 1. Lay down a thread base up to the bend of the hook, and bring the thread forward to within 1/4 inch behind the hook eye.

Step 2. Select a modest-size bunch (diameter of a pencil) of deer body hair fibers for the wings, and even the tips using a hair stacker. Tie in the stacked bunch of hair on top of the shank, with the tips facing forward (over the hook eye), while holding them in position to prevent them from spinning (wing length equal to length of hook).

Step 3. Lift the tips until they are perpendicular to the shank, and make a few tight wraps in front to keep them in the upright position. Using your thread, divide the tips into two equal parts with a couple of figure-eight wraps through the wings and a couple of turns around the base of each wing, and return the thread to the hook bend. Remove any excess material.

Step 4. Tie in a stacked sparse bunch of natural deer body hair tips or moose body hair as the tail at the bend on top of the shank. Snip off any excess.

Step 5. Tie in a piece of yellow floss, and going forward, wrap a tapered body up to the wings.

Step 6. Take a brown and a grizzly hackle with fibers equal to the body length, and tie them in at the stems just behind the wings. Secure the stems, and then use your hackle pliers to give the hackle two to three wraps behind and in front of the wings. After securing the hackles, snip off any excess material.

Step 7. Form a neat head with your thread, and tie off with a whip finish. Give the head a couple coats of head cement, and allow it to dry.

Stimulator

Origin: United States
Originator: Randall Kauffmann
Demonstrators: Len Eckerly 1987–88
Todd McCagg 1993–94
Used for: Trout

Excellent imitation of an adult stonefly that works well during caddis hatches (especially in quick water). The pattern can be tied in various colors (yellow, olive, or orange) and sizes from #6 to #16.

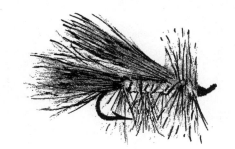

Thread	Fire orange		**Body**	Yellow Sparkle Dubbing
Hook	Tiemco TMC 300R, size 6 to 16		**Wing**	Elk hair
Tail	Elk hair		**Collar**	Grizzly or tan hackle
Rib	Fine gold wire		**Head**	Fire orange thread
Body hackle	Grizzly or tan			

Step 1. Lay down a thread base up to the bend of the hook and on top of the shank, and tie in a stacked bunch of elk hair as the tail. Hold on to the hair fibers while tying them in to prevent them from flaring. *Note: The length of the tail should be a gape length plus 1/8 inch.*

Step 2. Tie in a 6-inch-long piece of fine gold wire and a grizzly or tan saddle hackle at the bend and under the shank. *Note: Both will be used as a ribbing later in the pattern construction.*

Step 3. Going forward, dub in the body using yellow Sparkle Dubbing. The body should cover about three-quarters of the hook shank.

Step 4. Palmer the body using open spiral wraps with the grizzly or tan saddle hackle (secured with the thread), followed by the fine gold wire ribbing. After securing the hackles and the ribbing, snip off any excess material.

Step 5. Tie in the stacked elk hair wing (length should extend to the middle of the tail) on top of the shank in front of the body. *Note: Hold the hair fibers in position to prevent them from flaring.*

Step 6. Tie in another grizzly or tan saddle hackle by the butt end in front of the wing. Dub the area between the wing and one eye length behind the eye with more yellow Sparkle Dubbing. Then palmer the hackle, using tight, close wraps over the dubbing. Secure it with the thread, and remove any excess material.

Step 7. Form a neat head with your thread, and tie off with a whip finish. Give the head a couple coats of head cement, and allow it to dry.

Black Gnat

Origin: United Kingdom
Originator: Unknown
Demonstrators: Eric Heckman 1986–87
Robert Hetzke 1991–1992
Used for: Trout, panfish

This type of pattern is one of the oldest in existence. It's been around for hundreds of years, dating back to 1486 and maybe even earlier. It's an excellent trout pattern that can also be used as a panfish fly. There are many variations in the materials that are used in its construction, but for the most part, the recipe below is the traditional method used to tie it.

Thread	Black	**Body**	Dubbed black rabbit or synthetic material
Hook	Mustad 94840, size 12 to 20	**Hackle**	Black
Wings	Natural gray duck quill sections, tied upright and divided	**Head**	Black thread
Tail	Black hackle fibers		

Step 1. Select a pair of segments from a matched pair of gray duck quills for the wings (length equal to the hook shank). Pair up the segments with the shiny sides facing out, and place them over the shank approximately a hook eye behind the eye, with the butts toward the rear and the tips extending forward in front of the hook. Secure the segments on top of the shank with your thread, and lift the tips until they are perpendicular to the shank.

Step 2. Make a few wraps in front to keep them in the upright position. Using your thread, divide the tips with a couple of figure-eight wraps, and return the thread to the hook bend. Remove any excess butt end material.

Step 3. Tie in a sparse bunch of black hackle fibers (length equal to the hook shank) as the tail at the bend on top of the shank.

Step 4. Going forward, dub in a tapered body using black rabbit fur or a synthetic dubbing up to the wings.

Step 5. Take a black hackle with fibers equal to the body length, and tie it in at the stems just behind the wings. Secure the stem with a little more dubbing, and then use your hackle pliers to give the hackle a couple of wraps behind and in front of the wings. After securing the hackle, snip off any excess material.

Step 6. Form a neat head with your thread, and tie off with a whip finish. Give the head a couple coats of head cement, and allow it to dry.

Elk Hair Caddis

Origin: United States
Originator: Al Trout
Demonstrators: Bob Dulian 1985–86
George Cik 1996–97
Used for: Trout, panfish

Al Trout originated this pattern, which has become an all-purpose caddis imitation. The pattern is a very high floater that can be twitched, skittered, and popped. It can also be tied in gold, black, or green, which cover most caddisfly hatches.

Thread	Tan or brown	**Wing**	Tan elk-hair fibers
Hook	Mustad 94840, size 10 to 20	**Head**	Tan elk-hair fiber butt ends trimmed
Rib	Furnace or brown hackle		
Body	Dubbed hare's ear and mask dubbing or synthetic material		

Step 1. Wrap the shank with thread up to the bend of the hook, and tie in a furnace or brown hackle, which will be used as ribbing later in the pattern construction.

Step 2. Using hare's ear and mask dubbing or synthetic material, dub in the body, going forward to within one length of the hook eye.

Step 3. Palmer the body with the furnace or brown hackle, using equally spaced wraps. Secure it with the thread, and remove any excess material.

Step 4. Tie in a sparse bunch of evenly stacked tips of tan elk-hair fibers on top of the shank in front of the body as the wing. *Note: The length of the wing should be to the back bend of the hook.*

Step 5. Tie off with a whip finish, and trim the butt ends close to the tie-off point.

Catskill Mayfly

Origin: United States
Demonstrator: Todd McCagg 1990–91
Used for: Trout

A mayfly pattern that is found in most East Coast fishermen's fly boxes. Used extensively in the New York Catskills, the pattern has proven to be a great fish catcher. This type of pattern can be tied in a variety of color shades, which will cover most mayfly hatches.

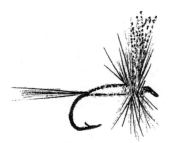

Thread	Black or cream		**Body**	Cream or brown dubbed rabbit or synthetic material
Hook	Mustad 94840, size 10 to 16		**Hackle**	Brown
Tail	Wood duck flank feather fibers		**Head**	Black or cream thread
Wing	Wood duck flank feather fibers, tied upright and divided			

Step 1. From one eye length behind the eye, lay down a thread base to the barb of the hook.

Step 2. Tie in a sparse bunch of wood duck flank feather fibers (length equal to one and a half times the body) as the tail on top of the shank. Return the thread forward to about one-third of the shank length behind the eye.

Step 3. Tie in the wood duck flank feather fibers (tips pointing forward) on top of the shank as the wing. The length of the fibers should be equal to the shank. Lift the fibers straight up, and make six wraps in front and directly at the base to keep them in the upright position.

Step 4. Divide the wing into equal parts, and secure them with figure-eight wraps. Then bring the thread back to the tail tie-in point.

Step 5. Using cream or brown dubbing, dub in a slightly tapered body, going forward to behind the wing.

Step 6. Tie in a brown hackle (dull side facing you), and advance the thread in front of the wing. Wrap the hackle around the shank, three or four turns behind the wing and three or four turns in front. Secure it with the thread, and remove any excess material.

Step 7. Form a neat head with your thread, and tie off with a whip finish. Give the head a couple coats of head cement, and allow it to dry.

Humpy

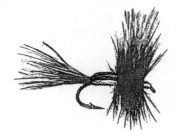

Origin: Western United States
Originator: Jack Horner
Demonstrators: Eric Heckman 1986–87
George Cik 1993–94
Roger Hetzke 1995–96
Bob Dulian 1997–98
Used for: Trout

The Humpy pattern is a takeoff of a pattern called Horner's Deer Hair, created by a fellow named Jack Horner. The pattern can be tied in many color and material variations, such as the Black, Blonde, Royal, Yellow, Poly, or Eastern Humpy. The construction for all of the above is basically the same, and the assembly can be done with little difficulty using the procedure below.

Thread	Tier's choice	**Wings**	Tips of cream-colored deer body hair fibers, tied upright and divided
Hook	Mustad 94840, size 8 to 18	**Hackle**	2 brown or a brown and a grizzly mixed
Tail	Moose, elk, or deer body hair fibers		
Shellback	Cream-colored deer body hair fibers	**Head**	Thread
Underbody	Thread		

Step 1. Lay down a thread base, and return the thread to midshank.

Step 2. Starting at midshank, tie in a sparse bunch of moose, elk, or deer body hair fibers by the butt ends, wrapping them in to the hook bend (length equal to the hook shank) as the tail.

Step 3. Wrap the thread (back and forth) over the butt ends of the tail to form the underbody. After the underbody is in place, return the thread to midshank.

Step 4. Stack a bunch of deer hair (about twice the hook eye diameter), and even up the butt ends. Tie in the deer-hair butt ends (with the tips extending back toward the bend) on top of the shank, starting at the midshank point back to the bend. Wrap back and forth over the deer-hair butt ends to further form the underbody.

Step 5. Bring the tips of the deer hair over the underbody, and secure them with the thread in front of the midshank point. After the tips are secured, lift the tips until they are perpendicular to the shank, and make a few tight wraps in front to keep them in the upright position. Using your bodkin, divide the tips into two equal parts. Then, with the thread, make a couple of figure-eight wraps through the wings to keep them divided, and a couple of turns around the base of each wing.

Step 6. Tie in the hackles, with the front hackle shiny side forward and the back hackle dull side forward. Wrap the hackles individually, giving each a couple of close wraps behind and in front of the wing. Secure them with the thread, and remove any excess material.

Step 7. Form a neat head with your thread, and tie off with a whip finish. Give the head a couple coats of head cement, and allow it to dry.

Goddard Caddis

Origin: United States
Originator: John Goddard and André Puyans
Demonstrator: George Cik 1984–85
Used for: Trout

This pattern has been around for a number of years and is an excellent choice for fishing for trout in fast or turbulent waters.

Thread	Brown	**Hackle**	2 brown hackle feathers
Hook	Mustad 94840, size 10 to 16	**Antennae**	Stripped stems from the 2 brown hackle feathers
Body	Natural gray deer hair, spun and trimmed	**Head**	Brown thread

Step 1. Tie in the thread at the hook bend.

Step 2. Starting at the bend, spin in tightly packed bunches of natural gray deer hair, covering the shank to just behind the hook eye, and tie off with a whip finish. *Note: Allow room for the antennae and head behind the hook eye.*

Step 3. Remove the hook from the vise, and secure it in a pair of forceps. Using scissors, trim the body to the adult caddisfly shape as follows: Starting under the shank, trim the bottom flat and as close to the shank as possible. From the bend, trim the sides and top, going forward on a slant toward the hook eye. Again from the hook bend (at an angle upward), trim the top and sides to about midshank or midbody.

Step 4. Return the hook to the vise.

Step 5. Strip about half the fibers from the stems of a pair of brown hackles. Tie in the hackles in front of the body, with the stems protruding over the hook eye. Using a couple of figure-eight wraps, divide the stems into a V shape. Then wrap the hackles in front of the body, secure them with the thread, and remove any excess material, returning the thread under the hackle stems.

Step 6. Form a small, neat head with your thread in front of the stems, and tie off with a whip finish. Trim the stems to about the body length. Give the head a coat of head cement, and allow it to dry.

Nelson's Caddis

Origin: United States
Originator: Nelson Ishiyama
Demonstrator: Jerry Wasil 1989–90
Used for: Trout

The pattern represents an adult caddisfly *(Trichoptera)* with a remarkable resemblance to the insect's tentlike wings. It was developed by a gentleman named Nelson Ishiyama, who used graduated lengths of deer hair for the wing construction.

Thread	Color to match body
Hook	Mustad 94840, size 12 to 20
Body	Synthetic or natural fur dubbing to match wing material

Wings	Natural deer-hair body fibers applied in 3 separate applications
Antennae	Stripped hackle stems
Hackle	Brown
Head	Thread

Step 1. Lay down a thread base up to the bend of the hook, and going forward, dub about one-third of the shank with synthetic or natural fur dubbing.

Step 2. Tie in a bunch of stacked natural deer-hair body fibers in front of the dubbing, with the tips extending slightly beyond the hook bend. *Note: Don't spin the deer hair; keep it on top of the shank.*

Step 3. Going forward, dub in a second body segment to about midshank.

Step 4. Tie in another bunch of stacked deer body hair in front of the dubbing.

Step 5. Repeat Steps 3 and 4 to add the third dubbing and hair segments, allowing about ¼ inch behind the hook eye.

Step 6. Strip about half the fibers from the stems of a pair of brown hackles. Tie in the hackles in front of the body, with the stems protruding over the hook eye. Using a couple of figure-eight wraps, divide the stems into a V shape. Then wrap the hackles in front of the body, secure them with the thread, and remove any excess material.

Step 7. Form a neat head with your thread, and tie off with a whip finish. Give the head a couple coats of head cement, and allow it to dry.

Neversink Skater

Origin: United States
Demonstrator: Bill Somerville 1984–85
Used for: Trout

Generally, skaters are patterns that use oversize hackles in their construction and are never tied with a wing or a tail. They are occasionally tied with a dubbed or peacock body under the hackles, but for the most part, only two hackles are used. They are excellent floaters that can be tied in a variety of colors.

Thread	White	**Hackle**	2 spade or saddle hackles with 1-inch (minimum) barbules
Hook	Mustad 94840, size 8 to 16	**Head**	Thread

Step 1. Lay down a thread base to the hook point.

Step 2. Tie in a spade or saddle hackle with 1-inch barbules, with the shiny side going forward, and wrap it around the shank using tight wraps. Secure it with the thread, and remove any excess material.

Step 3. Tie in another spade or saddle hackle with 1-inch barbules in front of the other hackle, with the shiny side going back toward the hook bend, and wrap it around the shank using tight wraps. Secure it with the thread, and remove any excess material.

Step 4. Form a neat head with your thread, and tie off with a whip finish. Give the head a coat of head cement, and allow it to dry.

Quill Gordon

Origin: United States
Originator: Theodore Gordon
Demonstrator: Ray Podkowa 1989–90
Used for: Trout

First tied just before the turn of the twentieth century by Theodore Gordon, the pattern was sometimes ribbed with fine gold wire. Also known as the Gordon Quill in parts of the Catskill region of New York, this pattern is still one of the most often used by local fishermen.

Thread	Gray	**Rib**	Fine gold wire (optional)
Hook	Mustad 94840, size 12 to 16	**Body**	Stripped peacock herl quill
Wing	Wood duck feather fibers, tied upright and divided	**Hackle**	Medium dun
Tail	Medium dun hackle fibers	**Head**	Gray thread

Step 1. Starting behind the hook eye, tie in a bunch of wood duck feather fibers (length equal to the hook shank), with the tips facing out toward the hook eye as the wing. Secure the fibers on top of the shank with your thread, and lift the tips until they are perpendicular to the shank. Make a few wraps in front to keep them in the upright position. Using your thread, divide the tips with a couple of figure-eight wraps, and return the thread to the hook bend. Remove any excess butt end material.

Step 2. Tie in a sparse bunch of medium dun hackle fibers (length equal to the hook shank) as the tail at the bend on top of the shank.

Step 3. (Optional) At the same tie-in point as the tail, tie in a short piece of fine gold wire, which will be used as ribbing later in the pattern construction.

Step 4. Strip the flues from the quill of a peacock herl by running the fibers between the fingernails of the forefinger and the thumb. After the quill is stripped, tie in the tip end at the tail tie-in point, and wrap it forward using close wraps to just behind the wing. Secure the quill with the thread, and remove any excess material.

Step 5. (Optional) If you tied in the fine gold wire, wrap it over the quill in the opposite direction from which you wrapped in the quill. Secure the wire with the thread, and remove any excess material.

Step 6. Take a medium dun hackle with fibers equal to the body length, and tie it in at the stems just behind the wing. Secure the stem with thread, and then use your hackle pliers to give the hackle a couple of wraps behind and in front of the wing. After securing the hackle, snip off any excess material.

Step 7. Form a neat head with your thread, and tie off with a whip finish. Give the head a couple coats of head cement, and allow it to dry.

Trico Spinner

Origin: United States
Demonstrators: George Carcao 1989–90
Todd McCagg 1991–92, 1994–95
Used for: Trout

This type of pattern represents a spentwing insect often found floating on the water surface. Spinner patterns in general are fairly easy to tie and are intended to ride the surface film when used.

Thread	Black	**Body**	Dubbed black rabbit, mole, or synthetic material
Hook	Mustad 94840 or 94843, size 18 to 24	**Wings**	Pearl Krystal Flash or Spinner Glass tied spentwing style
Tail	Black hackle fibers or Spinner Glass	**Head**	Black thread

Step 1. Lay down a thread base to the midpoint between the hook point and the barb, and tie in a small bunch of black hackle fibers or Spinner Glass (four to six) as the tail (length equal to the hook shank).

Step 2. Using black rabbit, mole, or synthetic dubbing material, dub in the body, going forward, stopping just behind the hook eye (two hook eye diameters).

Step 3. Take about six to eight strands of pearl Krystal Flash or Spinner Glass, and tie them in centered and flat on top of the shank in front of the body as the wings, using figure-eight wraps to secure them in place.

Step 4. Using more dubbing, dub over the wing tie-in area, covering the thread. Continue dubbing forward to the hook eye.

Step 5. Form a neat head with your thread, and tie off with a whip finish. Trim the spentwings to the desired length. Give the head a couple coats of head cement, and allow it to dry.

Extended Body Parachute Brown Drake

Origin: United States
Demonstrator: George Cik 1988–1989
Used for: Trout

This pattern was submitted by George Cik, who obtained the recipe from Paul Meichior, a member of the Northern Illinois Fly Tiers.

Thread	Tan or white		**Wing**	White calf-tail fibers
Hook	Mustad 94840, size 8 to 10		**Hackle**	Brown tied parachute style
Body	Natural-color elk, or deer-hair fibers folded back		**Head**	Natural color elk or deer hair folded back bullet style
Tail	Long fiber segment from a ring-necked pheasant tail feather			

Step 1. Tie in a bunch of stacked natural-color elk- or deer-hair fibers (about ⅛ inch thick) by the butt ends behind the hook eye, with the tip going forward and extending beyond the eye. *Note: The fibers should be around the entire hook shank (top, bottom, and sides), tied in at the butt ends as close to the hook eye as possible. The fibers will be folded over the shank to form a bullet head later in the pattern construction.*

Step 2. Bring the thread back to the hook bend, and tie in about eight to ten long fiber segments from a ring-necked pheasant tail feather as the tail. *Note: The fiber segments should extend about 2 inches beyond the hook bend.*

Step 3. Bring the thread forward to about ³/₁₆ inch behind the hook eye. Tie in a bunch of white calf-tail fibers on top of the shank as the wing. Secure them in an upright position (perpendicular to the shank) with the thread, then make a few wraps at the base of the fibers. The length of the wing should equal the hook shank length.

Step 4. Tie in a brown hackle at the same tie-in point, making a few wraps around the wing base parallel to the shank (parachute style), and securing the hackle with the thread. Remove any excess material, and bring the thread forward of the wing.

Step 5. Bring the elk- or deer-hair fibers back evenly over the hook eye, and secure them in front of the wing with a couple of wraps to form a folded-back bullet-style head.

Step 6. Using the thread, make a couple of wraps over the hair fibers behind the wing, being careful not to tie down the hackle. Continue making equally spaced wraps to the hook bend.

Step 7. Continue wrapping the thread over the tail area extending beyond the bend, using equally spaced wraps, until you reach the end of the hair fibers. Tie off the last wrap with a whip finish to complete the extended body. *Note: Keep the tail fibers in the center of the hair fibers as you wrap.*

Blue-Winged Olive

Origin: United States or United Kingdom
Demonstrators: Bob Dulian 1984–85
Eric Heckman 1986–87
Roger Hetzke 1991–92
Dave Alexander 1994–95
Used for: Trout, panfish

The origin of this pattern is questionable, because it is claimed by some that it originated in the United Kingdom and by others that it was created in the United States. All that really matters is the fact that it's a great pattern that continues to produce excellent catches.

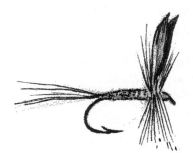

Thread	Olive	**Body**	Olive fur or synthetic dubbing material
Hook	Mustad 94840, size 14		
Wings	Matched gray mallard duck quill segments	**Hackle**	Light gray
		Head	Olive thread
Tail	Light gray hackle fibers		

Step 1. Select a pair of segments from a matched pair of gray duck quills for the wings (length equal to the hook shank). Pair up the segments with the shiny sides facing out, and place them over the shank approximately a hook eye behind the eye, with the butts toward the rear and the tips extending forward in front of the hook. Secure the segments on top of the shank with your thread, and lift the tips until they are perpendicular to the shank.

Step 2. Make a few wraps in front to keep them in the upright position. Using your thread, divide the tips with a couple of figure-eight wraps, and return the thread to the hook bend. Remove any excess butt end material.

Step 3. Tie in a sparse bunch of light gray hackle fibers (length equal to the hook shank) as the tail at the bend on top of the shank.

Step 4. Going forward, dub in a tapered body using olive fur or synthetic dubbing material up to the wings.

Step 5. Take a light gray hackle with fibers equal to the body length, and tie it in at the stems just behind the wings. Secure the stem with a little more dubbing, and then use your hackle pliers to give the hackle a couple of wraps behind and in front of the wings. After securing the hackle, snip off any excess material.

Step 6. Form a neat head with your thread, and tie off with a whip finish. Give the head a couple coats of head cement, and allow it to dry.

Blue Dun

Origin: United Kingdom
Demonstrator: Bob Dulian 1984–85
Used for: Trout, panfish

This pattern has been around for hundreds of years. It's an excellent trout pattern that can also be used for panfish. The materials can be varied. The recipe below is for the traditional method.

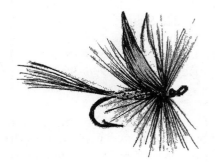

Thread	Gray	**Tail**	Medium dun hackle fibers
Hook	Mustad 94840, size 12	**Body**	Muskrat fur or synthetic dubbing material
Wings	Natural gray mallard duck wing quill sections, tied upright and divided	**Hackle**	Medium dun
		Head	Gray thread

Step 1. Select a pair of segments from a matched pair of gray mallard duck quills for the wings (length equal to the hook shank). Pair up the segments with the shiny sides facing out, and place them over the shank approximately a hook eye behind the eye, with the butts toward the rear and tips extending forward in front of the hook. Secure the segments on top of the shank with your thread, and lift the tips until they are perpendicular to the shank.

Step 2. Make a few wraps in front to keep them in the upright position. Using your thread, divide the tips with a couple of figure-eight wraps, and return the thread to the hook bend. Remove any excess butt end material.

Step 3. Tie in a sparse bunch of medium dun hackle fibers (length equal to the hook shank) as the tail at the bend on top of the shank.

Step 4. Going forward, dub in a tapered body using muskrat fur or synthetic dubbing material up to the wings.

Step 5. Take a medium dun hackle with fibers equal to the body length, and tie it in at the stems just behind the wings. Secure the stem with a little more dubbing, and then use your hackle pliers to give the hackle a couple of wraps behind and in front of the wings. After securing the hackle, snip off any excess material.

Step 6. Form a neat head with your thread, and tie off with a whip finish. Give the head a couple coats of head cement, and allow it to dry.

Henryville Special

Origin: United States
Originator: Hiram Brobst
Demonstrators: Eric Heckman 1986–87
Roger Hetzke 1998–99
Used for: Trout

The Henryville Special is a caddisfly imitation that was first introduced by Hiram Brobst while fishing the Henryville section of Brodhead Creek in Pennsylvania.

Thread	Olive	**Overwing**	Mallard duck wing quill segments tied down-wing
Hook	Mustad 94840, size 12 to 20	**Hackle**	Dark ginger
Rib	Grizzly hackle	**Head**	Olive thread
Body	Light olive floss		
Underwing	Wood duck flank feather fibers		

Step 1. Lay down a thread base to the bend of the hook, and tie in a grizzly hackle (fiber length shorter than the hook gap) as ribbing for the body.

Step 2. Tie in a short piece of light olive floss at the same tie-in point, and going forward, wrap the shank to within ¼ inch of the hook eye. Secure the floss with the thread, and remove any excess material.

Step 3. Palmer the grizzly hackle over the body, using equally spaced wraps. Secure it with the thread, and remove any excess material.

Step 4. Tie in a bunch of wood duck flank feather fibers on top of the shank in front of the body as the underwing.

Step 5. Tie in two matching mallard duck wing quill segments over the underwing. The lower side of each quill section should be parallel to the hook shank and body.

Step 6. Tie in the dark ginger hackle in front of the wing, and make three or four wraps. Secure it with the thread, and remove any excess material. *Note: The hackle fibers should be wider than the hook gap.*

Step 7. Form a neat head with your thread, and tie off with a whip finish. Give the head a couple coats of head cement, and allow it to dry.

Pale Evening Dun

Origin: United States
Demonstrator: Ray Podkowa 1988–89
Used for: Trout

This is one version of a few patterns that imitate the mayfly *Ephemerella dorothea*. Other patterns include the Pale Watery Dun, Sulfur Dun, and the Little Sulfur Dun.

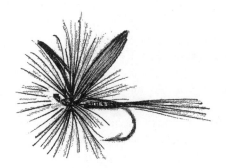

Thread	Cream or primrose	**Body**	Pale yellow fur or synthetic dubbing material
Hook	Mustad 94840, size 14 to 20	**Hackle**	Light blue dun
Wings	Light dun hackle tips, tied upright and divided	**Head**	Cream or primrose thread
Tail	Light blue dun hackle fibers		

Step 1. Select a pair of light dun hackle tips for the wings (length equal to the hook shank). Pair up the tips with the shiny sides facing out, and place them over the shank approximately a hook eye behind the eye, with the butts toward the rear and the tips extending forward in front of the hook. Secure the tips on top of the shank with your thread, and lift them until they are perpendicular to the shank.

Step 2. Make a few wraps in front to keep them in the upright position. Using your thread, divide the tips with a couple of figure-eight wraps, and return the thread to the hook bend. Remove any excess material.

Step 3. Tie in a sparse bunch of light blue dun hackle fibers (length equal to the hook shank) as the tail at the bend on top of the shank.

Step 4. Going forward, dub in a tapered body using pale yellow fur or synthetic dubbing material up to the wings.

Step 5. Take a light blue dun hackle with fibers equal to the body length, and tie it in at the stems just behind the wings. Secure the stem with a little more dubbing, and then use your hackle pliers to give the hackle a couple of wraps behind and in front of the wings. After securing the hackle, snip off any excess material.

Step 6. Form a neat head with your thread, and tie off with a whip finish. Give the head a couple coats of head cement, and allow it to dry.

Light Cahill

Origin: United States
Originator: Dan Cahill
Demonstrators: Ray Podkowa 1988–89
Dave Alexander 1993–94
Used for: Trout

This pattern is one of the most popular in existence. Originated by Dan Cahill, it imitates a variety of light-colored insects, making it a must for every fly fisher to carry in his or her fly box.

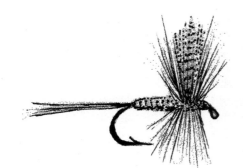

Thread	Cream or pale yellow	**Body**	Creamy yellow fur or synthetic dubbing material	
Hook	Mustad 94840, size 10 to 20			
Wings	Lemon wood duck flank feather fibers, tied upright and divided	**Hackle**	Dark cream	
		Head	Cream or pale yellow thread	
Tail	Dark cream hackle fibers			

Step 1. Starting behind the hook eye, tie in a bunch of lemon wood duck flank feather fibers (length equal to the hook shank) with the tips facing out toward the hook eye as the wings. Secure the fibers on top of the shank with your thread, and lift the tips until they are perpendicular to the shank. Make a few wraps in front to keep them in the upright position. Using your thread, divide the tips with a couple of figure-eight wraps, and return the thread to the hook bend. Remove any excess butt end material.

Step 2. Tie in a sparse bunch of dark cream hackle fibers (length equal to the hook shank) as the tail at the bend on top of the shank.

Step 3. Going forward, dub in a tapered body using creamy yellow fur or synthetic dubbing material up to the wings.

Step 4. Take a dark cream hackle with fibers equal to the body length, and tie it in at the stem just behind the wings. Secure the stem with a little more dubbing, and then use your hackle pliers to give the hackle a couple of wraps behind and in front of the wings. After securing the hackle, snip off any excess material.

Step 5. Form a neat head with your thread, and tie off with a whip finish. Give the head a couple coats of head cement, and allow it to dry.

Coffin Fly

Origin: United States
Originator: Walt Dette
Demonstrator: Ray Podkowa 1989–90

Used for: Trout

This fly was originated by Walt Dette back in 1930. It was designed to represent the spinner of the green drake *Ephemera guttulata*. There are a number of Coffin Fly recipes, which vary in the pattern construction.

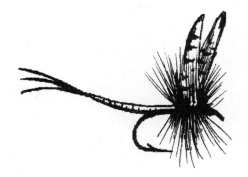

Thread	Black	**Wing**	Barred teal flank feather fibers
Hook	Mustad 79580 or 94831, size 10 to 14	**Hackle**	Badger
		Head	Black thread
Tail	Peccary or moose mane fibers		
Body	White deer-hair fibers		

Step 1. Lay down a thread base to the hook bend, and tie in two or three peccary or moose mane fibers (twice the length of the hook shank) as the tail at the hook bend on top of the shank.

Step 2. Bring the thread forward to about one-quarter of the hook shank behind the eye. Take some white deer-hair fibers that have been trimmed at both ends, and tie them in at the butt ends with the tips extending beyond the hook bend to the center of the tail. *Note: Use enough fibers to go completely around the shank.*

Step 3. Just in front of the deer-hair fibers, tie in a bunch of barred teal flank feather fibers (length equal to the shank) with the tips facing out toward the hook eye as the wing. Secure the fibers on top of the shank with your thread, and lift the tips until they are perpendicular to the shank. Make a few wraps in front to keep them in the upright position. Using your thread, divide the tips with a couple of figure-eight wraps, and return the thread behind the wing.

Step 4. Tie in a pair of badger hackles, and bring the thread forward of the wing. Wrap the two hackles individually in back and in front of the wing, and secure them with the thread. Remove any excess material. Make a neat head behind the hook eye with the thread, then return the thread through the hackles behind the wing.

Step 5. Using the thread, wrap over the deer-hair fibers, going back to the bend using evenly spaced wraps. When you reach the hook bend, continue wrapping the fibers over the tail, keeping the peccary or moose mane fibers in the center. When you make the last wrap (center of tail), tie off with a whip finish.

Irresistible

Origin: United States
Originator: Harry Darbee
Demonstrator: Scott Hodlmair 1986–87
Used for: Trout, bass

This pattern is credited to a gentleman named Harry Darbee. It has a distinctive profile and natural buoyancy because of the deer hair used in its construction.

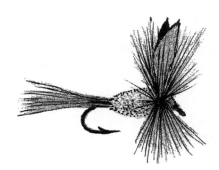

Thread	Gray	**Body**	Natural gray deer body hair, spun and clipped	
Hook	Mustad 94840, size 10 to 16			
Tail	Natural gray deer body hair fibers	**Hackle**	Medium dun	
Wings	Furnace hackle tips or white calf-tail fibers, tied upright and divided.	**Head**	Gray thread	

Step 1. Starting a little forward of the hook bend, tie in your thread and a sparse bunch of stacked natural gray deer body hair fibers, with the tips extending the length of the shank beyond the bend as the tail.

Step 2. Spin bunches of natural gray deer body hair fibers forward along the shank, covering two-thirds of the shank, compacting each bunch as you spin it. Make a half hitch when you spin in the last bunch, and remove the hook from the vise.

Step 3. Using scissors, trim the body to a bullet shape toward the hook bend and flat on the bottom of the shank.

Step 4. Return the hook to the vise. Tie in a pair of furnace hackle tips or white calf-tail fibers (length equal to the body) on top of the shank. Secure them with the thread, and lift the tips until they are perpendicular to the shank. Make a few wraps in front to keep them in the upright position. Using your thread, divide the tips or fibers in half with a couple of figure-eight wraps, and return the thread behind the wings. *Note: If you use calf-tail fibers, make a few wraps around the base of each wing.*

Step 5. Tie in a pair of medium dun hackles behind the wings, and advance the thread to the hook eye. Wrap the hackles individually in back and in front of the wings. Secure them with the thread, and remove any excess material.

Step 6. Form a neat head with your thread, and tie off with a whip finish. Give the head a couple coats of head cement, and allow it to dry.

Turck Tarantula

Origin: United States
Originator: Guy Turck
Demonstrator: Jerry Wasil 1994–95
Used for: Trout

This pattern was originated by Guy Turck in the summer of 1990. The pattern can be tied in various colors to match specialized hatches, such as salmon flies and golden stoneflies. It should be fished with a dead drift, using an occasional twitch to give the legs a little wiggle.

Thread	Tan		**Overwing**	Pearl Krystal Flash strands
Hook	Dai-Riki 710, size 4 to 12		**Legs**	White or brown medium Living Rubber hackle
Tail	Amherst pheasant tippet fibers		**Collar**	Deer body hair fibers
Body	Hare's mask or synthetic dubbing material		**Head**	Deer body hair fibers, spun and clipped to shape
Underwing	White calf-tail fibers			

Step 1. Lay down a thread base to the hook point, and tie in a few Amherst pheasant tippet fibers as the tail (length equal to the hook gap).

Step 2. Using hare's mask or synthetic dubbing material, dub a tapered body going forward to one-third of the hook shank behind the hook eye.

Step 3. Tie in a sparse bunch of stacked white calf-tail fibers as the underwing in front of the body (length should be to the tip of the tail).

Step 4. Tie in one strand of pearl Krystal Flash on each side of the calf tail, and trim it to the under-wing length.

Step 5. Tie in a stacked bunch of deer body hair fibers over the underwing on top of the shank, with the tips to the back as the collar. *Note: Keep the collar hairs from spinning and on top of the shank.*

Step 6. Tie in two short strands of white or brown medium Living Rubber hackle in front of the collar. Figure-eight the strands so that there are two legs on each side of the body.

Step 7. Spin bunches of deer body hair to fill the remainder of the shank. Tie off with a whip finish, and remove the hook from the vise.

Step 8. Trim the head to the desired shape with a pair of scissors. The head should angle back from the eye to the collar and should be flat on the bottom of the shank. Also trim the rubber legs to the desired length.

George's Extended Body Damsel

Origin: United States
Originator: George Cik
Demonstrator: George Cik 1997–98
Used for: Trout

One of George Cik's innovative creations (made from closed-cell foam), designed to represent the common damselfly. The pattern can be tied in assorted colors (blue, yellow, green, or black), utilizing various waterproof markers.

Thread	Color tier's choice	**Underbody**	Wool dubbing, color to match foam
Hook	Mustad 94840, size 10 to 12	**Eyes**	Black mono
Extended tail	Round white closed-cell foam, $^3/_{32}$ inch diameter by 1 $^3/_4$ inches long	**Overbody**	Round white closed-cell foam, $^3/_{32}$ inch diameter
Hackle	White saddle tied parachute	**Head**	Closed-cell foam

Step 1. Starting just ahead of the hook bend, tie in the round white closed-cell foam, using two or three close wraps, and secure the wraps with a half hitch. *Note: The back end of the foam should extend about 1 inch beyond the hook bend.*

Step 2. Tie in the white saddle hackle just in front of the extended tail.

Step 3. Using the wool dubbing, dub in the underbody to within $^1/_{16}$ inch of the hook eye, returning the thread back to the hackle tie-in point.

Step 4. Lift the front end of the white closed-cell foam, and wrap the hackle parachute style around the base of the foam. Secure the hackle with the thread, and remove any excess material.

Step 5. Bring the thread forward in front of the underbody just behind the hook eye, and tie down the forward end of the white closed-cell foam, which will be over the underbody. Secure the foam with a couple of close wraps and a half hitch.

Step 6. Tie in the black mono eyes at the same point on top of the foam, using figure-eight wraps, and tie off with a whip finish.

Step 7. Snip off any remaining foam material in front of the hook eye, and add the desired color markings using waterproof markers.

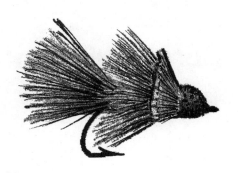

CHAPTER 9

Hair Patterns

Hare Waterpup

Origin: United States
Originator: Dave Whitlock
Demonstrator: Bob Dulian 1997–98
Used for: Largemouth bass

One of Dave Whitlock's innovative creations, designed to represent a mud puppy salamander, found in many lakes and streams throughout the United States. *Note: The pattern can be tied in various colors.*

Thread	Black 6/0 and single strand red nylon floss	**Throat**	15 strands of red Flashabou
Hook	Mustad 36890, size 1/0 and 4	**Gills**	Red dubbing
Rib	Copper wire	**Collar**	Deer hair (black, purple, green, or brown)
Body	Rabbit dubbing (black, purple, green, or brown)	**Head**	Spun deer hair (black, purple, green, or brown)
Tail	Rabbit strip (black, purple, green, or brown)	**Eyes**	Solid plastic (7mm), white with black centers

Step 1. Tie in your thread, and lay down a base starting about 5/16 inch behind the hook eye and ending above the hook barb. Then tie in the wire ribbing (which will be used later in the pattern) under the hook shank at the hook barb position.

Step 2. Dub a heavy tapered body to the front of the thread base (about 5/16 inch behind the hook eye).

Step 3. Tie in the rabbit fur strip at the front of the body. *Note: Prepare the rabbit fur strip prior to tying it in by removing about 1/16 inch of hair from the hide at the tie-in end and cutting the hide to a point.*

Step 4. Form a small tag with the copper wire ribbing, then stretch the fur strip back and, using equally spaced wraps, wrap the wire through the fur and around the body, going forward *Note: To simplify the wrapping process, moisten the fur first, then start the first wrap even with the back end of the body. Also use your bodkin to separate the hairs for each wrap.*

Step 5. Take about fifteen strands of red Flashabou, double them over, and cut them in half. Fold both bunches (thirty strands) again in half around the tying thread. Slide the Flashabou along the thread under the hook shank up against the front end of the body, tying the strands in with a few wraps and a half hitch. Trim the Flashabou ends so that they extend to the hook point.

Hare Waterpup continued

Step 6. Cover the tie-in area (the rabbit strip, the front of the body, and the Flashabou) with red dubbing, and tie off the black thread. At the same spot, tie in the red floss.

Step 7. Spin a stacked bunch of deer hair around the hook shank (tips to the back) up against the red dubbing to form the collar. *Note: The collar should extend to the hook point.* Secure it with a half hitch and a drop of cement.

Step 8. Take another bunch of deer hair, and trim off the tips. Spin the second bunch up against the first bunch (packing it tightly), and secure it with another half hitch and a drop of cement. Using the thread, form a small, neat head, and tie off with a whip finish.

Step 9. Trim the deer hair to the desired head shape (see pattern illustration), being careful not to cut away the collar. Also burn or cut out sockets for the eyes on each side of the trimmed head.

Step 10. Glue in the plastic eyes using Goop cement, and trim the rabbit strip so that it extends past the hook bend about twice the length of the body. Also trim the end tip of the rabbit strip to a point, and give the head a coat of cement.

Flash Dancer

Origin: United States
Originator: Dave Whitlock
Demonstrator: Bob Dulian 1997–98
Used for: Largemouth bass

One of Dave Whitlock's innovative creations, designed to represent a muddler minnow, found in lakes and streams throughout the United States. *Note: The pattern can be tied in various colors.*

Thread	White Kevlar		**Wing**	15 strands of gold Flashabou
Hook	Tiemco TMC 8090, size 2 to 6		**Collar**	Natural deer hair stacked on top of the hook shank
Tail	Red marabou			
Body	White chenille		**Head**	Spun natural deer hair trimmed to shape

Step 1. Lay down a thread base, then tie in the red marabou tail on top of the hook shank (tail length equal to hook length).

Step 2. Tie in a piece of white chenille at the tail tie-in point, and wrap about two-thirds of the shank, going forward, as the body. Remove any excess material.

Step 3. Tie in the gold Flashabou on top of the shank as the wing, and again remove any excess material. *Note: The Flashabou should extend out as far as the tail.*

Step 4. Form the collar on top of the shank, using bunches of natural deer body hair with the tips toward the bend of the hook. The collar should extend to the end of the body. *Note: When securing the hair, keep holding it in position when you pull down with the thread to prevent it from spinning around the shank.*

Step 5. Form the head up to the hook eye by spinning and compacting bunches of natural deer body hair. Tie off with a whip finish, and remove the pattern from the vise.

Step 6. Secure the pattern in a pair of forceps (hemostats) or use your fingers to hold it, and trim the head to the proper shape (see pattern illustration) using a pair of scissors.

Dahlberg Mini Diver

Origin: United States
Originator: Larry Dahlberg
Demonstrators: Bob Dulian 1993–94
Todd McCagg 1996–97
Used for: Largemouth bass

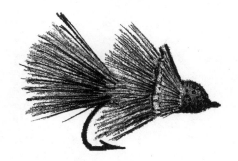

One of Larry Dahlberg's innovative creations, tied in a petite size. *Note: The pattern can be tied in various colors.*

Thread	6/0 thread (color tier's choice)	**Body**	Dubbing (color tier's choice) half the hook shank
Hook	Mustad 3366, size 10 to 14	**Collar**	Stacked deer hair (color tier's choice) extending to the bend
Tail	Calf tail with a layer of marabou over it, with a few strands of Flashabou or Krystal Flash over the marabou, topped by more marabou (color tier's choice)	**Diving collar**	Stacked deer hair (color tier's choice)
		Head	Spun deer hair (color tier's choice)

Step 1. Tie in your thread, and lay down a base starting about midshank, going back to the bend.

Step 2. Tie in the tail in the following order on top of the shank at the hook bend: Start with a small bunch of calf tail, then tie in a sparse layer of marabou over it, with a few strands of Flashabou or Krystal Flash over the marabou, topped by another layer of sparse marabou (color tier's choice).

Step 3. Using dubbing (color tier's choice), dub about 50 percent of the hook shank as the body.

Step 4. Tie in a bunch of stacked deer hair (color tier's choice) on top of the shank, extending to the bend as the collar. Using a contrasting thread, tie down the tip ends of the collar around the body. *Note: Even up the tips with a stacker prior to tying them in, and hold them in place while securing them to keep them from spinning around the shank.*

Step 5. Take another bunch of stacked deer hair (color tier's choice), and tie them in as the diving collar in front of the last stack.

Step 6. Pull all the hairs for the diving collar to the rear, and tie them down around the body, using another contrasting thread, as you did in Step 4. *Note: Tying the diving collar down at the body simplifies the head trimming during the finishing process.*

Step 7. Using more deer hair (color tier's choice), spin bunches around the shank up to the hook eye. Compact each bunch with your fingers as you tie it in. After the area between the diving collar and the eye is filled, tie off with a whip finish, and remove the pattern from the vise.

Step 8. Secure the pattern in a pair of forceps (hemostats) or use your fingers to hold it, and trim the head to the proper shape (see pattern illustration) using a pair of scissors. *Note: Trim the head to a cylindrical shape, using the tied-down diving collar as a guide, then to a conical shape from the eye to the diving collar.*

Step 9. Remove the thread used to tie down the diving collar. Slip a tubular sleeve (diameter about the same as diameter of tied-down hairs) over the hook eye and the hairs to about the hook point, and trim the hairs evenly against the sleeve edge.

Step 10. Remove the thread from the collar, releasing the tips of the deer hair, and fluff up both collars.

Feather Wing Sculpin

Origin: United States
Originator: Unknown
Demonstrator: Bob Dulian 1997–98
Used for: Most larger game fish species

A pattern designed to represent one of the many types of sculpin found in lakes and streams throughout the United States. *Note: The pattern can be tied in various colors.*

Thread	White Kevlar	**Pectoral fins**	Bunch of dyed brown arctic fox tied in on each side of the body
Hook	Tiemco TMC 9395, 4X long, size 4	**Gills**	Red dubbing
Weight	Lead wire tied on each side of shank and secured with Krazy Glue	**Collar**	Spun brown deer body hair
Tail	Bunch of dyed brown arctic fox	**Head**	Spun brown deer hair trimmed to shape
Body	White or cream-colored rabbit dubbing	**Eyes**	Solid plastic (7mm), amber with black centers
Dorsal fin	6 cree-colored neck feathers		

Step 1. Tie in your thread, and lay down a base covering two-thirds of the hook shank. *Note: Leave about one-third of the hook shank bare behind the hook eye.*

Step 2. Tie in a piece of lead wire on each side of the shank over the thread base. After the lead wires are in place, coat them with Krazy Glue.

Step 3. Tie in a bunch of brown arctic fox hair as the tail on top of the shank at the hook bend.

Step 4. Dub a fairly heavy tapered body using white rabbit dubbing, going forward over the lead wire and thread base.

Step 5. Tie in the six brown cree neck feathers at the front of the body on top of the shank as the dorsal fin. *Note: Make sure that the feathers are tied in so that they rest close to the body. Tip: A small ball of dubbing at the tie-in point will help keep the feathers from sticking up.*

Step 6. Tie in a bunch of brown arctic fox hair on each side of the body as the pectoral fins, extending to the hook point.

Step 7. Cover the area in front of the body where the feathers and pectoral fins were tied in with a small bunch of red dubbing as the gills.

Step 8. Tie in a bunch of brown deer body hair as the collar, with the tips toward the bend of the hook. Push the collar hair back toward the bend using your fingers, pull back the butt ends with your hand, and add a half hitch and a drop of cement to secure the hair in place. *Note: The collar can be tied in with the hair on top of the shank, or it can be spun a full 360 degrees.*

Step 9. Cover the remaining open area between the collar and the hook eye with tightly packed bunches of spun brown deer body hair for the head. *Note: Again, add a half hitch after each bunch, with a drop of cement.* After the bunches are secured, tie off and remove the hook from the vise.

Step 10. Trim the deer hair to the desired head shape (see pattern illustration), being careful not to cut away any of the collar tip ends. Also burn or cut out sockets for the eyes on each side of the trimmed head.

Step 11. Glue in the plastic eyes using Goop cement.

Newt Diver

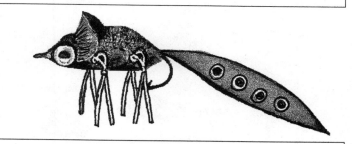

Origin: United States
Originator: Gene Kugach
Used for: Largemouth bass

This pattern was designed to represent a newt found in many lakes and streams throughout the United States.

Thread	Black	**Collar**	White deer hair coated with clear silicone cement
Hook	Mustad 3191, size 1/0 or 2/0	**Legs**	Green Living Rubber
Tail	Chamois material cut to shape	**Eyes**	Plastic doll eyes (7mm)
Body	Light green deer hair	**Markings**	Permanent markers in light green, yellow, and red

Step 1. Cut out the tail from the chamois material per the template below. Color the entire tail (both sides) light green, and add the yellow spots with red centers, using the permanent markers.

Tail Template (Actual Size)

Step 2. Place your hook in the vise, and tie in the tail on top of the shank at the bend of the hook. *Note: Use as little thread and space as possible when securing it.*

Step 3. Take a small bunch of light green deer hair, and carefully spin it over the area where the tail was tied in. Continue adding bunches of deer hair until you have at least a $^{1}/_{4}$-inch area of compact hair on the hook shank. *Note: Use your fingers to compact the hair by pushing it back along the shank.*

Step 4. Tie in two 6-inch-long strands of Living Rubber, with equal lengths on each side of the shank. Take the two strands on each side, and tie an overhand knot approximately $^{1}/_{2}$ inch below the shank. Trim the remaining ends to within $^{1}/_{2}$ inch of the knot.

Step 5. Continue adding bunches of spun deer hair to the shank until you fill three-quarters of the shank.

Step 6. Take another pair of strands of Living Rubber, and attach them to the shank as you did in Step 4. Spin a bunch of deer hair in front of them, and tie off with your thread.

Step 7. Remove the hook from the vise, and trim the hair on the back of the newt's body. Start with the hairs on the bottom, clipping away until they are flat and close to the shank. Then, starting at the bend, clip the top hairs at an angle going up and forward. Once you have shaped the rear portion of the body, place the hook back in the vise.

Step 8. Spin a couple bunches of white deer hair around the shank. Compact them toward the back of the hook, and then spread them evenly around the shank.

Step 9. Work some silicone into the white hair until you have a solid, sticky collar around the pattern. Allow the cement to dry.

Step 10. Continue spinning bunches of the green deer hair on the shank up to the hook eye. Tie off with a whip finish, and remove the hook from the vise.

Step 11. Starting behind the hook eye, trim the hair to form the head as shown in the illustration. Then trim the collar in a circular shape as shown.

Step 12. Using Goop cement, glue the plastic doll eyes on each side of the head. Color in the markings shown in the tail illustration, using the various color markers. Also add some red color to the top of the head and the body.

Gene's Diving Waterbug

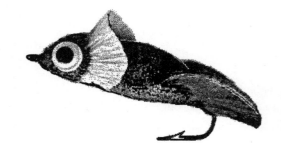

Origin: United States
Originator: Gene Kugach
Used for: Largemouth bass

This pattern was designed to represent any of the large aquatic waterbugs found in many lakes and streams throughout the United States.

Thread	Black	**Body**	Black deer hair
Hook	Mustad 3191, size 1/0 or 2/0	**Collar**	White deer hair impregnated with clear silicone cement
Tail	Black bucktail deer hair impregnated with silicone cement and cut to shape	**Head**	Red deer hair
		Eyes	Plastic doll eyes (7mm)

Step 1. Place your hook in the vise, and tie in a bunch of black deer hair (bucktail) on top of the shank at the bend of the hook with a couple of loose wraps. Pull back on the butt ends, and make a few more wraps in front of them so they stand up, then secure them with a few tight wraps.

Step 2. Take a small bunch of black deer hair (body hair), and carefully spin it over the area where the tail was tied in. Continue adding bunches of spun deer hair to the shank until you fill three-quarters of the shank. Tie off with a whip finish. *Note: Use your fingers to compact the hair by pushing it back along the shank.*

Step 3. To make things easier in the pattern construction, remove the hook from the vise. Using your fingers, apply a liberal amount of silicone cement to the tail, and work it into the tail fibers up to the hook shank. Spread the tail fibers out, and compress them to form a flat surface that is horizontal to the hook shank.

Step 4. Trim the hair on the back of the body, being careful not to cut the tail fibers. Start with the hairs on the bottom of the shank, clipping away until they are flat and close to the shank. Then, starting at the bend, clip the top hairs at an angle going up and forward, as shown in the pattern illustration. *Note: Be careful not to cut off the side hair.*

Step 5. Apply some more silicone cement to the rear half of the body side hairs and pull them back into the tail section, compressing the fibers to form a flat surface as you did in Step 3 to complete the tail.

Step 6. Continue shaping the rear portion of the body while leaving the tail to dry. After the tail dries, cut it to shape as shown in the pattern illustration, and place the hook back in the vise.

Step 7. Spin a couple of bunches of white deer hair around the shank. Compact them toward the back of the hook using your fingers, and then spread them evenly around the shank.

Gene's Diving Waterbug *continued*

Step 8. Work some silicone cement into the white hairs until you have a solid, sticky collar around the pattern. Allow the cement to dry.

Step 9. After the cement has dried, continue spinning bunches of the red deer hair on the shank up to the hook eye (again compacting the hair with your fingers). Tie off with a whip finish, and remove the hook from the vise.

Step 10. Starting behind the hook eye, trim the hair to form the head as shown in the pattern illustration. Then trim the collar in a circular shape as shown.

Step 11. Using Goop cement, glue the plastic doll eyes into position on each side of the head.

Water Crawler

Origin: United States
Originator: Gene Kugach
Used for: Largemouth bass

Designed as a fly-rod version of an old Heddon's plug called the Crazy Crawler. Retrieve it in short, quick jerks to create the desired action.

Thread	Black	**Side crawler paddles**	White deer body hair coated with clear silicone cement
Hook	Mustad 3261, size 1/0 or 2/0	**Head**	Red deer body hair
Weed guard (optional)	Mono line	**Eyes**	Plastic doll eyes (7mm)
Body	White deer body hair two-thirds of the hook shank		

Step 1. Place your hook in the vise, and starting just before the bend of the hook, secure your thread to the shank. If desired, tie in one end of the mono weed guard.

Step 2. Take a bunch of white deer body hair, and starting at the bend, spin it around the shank. Continue adding bunches of the white deer body hair until you have covered (with compacted hair) at least three-quarters of the hook shank. Tie off with your thread, and remove the hook from the vise. *Note: Use your fingers to compact the hair by pushing it back along the shank. Also add a drop of head cement to the shank where you tie in each bunch of deer hair.*

Step 3. Trim the hair for the back of the body. Start with the hairs on the bottom of the shank, clipping away until they are close to the shank. Then, starting at the bend, clip the top hairs at an angle going up and forward, as shown in the pattern illustration. After the rear of the body is complete, place the hook back in the vise.

Step 4. Spin a couple bunches of white deer hair around the shank. Compact them toward the back of the hook, using your fingers, and then spread them evenly around both sides of the shank. Tie off, and remove the hook from the vise.

Step 5. Work some silicone cement into the white hairs, until you have a solid sticky collar around the pattern. Then pull the top and bottom hairs to the sides, forming the side crawler paddles, and allow the cement to dry.

Step 6. When the cement is dry, trim the side crawler paddles to the desired shapes, and again place the hook in the vise.

Step 7. Spin in some bunches of the red deer hair in front of the paddles, compacting the hair up to 1/8 inch of the hook eye. Secure the last bunch with your thread. Then bring up the loose end of the mono weed guard material, and tie it in behind the eye on the bottom of the shank. Tie off with a whip finish, and remove the hook from the vise.

Step 8. Starting behind the hook eye, trim the hair to form the head as shown in the pattern illustration. Blend the area between the paddles (both top and bottom) into the rear body.

Step 9. Using Goop cement, glue the plastic doll eyes into position on each side of the head.

Tadpole Diver

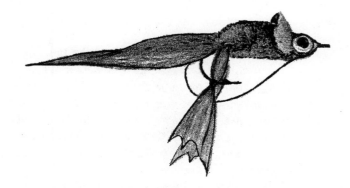

Origin: United States
Originator: Gene Kugach
Used for: Largemouth bass

This pattern was designed to represent tadpoles found in many lakes and streams throughout the United States. It requires silicone cement in construction of the collar, legs, and tail. It can be made weedless by addition of a mono weed guard.

Thread	Black	**Leg support**	Fine wire or any fine wire long shank hook cut off at the bend
Hook	Mustad 3261, size 1/0 or 2/0	**Collar**	White deer body hair coated with clear silicone cement
Tail	Light green bucktail coated with clear silicone cement	**Legs**	Light green and white bucktail tied on a wire support
Body	Light green deer body hair	**Eyes**	Plastic doll eyes (7mm)
Leg hinge	Fine wire		

Step 1. Make the leg assembly as follows:
- Starting with a piece of fine-gauge wire, form the leg hinge as shown in the hinge pattern.
- Form two wire leg supports as shown in the leg support pattern. Or, use two long shank hooks and, after constructing the legs, snip off the points at the hook bends.

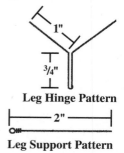

Leg Hinge Pattern

Leg Support Pattern

Step 2. To make the legs, place a leg support or a long shank hook in your vise, grasping the wire end, and tie in a bunch of white bucktail by the butt ends just behind the eye on one side of the wire. Repeat the procedure with a bunch of light green bucktail on the other side of the wire, and bring your thread back toward the vise. Fold the bucktail over (Thunder Creek style), secure it with your thread, and tie off with a whip finish. *Note: The leg should have a white side and a green side.* Put the completed legs and leg hinge aside until later.

Tadpole Diver continued

Step 3. Place your hook in the vise, and tie in a fair size bunch of the light green bucktail on top of the shank at the bend of the hook as the tail. *Note: When starting Step 3, a monofilament weed guard can be added to the pattern if desired. The following procedure can be done at this point or later, when the pattern is completed. Work some silicone cement into the tail hairs, until you can shape the tail to look like the tail in the pattern illustration. Allow the cement to dry.*

Step 4. Take a small bunch of light green deer hair. and carefully spin it at the tie-in point. Repeat, adding bunches of deer hair until you have at least a ¼-inch area of compact hair on the hook shank. *Note: Use your fingers to compact the hair by pushing it back along the shank.*

Step 5. Tie in the leg hinge on top of the shank (with the spread wires to the back), and continue adding bunches of spun deer hair over the leg hinge and the hook shank until you fill three-quarters of the shank.

Step 6. Remove the hook from the vise, and trim the hair for the back of the tadpole's body. Start with the hairs on the bottom of the shank, clipping away until they are flat and close to the shank. Then, starting at the bend, clip the top hairs at an angle going up and forward, as shown in the pattern illustration. Once you have shaped the rear portion of the body, place the hook back in the vise.

Step 7. Spin a couple bunches of white deer hair around the shank. Compact them toward the back of the hook using your fingers, and then spread them evenly around the shank.

Step 8. Work some silicone cement into the white hairs until you have a solid, sticky collar around the pattern. Allow the cement to dry.

Step 9. After the cement has dried, continue spinning bunches of the green deer hair on the shank up to the hook eye (again compacting the hairs with your fingers). Tie off with a whip finish, and remove the hook from the vise.

Step 10. Starting behind the hook eye, trim the hair to form the head as shown in the pattern illustration. Then trim the collar in a circular shape as shown.

Step 11. Attach the legs to the leg hinge by slipping the hinge wire through the leg eyes and then twisting the wire. Snip off any excess wire from both the hinge and in the legs, using wire cutters.

Step 12. Using Goop cement, glue the plastic doll eyes into position on each side of the head.

Hair Frog Diver

Origin: United States
Originator: Gene Kugach
Used for: Largemouth bass

A pattern designed to represent the common frogs found in many lakes and streams throughout the United States. Retrieve it with quick, short jerks to create a diving action. It can be made weedless by adding a mono weed guard.

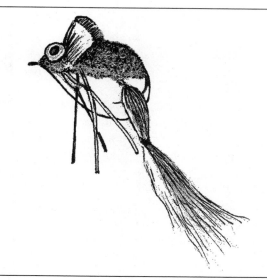

Thread	Black	**Collar**	White deer hair coated with clear silicone cement
Hook	Mustad 3261, size 1/0 or 2/0	**Legs**	Front: Green Living Rubber
Body	Light green deer hair		Rear: Light green and white bucktail tied on a wire support
Leg hinge	Fine wire	**Eyes**	Plastic doll eyes (7mm)
Leg support	Fine wire or any fine wire long shank hook with the point cut off at the bend.		

Step 1. Make the log assembly as follows:
- Starting with a piece of fine-gauge stainless steel wire, form the leg hinge as shown in the hinge pattern.
- Form two wire leg supports as shown in the leg support pattern. Or, use two long shank hooks and, after constructing the legs, snip off the points at the hook bends.

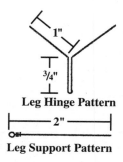

Leg Hinge Pattern

Leg Support Pattern

Step 2. To make the legs, place a leg support or a long shank hook in your vise, and tie in a bunch of white bucktail by the butt ends just behind the hinge eye on one side of the wire. Repeat the procedure with a bunch of light green bucktail on the other side of the wire, and bring your thread back toward the vise. Fold the bucktail over (Thunder Creek style), secure it with your thread, and tie off with a whip finish. *Note: The leg should have a white side and a green side.* Put the completed legs and leg hinge aside until later.

Hair Frog Diver continued

Step 3. Place your hook in the vise, and tie in at the bend of the hook. *Note: When starting Step 3, a monofilament weed guard can be added to the pattern if desired.* Take a small bunch of light green deer hair, and carefully spin it at the tie-in point. Repeat, adding bunches of deer hair until you have at least a ¼-inch area of compact hair on the hook shank. *Note: Use your fingers to compact the hair by pushing it back along the shank.*

Step 4. Tie in the leg hinge on top of the shank (with the spread wires to the back), and continue adding bunches of spun deer hair over the leg hinge and the hook shank until you fill three-quarters of the shank.

Step 5. Tie in two 6-inch-long strands of Living Rubber, with equal lengths on each side of the shank. Take the two strands on each side, and tie an overhand knot approximately ½ inch below the shank. Trim the remaining ends to within ½ inch of the knot.

Step 6. Remove the hook from the vise, and trim the hair for the back of the frog's body. Start with the hairs on the bottom of the shank, clipping away until they are flat and close to the shank. Then, starting at the bend, clip the top hairs at an angle going up and forward, as shown in the pattern. *Note: Be careful not to cut off the Living Rubber legs.* Once you have shaped the rear portion of the body, place the hook back in the vise.

Step 7. Spin a couple bunches of white deer hair around the shank. Compact them toward the back of the hook using your fingers, and then spread them evenly around the shank.

Step 8. Work some silicone cement into the white hair until you have a solid, sticky collar around the pattern. Allow the cement to dry.

Step 9. After the cement has dried, continue spinning bunches of the green deer hair on the shank up to the hook eye (again compacting the hairs with your fingers). Tie off with a whip finish, and remove the hook from the vise.

Step 10. Starting behind the hook eye, trim the hair to form the head as shown in the pattern illustration. Trim the collar in a circular shape as shown.

Step 11. Attach the legs to the leg hinge by slipping the hinge wire through the leg eyes and then twisting the wire. Snip off any excess wire from both the hinge and in the legs, using wire cutters.

Step 12. Using Goop cement, glue the plastic doll eyes into position on each side of the head.

George's Bluegill

Origin: United States
Originator: George Cik
Used for: Largemouth bass, pike

George's Bluegill was created to represent a small bait-fish used for bass or pike fishing. George's expertise and innovations in the use of materials and his tying techniques produce some of the best-looking patterns you will ever see. This is just one of his many creations.

Thread	Tan	**Eyes**	Plastic doll eyes (4mm) with the stems removed, red with black centers
Hook	Mustad 9674, size 6	**Markings**	Permanent markers in red, yellow, black, and light blue
Tail	Grizzly marabou plume		
Body/head	Natural-color spun deer body hair		

Step 1. Starting at the hook bend, tie in two grizzly marabou plumes extending a hook shank beyond the hook bend.

Step 2. Cut off the tips and even up the butt end of small bunches of natural-color deer body hair, and completely fill the shank, spinning and compacting the hair bunches up to the hook eye. When you reach the eye, tie off and remove the hook from the vise.

Step 3. Place the hook in a pair of forceps, and starting under the shank, trim the hairs as close as possible with a pair of scissors.

Step 4. Trim the sides as close to the shank as possible. *Note: At this point, you should have a thin body about 3/16 inch wide.*

Step 5. Trim the top, starting up from the hook eye, to create a rounded shape for the head. Also slightly round off the bottom hairs. Continue trimming the top toward the hook bend with a slight taper.

Step 6. Glue the 4mm plastic doll eyes with the stems removed on each side of the head, using five-minute epoxy cement.

Step 7. After the glue is dry, color the pattern with the permanent markers, putting colored stripes down each side in the following order: Starting just behind the eye, put in a thin red stripe, followed by a thin yellow stripe, then a thin black stripe, followed by a thin light blue stripe. *Note: At this point you should be at about midshank.* Now allow a natural thin stripe of deer hair, followed by a thin light blue stripe, followed by another thin natural deer hair stripe, with thin black and yellow stripes behind it to finish the pattern.

Gene's Mouse

Origin: United States
Originator: Gene Kugach
Used for: Largemouth bass, pike

This pattern is a variation of the common hair mouse pattern that works well for bass or pike. It can be made weedless with the addition of a mono weed guard.

Thread	Black	**Ears**	White deer body hair coated with clear silicone cement and cut to shape
Hook	Mustad 3191, size 1/0 or 2/0	**Eyes**	Seed beads glued onto copper wire
Tail	Thin chamois material cut to shape, $^1/_{16}$ inch wide by 3 inches long	**Head**	Natural-color deer body hair
Body	Natural-color deer body hair	**Whiskers**	Brown hackle

Step 1. Cut out a tail $^1/_{16}$ inch wide by 3 inches long from the chamois material.

Step 2. Place your hook in the vise, and tie in the tail on top of the shank at the bend of the hook.

Step 3. Take a small bunch of natural-color deer body hair (with the tips and butt ends evened up), and carefully spin it over the area where the tail was tied in. Continue adding bunches of deer hair until you cover two-thirds of the hook shank. *Note: Use your fingers to compact the hair by pushing it back along the shank each time you add a bunch.*

Step 4. To simplify shaping the body, tie off with a whip finish, and remove the pattern from the vise.

Step 5. Start with the hairs on the bottom of the shank, clipping away until they are flat and close to the shank. Then, starting at the bend, clip the top hairs at an angle going up and forward, as shown in the pattern illustration.

Step 6. Place the hook back in the vise. Spin a couple bunches of white deer body hair around the shank. Compact them toward the back of the hook using your fingers, and then spread them evenly around the shank.

Step 7. Work some silicone cement into the white hair until you have a solid, sticky collar around the pattern. Allow the cement to dry.

Step 8. Using 5-minute epoxy cement, glue a pair of black seed beads onto a piece of copper wire, with a $^1/_2$-inch or $^3/_4$-inch space between the beads, for the eye stems. After the glue is dry, fold the wire in half, and tie the seed bead eyes onto the shank about midpoint between the white collar and the hook eye.

Step 9. Return the thread to the collar, and continue spinning bunches of the natural-color deer body hair on the shank up to the hook eye. Tie off with a whip finish, and remove the hook from the vise.

Step 10. Starting behind the hook eye, trim the hair to form the head so it blends into the body. *Note: Be very careful not to cut off the eyes as you trim the head.* Also trim the collar around the sides to blend it into the body and head. Then form two distinct ears out of the remaining white deer hair collar on top of the head with the scissors.

Step 11. Place the hook back in the vise, and tie in the brown hackle for the whiskers just behind the hook eye. Make a couple of close wraps behind the eye, secure the hackle with the thread, and remove any excess material. Tie off with a whip finish.

Rabbit Muddler

Origin: United States
Demonstrator: Scott Hodlmair
Used for: Largemouth bass

A simple rabbit and deer-hair pattern designed to represent a muddler baitfish. The pattern can be tied in assorted colors, such as brown, white, green, or black.

Thread	Color to match body	**Head**	Spun deer body hair (color to match body)
Hook	Mustad 37189, size 2 to 6		
Tail	Rabbit fur strip (color tier's choice)	**Eyes**	Movable plastic doll eyes (7mm)
Body	Rabbit fur strip palmered around the shank		

Step 1. Starting about $\frac{1}{2}$ inch behind the hook eye, lay down a thread base up to the start of the hook bend.

Step 2. Tie in a 6-inch-long rabbit fur strip at the bend on top of the shank, with about 2 inches extending beyond the hook as the tail. *Note: Use a couple of close wraps at the hook bend when tying in the tail.* Then bring the thread forward to about $\frac{1}{2}$ inch behind the hook eye.

Step 3. Using the remaining rabbit fur strip in front of the tail, palmer it forward around the shank to within $\frac{1}{2}$ inch of the hook eye to form the body. Secure it with the thread, and remove any excess material.

Step 4. Using deer body hair with the tips and butt ends evened up, spin enough bunches onto the shank to fill the remaining $\frac{1}{2}$ inch of open shank. *Note: Compact the bunches with your fingers as you tie them in.* After you tie in the last bunch, tie off with a whip finish.

Step 5. Remove the pattern from the vise, and place the hook in a pair of forceps. Using scissors, trim the head to shape, making the head flat under the shank and ball shaped on the top and sides.

Step 6. Glue the 7mm movable plastic doll eyes on each side of the head using Goop cement.

Mega Diver

Origin: United States
Originator: Bob Dulian
Demonstrator: Bob Dulian 1989–90
Used for: Bass

This pattern is a large, excellent bass lure that can be tied in an assortment of color combinations and sizes. It is one of the many examples of Bob Dulian's creative tying ability, using a variety of new materials. It can be used for most freshwater and many saltwater species.

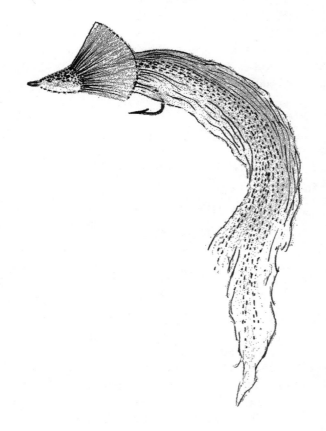

Thread	Color tier's choice
Hook	Mustad 3366 or 34007, size 1/0 to 5/0
Weed guard (optional)	.012 to .018 stainless steel wire
Tail	Hairabou and Flashabou 5 to 8 inches long
Body	Thread base over weed guard
Collar	Deer body hair fibers, color to match Hairabou
Head	Deer hair, clipped

Step 1. (Optional) Using a small pair of pliers, cut and shape a wire weed guard to fit the hook as shown below. Secure the weed guard on the hook with thread, and bend the guard wires forward to clear the thread for tving.

Weed Guard

Step 2. Secure about a dozen strands of Hairabou (5 to 8 inches long) at the rear bend of the hook.

Step 3. Tie in a dozen strands of Flashabou (same length) at the same tie-in point.

Step 4. Repeat Steps 2 and 3 until you have the tail you desire.

Step 5. Stack and tie in a couple of bunches dyed deer body hair at the tail tie-in point with the tips extending toward the rear of the hook as the collar. *Note: Try to keep the hair on top of the shank when you tie it in. Also, wrap down the tips with a piece of thread to make trimming the head easier.*

Step 6. Add more tightly compacted bunches of hair in front of the collar up to the hook eye for the head. Tie off with a whip finish.

Step 7. Place the hook in a pair of forceps, and trim the head to the proper shape, making sure it is as symmetrical as possible.

Step 8. Release the thread holding down the collar, and trim the collar if necessary. If you used a weed guard, bend back the weed guard wire over the hook guard.

Dulian Diver

Origin: United States
Originator: Bob Dulian
Demonstrator: Bob Dulian 1997–98
Used for: Largemouth bass

Bob Dulian is a member of the Chicago Fly Fishers and an expert tier. The Dulian Diver is one of Bob's diver variations developed for bass or pike fishing. His expertise and innovations in the use of materials and tying techniques improve many of the patterns tied today and produce some of the best-looking patterns you will ever see.

Thread	White 6/0 and singe-strand nylon floss	**Wing**	Chartreuse marabou
Hook	Tiemco TMC 9395, size 2 to 6	**Gills**	Red dubbing
Tail	Red Schlappen fibers	**Skirt**	White deer hair, stacked on top of shank
Body	Silver tinsel braid	**Collar**	White and chartreuse deer hair
Underwing	White marabou and pearl Flashabou	**Head**	White deer hair

Step 1. Lay down a thread base, starting $^3/_8$ inch in back of the hook eye and ending above the hook barb.

Step 2. Tie in the Schlappen fibers for the tail at the hook bend, extending one hook gape beyond the tie-in point. Bring the thread forward over the butt ends up to the front of the thread base, and remove any excess material.

Step 3. Tie in the tinsel braid at the front of the thread base, extending the braid toward the rear of the hook, and spiral the thread over the braid and hook shank up to the hook bend and back again to the front of the thread base. Leave the thread hanging by the bobbin at this point.

Step 4. Wrap the tinsel braid forward to form the body. Secure it with the thread and remove any excess material.

Step 5. Tie in the white marabou underwing at the front of the thread base, and remove the butt ends from the marabou. The marabou should be about two hook lengths long. After the marabou is in place, tie in six strands of pearl Flashabou on top of the underwing by doubling over the Flashabou, with the tips extending about $^1/_2$ inch past the underwing. *Note: Maintain a space of $^5/_{16}$ inch between the hook eye and the wing tie-in for the skirt, collar, and head.*

Step 6. Tie in the chartreuse marabou wing at the same tie-in point on top of the Flashabou, and snip off the excess material. The wing length should be equal to the underwing length.

Step 7. Cover the wing tie-in point with red dubbing for the gills, and tie off with a whip finish. *Note: Remember to maintain the $^5/_{16}$-inch space for the rest of the pattern construction.*

Dulian Diver continued

Step 8. Tie in the single strand floss, then cut, clean, and stack a bunch of white deer hair for the skirt. Tie in the skirt on top of the shank, with the tips extending as far back as the hook barb. *Note: Do not spin this bunch around the shank. Hold it in position with your hand, and secure it on top of the shank with the floss.*

Step 9. Cut, clean, and stack a bunch of white and chartreuse deer hair for the collar. Cut off the tips, and stack this bunch in front of the skirt. *Note: Do not spin this bunch around the shank. Hold it in position with your hand, and secure it on top of the shank with the floss.*

Step 10. Using thread, wrap down the skirt and collar hair fibers along the body to simplify trimming the head after it's tied in.

Step 11. Cut, clean, and trim the tips off a bunch of white deer hair, and this time spin the hairs around the shank to form the head. Continue adding bunches of white deer hair until the remaining front section of the hook shank is filled. Tie off with a whip finish, and coat the tie-off area with head cement.

Step 12. Remove the pattern from the vise, and trim the head to shape. Then remove the thread from around the skirt and collar, and trim the collar to shape. Apply Flexament to the head and collar.

Black and Yellow Hair Bug

Origin: United States
Demonstrator: George Cik 1991–92
Used for: Largemouth bass

A simple-to-tie popper hair bug that can be tied in an assortment of sizes and colors. The color combination can be black/yellow/black, yellow/black/yellow, white/red/white, red/white/red, green/yellow/green, or yellow/green/yellow.

Thread	Tier's choice	**Body**	Spun deer body hair clipped to shape
Hook	Mustad 36890, size 1/0 to 10	**Eyes** (optional)	Plastic doll eyes (7mm)
Tail	Bucktail to match one of the body colors		

Step 1. Starting at the hook bend, tie in a sparse bunch of bucktail hair fibers as the tail. Fibers should extend about a hook shank length beyond the back of the hook.

Step 2. Using bunches of dyed deer body hair (color tier's choice), spin in the bunches, covering one-third of the shank.

Step 3. Select another color of deer body hair that is compatible with the first color you used, and spin in enough bunches to reach midshank.

Step 4. Using the first color deer body hair, continue spinning bunches until you fill the shank completely. Tie off with a whip finish, and remove the hook from the vise.

Step 5. Place the hook in a pair of forceps, and trim the body to a bullet shape toward the back of the hook. *Note: Trim the front end of the body flat.*

Step 6. Coat the front surface with a little silicone cement, and allow it to dry. If desired, you can also glue on some 7mm movable doll eyes using a little Goop cement.

Steve's Green and White

Origin: United States
Originator: Steve Almgreen
Used for: All species

Created by Steve Almgreen, a member of the Chicago Fly Fishers, as a bass pattern that can also be used for most other species, including saltwater game fish. It can be tied in a variety of color combinations.

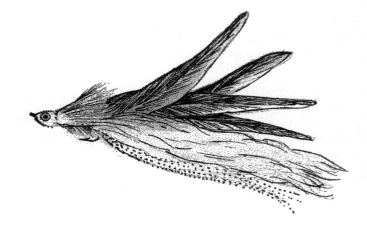

Thread	Black	**Collar**	White reindeer hair
Hook	Mustad 90240, size 6	**Head**	White reindeer hair
Tail	Silver Krystal Flash, topped by Icelandic wool, topped by 4 bright green or chartreuse saddle hackles	**Eyes**	Plastic doll eyes, yellow with black centers

Step 1. Tie in your thread at the hook point.

Step 2. Tie in four to six strands of silver Krystal Flash doubled over (about 4 inches long) on top of the hook shank, followed by a bunch of Icelandic wool (also about 4 inches long) over the Krystal Flash.

Step 3. Tie four bright green or chartreuse saddle hackles (two per side), spraying out on top of the Icelandic wool.

Step 4. Tie in a couple bunches of white reindeer hair, with the tips to the back of the hook, in front of the tail to form the collar. *Note: Keep the collar bunches on top of the shank.*

Step 5. Using white reindeer hair, fill the shank by spinning tightly packed bunches up to the hook eye. Tie off with a whip finish.

Step 6. Remove the hook from the vise, and using scissors, trim the head to the desired shape (Dahlberg Diver style), being careful not to cut off the collar.

Step 7. Burn out the eye sockets on each side of the head. Remove the long stems from the doll eyes, and hot glue or cement the eyes in place.

Swimmin' Deer Hair Frog

Origin: United States
Originator: Jeff Norberte
Used for: Bass, pike

A great bass and pike pattern that can be tied weedless. Jeff recommends that it be used among the lily pads early in the morning or just before sundown. Developed by Jeff Norberte of the Chicago Fly Fishers, it's one of his many creations that have proven to be excellent producers.

Thread	Kevlar or 3/0 Monocord and 6/0 Olive Uni-Thread	**Body**	Spun olive deer body hair with 4 bands of chartreuse hair on top
Hook	Mustad 3366, size 2 to 3/0	**Front legs**	Green rubber hackle
Weed guard	30-pound mono 6 inches long	**Head**	Spun olive deer body hair with a red band under the head
Butt	Dark green deer body hair	**Eyes**	Plastic stem doll eyes (3mm or 5mm), white or yellow with black centers
Back legs	Green rubber hackle		

Step 1. Attach the weed guard at the halfway point of the shank, and wrap one-third of the way back into the curve of the hook. Return the thread to a point just above the hook barb.

Step 2. Spin a couple bunches (about the diameter of a pencil) of green hair around the shank, packing them tightly by using your thumbnail to form the butt.

Step 3. Using stacked bunches of olive deer body hair, spin a couple bunches in front of the butt.

Step 4. Take a ten-strand section of green rubber hackle material about 5 inches long, and make a knot about 1 inch above each end. Center the rubber hackle on top of the shank above the hook point, and tie it in as the rear legs with a few figure-eight wraps.

Step 5. Stack a bundle of olive hair on top of the shank, and leave the thread hang in the middle of the bundle.

Step 6. Stack a smaller bundle of chartreuse hair in the center on top of the olive hair bundle, then wrap in front of the bunch while pulling the hair back. Secure the bundle with a hitch, and repeat the same process three more times, up to about 3/4 inch behind the hook eye.

Step 7. Repeat Step 4 with a 4-inch-long, six-strand section of green rubber hackle at the 3/4-inch location for the front legs.

Step 8. Spin in another bundle of olive hair in front of the legs, then take another bundle of olive hair and stack it on top of the shank with a smaller bundle of red hair underneath it, and secure the bunch while pulling the hairs back.

Step 9. Continue spinning olive bunches of hair until you fill the shank to just behind the hook eye. Tie off with a whip finish.

Swimmin' Deer Hair Frog continued

Step 10. Remove the hook from the vise, and trim the body into a torpedo shape, taking care not to clip the legs off. Place the hook back in the vise, and attach the olive thread behind the hook eye.

Step 11. Bring the free end of the weed guard forward through the hook eye, and bend it back over the shank. Secure it behind the hook eye, using close, neat thread wraps (removing any excess material), and tie off with a whip finish.

Step 12. Burn some eye sockets in the head, taking care not to burn the thread. Clip the stems off the plastic doll eyes, and Krazy Glue the eyes into the sockets by putting a small dab of glue into each socket and pressing an eye in carefully. Separate the strands below the knot of each rubber leg, and trim them if necessary.

CHAPTER 10

Crustacean and Leech Patterns

George's Crayfish

Origin: United States
Originator: George Cik
Used for: All species

One of George Cik's original patterns designed to represent a crayfish. A very realistic imitation that works well for both smallmouth and largemouth bass.

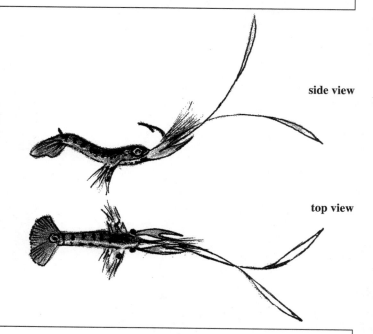

side view

top view

Thread	Black		**Claws**	Ring-necked pheasant church feathers
Hook	Mustad 336620, (bent), size 2 to 6		**Legs**	Ring-necked pheasant tail feather segment
Whiskers	Black squirrel tail fibers		**Underbody**	Green latex over lead wire base
Feelers	Furnace saddle hackles		**Tail**	Brown bucktail fibers
Carapace/tail	Brown bucktail fibers		**Coating**	5-minute epoxy cement
Weight	Lead wire			
Eyes	Black seed beads glued onto monofilament line			

Start by preparing various items to be used in the construction of the pattern as follows:

Feelers: Take two furnace saddle hackles, and strip off the barbules on both sides of the stem until approximately 1 inch remains at the tip.

Stripped Furnace Saddle Hackle

Pinchers: Take two ring-necked pheasant church feathers, and strip off the fuzz at the base of the stems. Coat each side of each feather with head cement, stroking it with your fingers until the feather narrows. After the cement dries, cut a V wedge at the tip of each feather, and trim off some of the barbules at the base on each side of the stem.

Ring-necked Pheasant Church Feather

Legs: Cut a ¹/₂-inch-wide section out of a ring-necked pheasant tail feather. *Note: Barbules should be equal in length on both sides of the stem.*

Ring-necked Pheasant Tail Feather Segment

Eyes: Take two black seed beads, and insert a piece of monofilament line about ¹/₂ inch long into the hole in one of the beads. Melt the mono tip protruding out of the bead using a match or a lighter. Repeat the process with the second bead at the opposite end of the mono.

Black Seed Beads and Monofilament Eyes

George's Crayfish continued

Step 1. Lay down a thread base to the bend of the hook, and tie in a sparse bunch of fine black (stacked) squirrel tail fibers on top of the hook shank, extending 1 inch beyond the bend. Wrap the butt ends down along the shank to build up the body, and return to the tie-in point.

Step 2. Tie in the two furnace saddle hackles at the same tie-in point as the squirrel with approximately 2 to 2½ inches extending beyond the bend. *Note: Tie them in so that the tips curve out.*

Step 3. Using your thread, wrap both the squirrel fibers and the hackle stems slightly around the hook bend, and return the thread to the tie-in point.

Step 4. Tie in a ¼-inch-thick bunch of natural brown bucktail fibers (about 3 inches long) under the shank, wrapping the butt ends back toward the hook eye, and return the thread to the tie-in point.

Step 5. Using lead wire, start about ¼ inch behind the tie-in point, and wrap about three-fourths of the shank. Flatten the lead wire with a pair of pliers, secure it with the thread, and return to the tie-in point.

Step 6. Tie in a ¼-inch-wide by 6-inch-long piece of light green latex under the shank at the tie-in point, and advance your thread about ¼ inch toward the hook eye.

Step 7. Tie in the mono bead eyes under the shank and the pinchers on each side of the shank. Also tie in one end of the leg feather at the same tie-in point under the shank, and advance the thread about ½ inch.

Step 8. Wrap the body going forward with the green latex strip, crisscrossing between the eyes, and wrapping the shank up to the point where you stopped the thread.

Step 9. Pull down the other end of the leg feather, and secure it with the thread, advancing the thread to the hook eye. Continue wrapping the latex up to the hook eye, and secure it with the thread. Remove any excess, and tie off with a whip finish.

Step 10. Remove the hook from the vise, turn it over, and place it back in the vise.

Step 11. Tie in your thread in front of the leg feather, and pull down the natural brown bucktail fibers on top of the shank that you tied in in Step 4. Secure the bucktail at the front of the leg feather with close tight wraps, and advance the thread to the center of the leg feather (about ¼ inch). Again wrap down the bucktail with another three to four close wraps, and continue the wrapping process every ¼ inch until you reach the eye. At this point, pull down on the bucktail extending beyond the eye, and add some more wraps behind the eye to force the bucktail below the eye. Then tie off with a whip finish. *Note: At this point, the bucktail fibers should extend beyond the hook eye; these will be used to make the tail.*

Step 12. Bend the hook shank at the midway point upward toward the hook point, until the eye is even with the point.

Step 13. Mix up a liberal amount of five-minute epoxy cement, and cover the bucktail on top of the body with the cement. Also cover about a ½-inch area of the bucktail that extends beyond the hook eye.

Step 14. While the cement is setting up, spread the bucktail fibers that extend out beyond the eye into a fan shape, and allow the cement to dry.

Step 15. After the cement is dry, trim the fibers to form the tail, and give the body and the tail another coat of epoxy cement. *Note: Also coat the body thread wraps on the underside of the body.*

Scud

Origin: United States
Demonstrator: Bob Dulian 1984–85
Used for: Trout, panfish

One of many patterns designed to represent a freshwater crustacean called a scud or freshwater shrimp, found in streams, rivers, and lakes throughout the world.

Thread	Olive	**Carapace (shell)**	Plastic bag strip
Hook	Mustad 3906B, size 12	**Body**	Olive rabbit dubbing
Feelers	Olive hen hackle fibers	**Legs**	Picked-out body dubbing
Rib	Fine silver tinsel or wire	**Head**	Olive thread

Step 1. Lay down a thread base to the bend of the hook, and tie in a sparse bunch of olive hen hackle fibers as the feelers. Snip off any excess material.

Step 2. Tie in a 6-inch-long piece of fine silver tinsel or wire under the shank at the same tie-in point. The wire will be used later in the pattern construction.

Step 3. Cut out a 6-inch-long by ¼-inch-wide strip from a plastic sandwich bag. Tie in the strip on top of the shank at the same location as the tail and the ribbing.

Step 4. Dub in a full body, using the olive rabbit dubbing, up to a hook eye diameter behind the hook eye.

Step 5. Pull the plastic bag strip over the top of the dubbed body, and secure it behind the eye with your thread. Snip off any excess material.

Step 6. Rib the body with the fine silver tinsel or wire, using equally spaced wraps. Secure the wire behind the eye with your thread, and remove any excess material.

Step 7. Form a neat, small head with your thread, and tie off with a whip finish. Give the head a coat of head cement, and after it dries, use your bodkin to pick out some of the dubbing on the underside to create the legs.

Clouser's Crayfish

Origin: United States
Originator: Bob Clouser
Demonstrator: Todd McCagg 1992–93, 1994–95
Used for: All species

Clouser's Crayfish, named after its originator, Bob Clouser, is an all-purpose fly that has taken more than its share of rainbow, brown, and brook trout; smallmouth and largemouth bass; panfish; and even carp and catfish.

Thread	White	**Carapace**	Olive Furry Foam
Hook	Mustad 79580, size 6	**Under carapace**	Closed-cell Ethafoam
Weight	.025 lead wire	**Underbody**	Cream Hare-Tron dubbing
Antennae	Bronze golden pheasant tail fibers	**Pincers**	Hen back or pheasant rump feathers, notched
Nose	Tip of golden pheasant church feather one-quarter antennae length	**Feelers**	Ginger saddle hackle

Step 1. Lay down a thread base from one eye length to the point of the hook and back to the hook eye. Tie in a piece of lead wire (shank length) under the shank to weight the pattern. Secure the wire with the thread, and return to the hook point.

Step 2. Tie in the bronze golden pheasant tail fibers as the antennae, and the tip of a golden pheasant church feather (one-quarter antennae length) on top of the antennae as the nose.

Step 3. Tie in a 2-inch-long by a hook-gap-wide strip of olive Furry Foam at the same tie-in point, and let it hang.

Step 4. Take a piece of round closed-cell Ethafoam about one-third the shank length, and cut a slit in the bottom for the hook shank. Tie it in on top of the shank at the bend, securing the entire length with your thread.

Step 5. Using the cream Hare-Tron dubbing, dub back over the foam to the hook point.

Step 6. Notch out four hen back or pheasant rump feathers, and tie in two per side as the pincers in an X pattern on top of the hook. Dub over the tie-in point back to the hook bend, and return the thread to the end of the under carapace.

Step 7. Pull the olive Furry Foam over the under carapace, and secure it with a couple of close wraps.

Step 8. Tie in the ginger saddle hackle, and bring the thread back to the hook eye. Using the cream Hare-Tron dubbing, cover the shank back to the hackle tie-in point with the dubbing to form the underbody.

Step 9. Using hackle pliers, palmer the hackle over the underbody back to the hook eye, and let the pliers hang.

Step 10. Bring the olive Furry Foam over the underbody, and secure it by ribbing it with the thread to behind the hook eye. Secure the hackle with the thread, and remove any excess hackle material.

Step 11. Tie off under the remaining Furry Foam with a whip finish, and trim the Furry Foam to a tail shape.

Kankakee Lectric Leech

Origin: United States
Demonstrator: Scott Hodlmair 1986–87
Used for: Walleye, smallmouth and largemouth bass

The Kankakee Lectric Leech pattern was originated by a fellow fisherman (name unknown) who fishes the Kankakee River in northern Illinois. It's designed to represent a leech, which is a major food source for bass and walleyes found in the Kankakee River, one of the best fisheries in the state of Illinois.

Thread	Black and bright red	**Body**	Peacock herl
Hook	Mustad 37187 (bent), size 6	**Eyes**	Silver bead chain
Weed guard (optional)	Mono loop	**Head**	Peacock herl, figure-eight wraps around eyes
Tail	Black marabou	**Nose**	Bright red thread
Side stripe	Silver mylar strip		
Hackle	Black saddle, palmered		

Step 1. Lay down a thread base to the bend of the hook, and tie in a piece of monofilament on top of the shank for the weed guard. Wrap the mono around the bend, and return your thread back to the tie-in point.

Step 2. Tie in a bunch of black marabou about twice the length of the hook shank as the tail at the tie-in point. *Note: Wrap the butt ends forward to within ¼ inch behind the hook eye and return your thread to the tie-in point. The butt ends are used to build up the body.*

Step 3. Tie in a 6-inch strip of silver mylar on each side of the hook shank and a black saddle hackle under the shank at the same tie-in point. Both will be used later in the pattern construction.

Step 4. Form a dubbing loop, holding the end of the loop with your hackle pliers. Tie in three to four peacock herls, placing them in between the loop and twisting the loop with the pliers to form a noodle. Wrap the shank going forward to about ¼ inch behind the hook eye. Secure the noodle with your thread, and snip off any excess material.

Step 5. Bring the silver mylar strips forward along each side and secure them with your thread. Remove any excess material.

Step 6. Palmer the body going forward with the black saddle hackle, using equally spaced wraps. Secure the hackle with your thread, and remove any excess material.

Step 7. Tie in the silver bead chain eyes on top of the shank in front of the body, using figure-eight wraps to secure them to the shank.

Step 8. Tie in a couple of peacock herls behind the eyes, and wrap them around the eyes using figure-eight wraps to form the head. Secure the herls in front of the eyes with your thread, and remove any excess material. Tie off with a whip finish.

Step 9. Tie in the bright red thread in front of the eyes. Bring up the opposite end of the mono weed guard, and wrap it in under the shank in front of the eyes using the red thread. Form a neat nose about 3/16 inch long with your thread, and tie off with a whip finish. Give the head a coat of head cement. After it dries, bend the hook shank slightly upward about midshank.

Ray's Marabou Leech

Origin: United States
Originator: Ray Podkowa
Demonstrator: Ray Podkowa 1987–88
Used for: Walleye, bass

The following pattern was designed by Ray Podkowa of the Chicago Fly Fishers. It's one of his own creations, which he developed to simulate a leech when he fishes for walleyes. Ray suggests that when it's used, it should be fished deep with a slow, jerking motion. It can also be used for most any game fish.

Thread	Black	**Body**	A black marabou blood feather and a yellow marabou blood feather
Hook	Mustad 34007, size 2/0	**Collar**	Black marabou blood feather
Tail	8 strands of gold Flashabou	**Head**	Black thread

Step 1. Wrap one-third of the hook shank with thread just behind the hook eye.

Step 2. Tie in eight stands of gold Flashabou at the back of the threaded area as the tail.

Step 3. Tie in a single black marabou blood feather (stem end), bringing your thread forward to about one-half of the threaded area on the hook shank.

Step 4. Palmer the marabou feather forward around the shank to the thread, and secure the feather with a half hitch. Collar it back with the thread, and snip off the excess.

Step 5. Tie in a yellow marabou blood feather, in front of the black feather, and again bring your thread forward to within 1/8 inch of the hook eye.

Step 6. Palmer the yellow feather forward to the thread, the same as you did with the black, and secure it with a half hitch. Collar it back, and snip off the excess. Tie in a second black marabou blood feather in front of the yellow.

Step 7. Wrap the black marabou feather around the shank in front of the yellow body feather. Secure it with the thread, and remove the excess. Then collar the black feather back over the yellow feather with your thread.

Step 8. Form a nice head with the thread, and tie off with a whip finish. Trim back the Flashabou tail to the desired length, and give the head a coat of head cement.

RB Leech

Origin: United States
Originator: Robert Brown
Demonstrator: Clay Rawn 1997–98
Used for: All species

The RB Leech pattern was originated by Robert Brown, utilizing a new type of material currently available from various fly shops and catalog houses called Ice Chenille or Cactus Chenille, which is basically short pieces of Flashabou attached to a thread, forming a chenille-type noodle. The pattern can be tied in assorted sizes and can be used for most any species of game fish.

Thread	Color to match body material	**Body**	Ice or Cactus Chenille (color tier's choice), clipped flat on both sides
Hook	Dai-Riki 700B, size 12	**Head**	Thread (color tier's choice)
Weight (optional)	Lead wire (half shank)		
Tail	Marabou (color to match body)		

Step 1. Lay down a thread base to the bend of the hook, and, if desired, wrap the forward half of the shank with lead wire to weight the pattern. Secure the wire with the thread, and return to the hook bend.

Step 2. Tie in a bunch of marabou about the length of the hook shank as the tail at the hook bend on top of the shank.

Step 3. Tie in a 6-inch strip of Ice Chenille or Cactus Chenille at the bend, and going forward, wrap a full body (tapered forward), covering the entire shank. Secure the chenille behind the hook eye with your thread, and remove any excess material.

Step 4. Form a small, neat head with the thread, and tie off with a whip finish. Give the head a coat of cement.

Step 5. Remove the hook from the vise, and using a pair of scissors, trim the chenille flat on each side of the body.

Translucent Wiggler

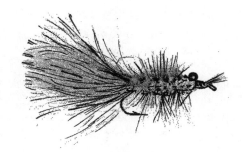

Origin: United States
Originator: Dan Pieczonka
Demonstrator: Dan Pieczonka 1997–98
Used for: Walleye, smallmouth and largemouth bass

The Translucent Wiggler is a leech pattern originated by Dan Pieczonka. It was designed to represent a leech, which is a major food source for bass and walleyes found in many rivers throughout the United States.

Thread	Camel	**Tail**	Bleached brown (coffee) marabou plume with 20 long strands of Luneflash translucent fibers on top
Hook	Dai-Riki 700, size 8		
Eyes	Black mono $^3/_{16}$ inch behind hook eye	**Rib**	Light brown saddle hackle, palmered over body, and brown medium chenille
Weight	.025 lead wire wrapped from the hook point to behind the eyes		
		Head	Camel-colored thread
		Nose	Luneflash translucent fibers

Step 1. Starting $^3/_{16}$ inch behind the hook eye, tie in the black mono eyes using a few figure-eight wraps.

Step 2. Starting at the hook point, wrap the shank with the lead wire up to the eyes. Secure the wire with the thread, and return the thread to the hook bend.

Step 3. Tie in a bleached brown (coffee) marabou plume, extending about a hook shank beyond the bend as the tail, with twenty long strands of Luneflash translucent fibers on top of the marabou. *Note: One end of the Luneflash translucent fibers should extend out as long as the tail.*

Step 4. Tie in a light brown saddle hackle and a short piece of brown medium chenille at the same tie-in point, bringing the thread forward to in front of the mono eyes.

Step 5. Wrap the shank with the brown medium chenille up to and through the eyes, using a figure-eight wrap. Secure the chenille with the thread, and remove any excess material.

Step 6. Palmer the body going forward with the light brown saddle hackle up to the mono eyes, using equally spaced wraps. Secure the hackle with your thread, and remove any excess material.

Step 7. Pull the remaining Luneflash translucent fiber stands over the top of the body and between the eyes, and secure them with the thread.

Step 8. Form a neat head with the thread, and tie off with a whip finish. Trim the Luneflash translucent fibers in front of the hook eye to form the nose.

Black Keel Leech

Origin: United States
Demonstrator: Len Eckerly 1987–88
Used for: Walleye, smallmouth and
largemouth bass

A simple leech pattern that resembles a black Woolly Bugger. Tied on a keel hook, it works well when fishing fast or deep water. When tied in smaller sizes, it is very effective on crappies and other panfish.

Thread	Black		Weight	.025 lead wire wrapped around the front diagonal section of the shank
Hook	Mustad 79666, size 8		**Hackle**	Soft black hen
Tail	Black marabou plume 1 inch long		**Head**	Black thread
Body	Black fuzzy mohair yarn			

Step 1. Starting at the bend of the hook, tie in your thread and a black marabou plume extending about 1 ½ inches behind the hook bend.

Step 2. Tie in a short (6-inch-long) piece of black fuzzy mohair yarn, which will be used for the body, and let it hang. Then bring your thread forward to the diagonal bend of the hook.

Step 3. Wrap the lead wire around the diagonal section of the shank to about ³/₁₆ inch behind the hook eye. Secure the lead wire with your thread by wrapping over, in back of, and in front of the wire.

Step 4. Wrap the black fuzzy mohair yarn forward, covering the entire shank and the lead wire to behind the hook eye. Secure the yarn with the thread, and remove any excess material.

Step 5. Tie in a soft black hen hackle in front of the body, and give it a couple of wraps. Secure it with the thread (collaring it back), and remove any excess material.

Step 6. Form a neat head with the thread, and tie off with a whip finish. Give the head a coat of cement.

Tochihara's OTR

Origin: United States
Originator: Jeff Norberte
Used for: Trout

A simple and deadly annelid (segmented marine worm) pattern used very successfully on the San Juan River in March 1999 while nymph fishing in relatively clear water. It was used as a dropper fly about 18 inches below a size 20 Pheasant Tail Nymph and was preferred by the San Juan rainbows 90 percent of the time.

Thread	6/0 Red Uni-Thread	**Rib**	Small silver wire or French tinsel
Hook	Daiichi 1273 (red), size 18 to 24	**Body**	Red Uni-Thread
Head	15/0 red glass bead from Umpqua		

Step 1. With a pair of flat pliers, smash the small barb down to make the hook barbless.

Step 2. Thread the glass bead onto the hook against the hook eye, and place the hook in the vise.

Step 3. Attach the thread directly behind the glass bead with a few wraps. Then, in a smooth and even fashion, cover the hook shank with a layer of thread to about one-third of the way down the bend of the hook.

Step 4. Wrap the thread back up to the glass bead using smooth and even wraps.

Step 5. Tie in about a 2-inch-long piece of ribbing, and secure it to the hook by taking a second layer of thread back one turn farther than the previous layer. Wind the thread back up to the glass bead, and use a half hitch to secure the thread behind the bead.

Step 6. Palmer the ribbing up the shank in a clockwise direction, using six or seven evenly spaced turns. Secure the ribbing with two wraps of thread, and cut away any excess material.

Step 7. Tie off with a whip finish, and coat the entire fly with head cement, taking care not to plug the hook eye.

Gene's Cactus Leech

Origin: United States
Originator: Gene Kugach
Used for: Walleye, smallmouth and largemouth bass

A simple leech pattern that can be tied in a variety of collar combinations by varying the color of the Krystal Flash, Cactus Chenille, marabou tail, and hackle collar.

Thread	Black	**Body**	Black Cactus Chenille
Hook	Mustad 36890, size 2	**Eyes**	Bead chain
Tail	Black marabou plume 1 1/2 inches long, with 10 to 12 strands of green Krystal Flash on each side	**Hackle**	Soft black hen, collared back
		Head	Black thread

Step 1. Lay down a thread base up to the hook bend, and tie in a black marabou plume 1 1/2 inches long with ten to twelve strands of Krystal Flash on each side.

Step 2. Tie in a short (6-inch-long) piece of black Cactus Chenille, which will be used for the body, and let it hang. Then bring your thread forward to about 3/16 inch behind the hook eye.

Step 3. Tie in the bead chain eyes, using figure-eight wraps on top of the shank, returning the thread behind the eyes.

Step 4. Wrap the black Cactus Chenille forward, covering the entire shank to behind the hook eye. Secure the yarn with the thread, and remove any excess material.

Step 5. Tie in a soft black hen hackle in front of the body, and give it a couple of wraps. Secure it with the thread (collaring it back), and remove any excess material.

Step 6. Form a neat head around and between the eyes using the thread, and tie off with a whip finish. Give the head a coat of cement.

Bluegill Leech

Origin: United States
Originator: Jim Pearce
Demonstrator: George Cik 1993–94
Used for: Panfish

A simple leech-type pattern using black marabou, designed by a Chicago-area tier named Jim Pearce

Thread	Black and fluorescent chartreuse	**Wing**	Several bunches of black marabou tied on top of the hook
Hook	Mustad 9672, size 6 to 10	**Head**	Fluorescent chartreuse thread
Tail	Black marabou plume		
Body	Thread and black marabou bunches		

Step 1. Lay down a thread base up to the hook bend, and tie in a black marabou plume extending the length of the shank beyond the bend.

Step 2. Tie in a bunch of black marabou fibers (length extending to the middle of the tail) on top of the shank in front of the tail, securing them with the thread.

Step 3. Continue adding bunches of black marabou fibers on top of the shank, forming the wing and body, until you fill the shank to within $1/16$ inch of the hook eye.

Step 4. Tie off the black thread with a whip finish, and tie on the fluorescent chartreuse thread.

Step 5. Form a neat oversize head with the fluorescent chartreuse thread, and tie off with a whip finish. Give the head a coat of cement.

Jim's Crayfish

Origin: United States
Demonstrator: Jerry Wasil 1989–90
Used for: All species

A simple crayfish pattern from the *Western Fly Tying Manual, Vol. II,* by Jack Dennis (Snake River Book Co., 1995).

Thread	Black or brown	**Pincers**	Fox squirrel tail fibers
Hook	Mustad 3665A or 79580, size 2 to 6	**Legs**	Brown saddle hackle
Weight	Heavy lead wire	**Carapace**	Fox squirrel tail fibers
Antennae	2 stripped brown hackle stems	**Body**	Reddish brown dubbing
Eyes	30-pound-test mono burned at both ends	**Tail**	Fox squirrel tail fibers

Step 1. Lay down a thread base to the hook bend, and starting forward of the hook point, wrap in the lead wire around the shank to about the mid-point of the shank. Secure the lead wire with your thread, and return the thread to the hook bend. Make a small thread ball at the bend.

Step 2. Tie in a stripped brown hackle stem (length equal to the hook length) on the side of the shank behind the ball as the antennae.

Step 3. Take a 30-pound-test piece of mono, and using a lighter or a match, burn one end until it balls and turns black. Do the same to the opposite end, until you have a pair of eyes with approximately ¼ inch between them.

Step 4. Tie in the eyes on top of the shank about midway between the barb and the point, using figure-eight wraps, then bring the thread back to the antennae tie-in point.

Step 5. Tie in a sparse bunch of stacked fox squirrel tail fibers (slightly shorter than the antennae) on each side of the shank as the pincers.

Step 6. Tie in the brown saddle hackle under the shank at the same tie-in point as the pincers.

Step 7. Tie in a thicker bunch of stacked fox squirrel tail fibers by the butt ends on top of the shank, with the tips extending over the hook bend.

Step 8. Cover the shank with reddish brown dubbing, going forward with the dubbing to within ¹⁄₁₆ inch of the hook eye.

Step 9. Palmer the brown saddle hackle over the dubbed body, using equally spaced wraps. Secure it with the thread, and remove any excess material.

Step 10. Pull the thicker bunch of stacked fox squirrel tail fibers over the body, and secure them behind the hook eye with the thread. Tie off with a whip finish.

Step 11. Trim the tail to the desired length.

INDEX

Pattern Index

PATTERN DEMONSTRATORS

PATTERN ORIGINATORS